On Roads

'A warm-hearted, ingenious, endlessly fascinating exploration of our complicated relationship with the road. Joe Moran is single-handedly transforming the history of everyday life in modern Britain.' David Kynaston, author of *Austerity Britain*

'Joe Moran has a genius for turning the prosaic poetic – this is a tone poem in tarmac. Motorway journeys will never be so dull again. A treat.' Peter Hennessy, author of *Having It So Good*

'Wonderful. Joe Moran is the master of turning the mundane realities of everyday life into the stuff of history, and in this book he has surpassed himself. From speed limits to Travelodges, nothing escapes his forensic examination, and almost no page is without some surprising insight. Whoever could have known that roads were so fascinating?' Dominic Sandbrook, author of *White Heat*

'Truly wonderful ... every minute devoted to this book is richly rewarded. It is hard to say which is the more remarkable here: the astonishing range and variety of what Joe Moran knows, or the easeful, evocative, luxuriously entertaining way he parcels it up and puts it across.' David McKie, author of *Great British Bus Journeys*

'Joe Moran is one of the most interesting and original observers of the minutiae of British life to emerge in a long while.' Matthew Engel, author of *Eleven Minutes Late*

'A delightful look at the cultural history of our roads ... Moran's reflections on traffic jams are also illuminating: after reading them the prospect of congestion is really quite alluring.' Editor's Pick, *The Bookseller*

'Entertaining stuff, a blend of history, cultural and social observation and travel writing which motors along nicely. Quirky, funny and a great gift buy for Father's Day.' Booksellers Choice, *The Bookseller*

On Roads

A Hidden History

Joe Moran

PROFILE BOOKS

1 3 5 7 9 10 8 6 4 2

A CIP catalogue record for this book is available
from the British Library.

ISBN 978 1 84668 052 6

Typeset in Sabon by MacGuru Ltd
info@macguru.org.uk

Printed and bound in Great Britain by
Clays, Bungay, Suffolk

The paper this book is printed on is certified by the © 1996 Forest Stewardship Council A.C. (FSC). It is ancient-forest friendly. The printer holds FSC chain of custody SGS-COC-2061

FSC
Mixed Sources
Product group from well-managed
forests and other controlled sources

Cert no. SGS-COC-2061
www.fsc.org
© 1996 Forest Stewardship Council

For all my friends on Cable Road

CONTENTS

1

IN ROAD COUNTRY

My idea of a piece of sculpture is a road. That is, a road doesn't reveal itself at any particular point or from any particular point. Roads appear and disappear. We either have to travel on them or beside them. But we don't have a single point of view for a road at all, except a moving one, moving along it.

Carl Andre[1]

If you walk down to the bottom of the street on which I grew up, you turn into one of the most famous roads in Britain: the Snake Pass, the winding route over the Pennines in Derbyshire's Peak District. Built by Thomas Telford, the Snake looks as though it has been there for ever, as much a part of the landscape as the millstone grit. But like most roads it is a palimpsest, laid on top of earlier versions like overwritten text. It used to start in Ashopton, a small village now buried at the bottom of the Ladybower reservoir. So the new road begins on the reservoir viaduct, then climbs slowly up to the barren plateaux of Kinder Scout and Bleaklow, before beginning its snaking, vertiginous descent into my hometown of Glossop. As you pass the final few hairpins, the Longdendale Valley spreads out beautifully along your windscreen – almost as though the road came first and the view has been supplied for the benefit of motorists by its benevolent engineers.

When I was young, I overheard a grown-up saying that the Snake was a great 'driving road', and I was puzzled by the adjective. Weren't all roads for driving on? Eventually I came to realise that the Snake, like all great driving roads, existed as much in the mind as on the earth. It was a fantasy road – the lovely, desolate, winding one in the motoring programmes and car commercials. The Snake also had an exciting air of mystery and danger, because it was always being blocked by snow and landslips, cutting Glossop off from civilisation – or, at least, from Yorkshire. It had, and still has, only one phone box along its entire length (and it's now one of the last frontiers of the mobile phone signal) so if you broke down or crashed you might have to walk for hours to get help. Hairy bikers came from miles around to race along its open straights and career around its sinuous curves in search of the perfect cornering line, before rewarding themselves with an all-day breakfast in the greasy spoon at the bottom of our road. Nowadays they film the ride from their handlebars and post the results on YouTube, for the envy and delectation of other members of the biker fraternity. The Snake remains a collective work of fiction, driven mainly in anticipation and remembrance.

An ordinary road is nothing like that: it is just part of the invisible landscape of the everyday. You will probably see those white lines stretching into the distance, and hear the sound of tyres on tarmac, every day of your life. Everyone eats, sleeps, talks, works and loves within about a hundred feet of a road. But a road is not there to be dreamt about, feared or remembered; it is there to be driven along forgetfully on the way to somewhere else. A road is overlooked and taken for granted because its shared routines seem to offer little opening for individual creativity or invention. We see most of our journeys on roads as dead time, just a rude interruption of the proper business of living. These everyday roads have penetrated our imaginations obliquely, not through the myth and folklore of the great driving roads but through the compulsive habits and accidental poetry of the commonplace – or a reflex moan about the M4 bus lane.

→

All roads lead to other roads. The Snake is part of the A57, which runs across the width of the north of England, all the way from Lincoln's railway station to Liverpool's dock road. These long A-roads are like the road system's unconscious, often stretching for miles without being signposted or acknowledged, disappearing into street names and getting caught up in one-way systems but still always there, connecting up different areas of our lives serendipitously. If you follow the A57 into Manchester, for instance, it becomes the first edifice I remember actually noticing as a road. During school holidays, my dad often had to take me into his office at work, and the walk from Piccadilly Station involved us going under an urban flyover. I must have said something about how odd it was to have a road suspended in midair, because I remember him telling me that this was a special kind of road, a 'motorway'.

Some years later, this road – the A57(M), or Mancunian Way – played a key role in the first episode of the BBC's time-travelling drama series, *Life on Mars*. DCI Sam Tyler (John Simm) is run over by a car on a slip road of the Mancunian Way and knocked unconscious, before waking up in 1973 on a motorway construction site. Leaving the site in a state of shock, he passes a hoarding that marks his entry into the past: 'Coming Soon! Manchester's Highway in the Sky.' It is clear straightaway what this exercise in historical surrealism means: we're being primed to enter a recent era that now seems quite remote in its blind faith in novelty, its naïve hope that a sunlit future can simply be planned and built. 'Am I mad, in a coma, or back in time?' asks Tyler. 'Whatever's happened, it's like I've landed on a different planet.' The Mancunian Way is treated as a dead fashion, a piece of embarrassing 1970s kitsch, the concrete equivalent of loon pants and lava lamps.

History, as usual, is more complicated. The local press did indeed once call the Mancunian Way a 'highway in the sky', even though it rises less than 30 feet from the ground. But not even in the salad days of flyover building did they announce new roads like forthcoming cinema attractions. And anyway, the Mancunian Way was built in 1967. If they had waited until 1973, it would probably not have been built at all.

When it comes to roads, it's hard to separate the facts from the folk memory. Every modern road carries a freight of ideas and meanings about postwar British history – none more so than these urban flyovers, lumbering overhead sculptures that seem to symbolise the mistakes of 1960s planning and the car-clogged world it bequeathed us. Our addiction to roads comes with some of the self-disgust and self-delusion more associated with chemical dependencies. Like many addicts we like to weave stories that blame our habit on something outside ourselves: in this case, we rely on a plausible but partial narrative about the errors of our immediate ancestors.

The real story of the Mancunian Way begins with the City of Manchester Plan, published a month after VE Day in June 1945. This aimed to rebuild Manchester over the next fifty years, sweeping away its obsolete Victorian infrastructure and allowing the city to enter 'a nobler, braver age in which the human race will be master of its fate'. The most ambitious part of the plan was a massive new road system that would set the traffic free and defer for ever 'the evil day of complete strangulation'.[2] The city would be threaded with a vast network of orbital and radial roads – mostly elegant parkways, lined with trees and flowers – including an inner ring road reaching right into the centre. The River Irwell would be covered over with a giant roundabout, and whole streets flattened to make a processional route to the town hall, as grandly elegant as one of Baron Haussman's Parisian boulevards.

But the council was broke, and carried on being broke, and none of these roads was ever built. The first major road to be constructed in the city after the war was the A57(M), and it was meant as a stopgap, relieving the city centre until the inner ring road was built. In an inter-school competition to name it, five children came up separately with 'Mancunian Way' and, on 5 May 1967, they all met the prime minister, Harold Wilson, at the official opening. The road was made of state-of-the-art prefab sections that could be hoisted into place with cranes and snapped together like Scalextric, a popular slot-car racing game of the time. In 1968 the newly formed Concrete Society (motto: *Concreti Corroboramus*, or 'having come together we strengthen') chose the Mancunian Way as the recipient of its first annual award for 'outstanding merit in the use of concrete'.[3]

The inner ring road remained on the drawing board well into the 1970s, by which time it was nicknamed the 'eternity ring' and urban motorways were terminally passé anyway. Unborn roads weigh invisibly on the landscape like stories without endings. Manchester's unbuilt inner ring road created a city centre scarred with derelict sites, as the land remained in limbo until the plans were officially cancelled in the 1980s. Some buildings in the city centre are still set back from the road line, awaiting the ring road's arrival, like a planning-blight version of *Waiting for Godot*.[4]

You can learn to read roads like any other part of the landscape, but often what is most revealing is what isn't there. The British road system is an unfinished symphony, made up of the modest remnants of never-realised utopian schemes. At the eastern end of the Mancunian Way, for instance, one of the ramps comes to a sudden stop in thin air. This bit of the road was meant to lead all the way into the city centre, sweeping away much of Chinatown in the process. Now the stump is half-hidden by an advertising hoarding and its thick iron bars cut short any motorist who has been cruelly misinformed that it leads somewhere.

The space beneath the A57(M) used to be common ground open to everyone. The road's undercarriage had a vast network of pedestrian subways and the grassy bits in-between were meant to be mini-parks, little oases where inner-city residents and students from the nearby Polytechnic could bask together in the road's bountiful shade. But the subways soon declined into dank, piss-stained, graffiti-sprayed theatres for casual muggings that symbolised the failures of urban planning from that era. Now the undercarriage is mostly cordoned off by railings and chain-link fencing, and has been recycled as a giant private car park, protected by CCTV cameras and anti-intruder paint, with room for a few tiny football pitches and skateboard runs.

There is another symbol of changing social attitudes to roads at the western end of the Mancunian Way: a horseshoe-shaped pedestrian bridge, a piece of post-millennial signature architecture meant to heal the rift made by the motorway between the rejuvenated city centre and the stranded ghetto of Hulme. In another sign of the times, it has been built not from concrete but Cumaru, a sustainable Brazilian hardwood. Underneath the bridge are the remains of a subway, now walled in with concrete blocks and clumsily plastered over.

The Mancunian Way may not be a great driving road, but ten yards of it will tell you more about recent British history than all 14 miles of the Snake Pass. Its tapered stanchions and flowing cantilevers are part of our cultural mythology, a cautionary tale in concrete and steel. Even people who have never heard of this road know the story, because every British city has a similar one to tell. When, a few years ago, the Birkenhead MP Frank Field championed a scheme for anti-social families to be moved into vandal-proof steel containers, he volunteered his own constituency for the pilot scheme. 'They can put them up underneath the motorway flyover,' he suggested.[5] Everyone knew what he meant: 'underneath the motorway flyover' was universal shorthand for the abandoned and godforsaken. There used to be a National Lottery television gameshow, *Winning Lines*, in which the booby prize for answering only one question correctly was a holiday to Spaghetti Junction. I don't know if anyone ever won the prize, or claimed it, but the conceit was clear enough: this convoluted maze of airborne concrete was the last place anyone would choose to linger.

You will look in vain on an *A-Z* for help in guiding you through the *terrain vague* underneath and around our urban motorways. Exploring this liminal land on foot may mark you out as a dangerous eccentric, an unauthorised person – although it is more likely you will simply be ignored because everyone else is inside a vehicle, looking only ahead. The land surrounding rural motorways is even more vast and unknown. If you're ever on the run from the law, I would strongly recommend that you hide in the wooded motorway verges of our oldest motorways, like the M1 or M6. There is just enough room for a tent in the half-century of undergrowth and you could surely live like Stig of the Dump, undisturbed for months or years, in this uninhabited wilderness just a cone's throw from the road.

According to the Department for Transport there are 245,366 ½ miles of motorable road in Britain,[6] and most of us spend large parts of our lives moving along them. If you drive an average of 10,000 miles a year, at an average speed of 40 miles per hour, then you will spend the equivalent of four-and-a-half working weeks on roads. In origin and destination surveys, traffic experts use the term 'desire lines' to describe these daily movements of drivers along roads. The term derives from the shortcuts made by pedestrians between paved pathways. When applied to motorists the phrase is pleasingly poetic but quite misleading, because so many road journeys are necessary rather than desirable ones. When computer programmers draw thousands of these motoring desire lines on to a single map, they show patterns that seem as silently inevitable as the mass migrations of birds, albeit ones driven by everyday obligation rather than the seasons.

As the Oxford zoologists Tim Guilford and Dora Biro have shown in their studies of homing pigeons, birds use roads as tracking devices on their migratory journeys. Although they have inbuilt magnetic compasses, they tend to fall back on the known landscape when they are in familiar territory. They follow the lines of motorways and trunk roads, almost as though they have checked the route beforehand on the *AA Route Planner* – and even if it means going miles out of their way. Working with the BBC's natural history unit, Guilford and Biro strapped tiny cameras and GPS devices to pigeons' backs with a Velcro strip and tracked them as they followed the A34 Oxford Bypass, turning at traffic lights and curving round roundabouts just like motorists. So homing pigeons do not make their way as the crow flies – and the jury is still out on whether crows do. In fact, you don't need a mini-GPS to find the circumstantial evidence. You will often see seagulls in landlocked Birmingham because they have flown up the Bristol Channel and followed the M5, mistaking it for a river. Drive north on the same motorway on a Saturday and you may be tailed by flocks of pigeons who have just been released from the Royal Pigeon Racing Association's Cheltenham HQ on racing day.

As with homing birds, so it is with motorists. After a fashion, roads allow us to follow our desires, but these personal itineraries amass to produce collective configurations as striking as any in nature. Look at a road from the window seat of a plane and you will see the compelling patterns made by converging cars; or take a picture of a motorway from an overbridge at night with a shutter delay and it will show trails of red and white light tracing the road's curvature, the visual remnant of countless identical journeys. If we are ever visited by aliens from other planets, and there are any natural scientists among them, they will surely find parallels between these human movements on roads and the behaviour of shoaling fish or flocking birds – those spellbindingly synchronised patterns that look like the work of superorganisms, but are just lots of individual animals following their own self-absorbed agendas. Motorists similarly behave like a micro-society, without ever imagining themselves as one.

The road is almost a separate country, one that remains under-explored not because it is remote and inaccessible but because it is so ubiquitous and familiar. Some roads are literally enclaves, like the checkpointed autobahn from Helmstedt to West Berlin that was an umbilical cord to the walled city during the Cold War. But even without passport controls or border police, a road has rules and often a price of admission. In Britain, there are not many tolls (yet) and the motorway's entry requirements aren't very exacting: as long as you've passed your driving test and aren't driving a moped or a Reliant Robin, you're in. But once you are inside the road system you will find that there are laws, rituals and codes of behaviour, many of them unwritten and unspoken. Roads are mapped as carefully as countries, while retaining their uncharted outposts like verges and the insides of roundabouts. There have been wars over road country – the fractious but usually non-violent ones about whether it should have its frontiers pegged back, and the often fatal, undeclared ones between the people who occupy it. Like most countries, the road is a synthetic and recent creation that its inhabitants have come to see as natural and eternal.

The anthropologist Marc Augé, a diligent student of the French autoroutes, argues that we should explore daily life in the western world with the same kind of careful attention that ethnographers once reserved for tribes in remote societies. For him, the toll-road habitats of French car commuters are as rich an environment for anthropologists as the tribal villages he stayed in on his field trips to the Ivory Coast in the 1960s and 1970s. What would we discover if we applied what Augé calls the 'anthropology of the near' to the British road?[7] Could we look beyond its surface sameness and re-imagine it not as a monotonous line interrupted occasionally by Little Chefs, but as the real, concrete space in which we spend much of our lives?

→

Most of us contemplate roads only when we're in motion, and we simply want them to be smooth, unvarying and amenable to distracted driving. Although cars are one of the most semiotically rich objects we own – loaded with the symbolic baggage of money, status, sexual competitiveness and aesthetic pleasure – roads, without which the cars would be almost useless, are simply part of our unnoticed collective life. But this ignoring of the road is a modern luxury. Before Thomas Telford and John Macadam's revolutionary roadbuilding techniques solved the problem of bogs and wheel ruts, British travellers complained unremittingly about what Daniel Defoe called 'the exceeding badness of the roads'. When the historian Edward Gibbon made his last journey in 1794 to see his surgeon, along what is now the A22 from East Grinstead to London, the road nearly saved his surgeon the trouble because he was 'almost killed ... by hard, frozen, long, and cross ruts, that would disgrace the approach to an Indian wigwam'.[8]

In its early days, the motor car made the road horribly visible again by turning its untarred surface into a dustbowl. In *The Wind in the Willows*, Ratty, Mole and Toad first encounter the motor car as 'a small cloud of dust, with a dark centre of energy, advancing on them at incredible speed, while from out of the dust a faint "poop-poop" wailed like an uneasy animal in pain'.[9] Virtually all Britain's roads were tarmacked after the First World War, the Tarmac company having perfected its methods in France, helping to build semi-permanent roads to supply the motionless trenches. Roads that had once assumed the colours of their local geology, from Devon's pinkish soil to Lancashire's grey grit, were buried under anodyne tar. But the load-bearing surfaces of tyre and road remained in treacherous misalignment until the ingenious design of the radial-ply tyre after the Second World War. Its intricate zigzags solved the eternal problems of skidding and aquaplaning and finally brokered the peace between rubber and road that we now take for granted.

The arrival of the motorways transformed the road into a place of pure mobility. The first section of the M1, opened in 1959, had maintenance depots spaced about 15 miles apart. Legions of workers emerged from them, using secret junctions and dive-under tunnels, to tidy up the road and its edges invisibly and thanklessly, like real-life Wombles. Their job was to keep the motorway free of litter or objects falling from lorries, and, when the road froze over, to decant rock salt from huge hoppers and spread it over the tarmac. The point of the motorway was to banish idiosyncrasy, to create uniform spaces for the ceaseless flow of traffic. When a new section of the M6 opened in 1963, the architect W.G. Howell complained that 'unless you are a connoisseur of bridge design, you could be anywhere from Watford to Preston'. The pleasant drive in which 'we look out through our windscreen and see the drunken English road-geometry staggering away in perspective' was 'more and more becoming a fantasy'.[10]

For drivers, the new motorways were a strange mix of the perilous and the tedious, of jangled nerves and straight-line monotony. Like fighting in a war, driving on a motorway consisted of long periods of boredom punctuated by brief moments of life-threatening danger. Ambient music suited this day-dreamy mode of driving – before the motorways arrived, only 4 per cent of British cars had radios but by the time a thousand miles of motorway were completed in 1972, about 30 per cent did.[11] The growing reliability of cars also meant that drivers were less likely to have this semi-hypnotic experience interrupted. Even after 1961, when the MOT test was introduced because our half-timbered, superannuated cars could not cope with fast roads, cars were regularly beached on hard shoulders. But today's cars are so dependable that drivers are almost as likely to stop on the hard shoulder as they are to camp on a roundabout.

It is no accident that the coming of the motorways coincided with the rise of that fluorescent orange symbol of the mundanity of the modern road: the traffic cone, designed to keep the cars moving while part of the road was repaired. The earliest cones were either too heavy to be easily moved, or too light and liable to wobble slowly across roads on the backdraughts of lorries. Then in 1961 a young ICI plastics engineer called David Morgan was experimenting with spinning liquid polythene inside rotating metal moulds. He was meant to be producing toy elephants, but removing the trunk proved tricky, so he hit on the ideal shape for getting out of a mould: a cone. Morgan's model prevailed and there were soon hundreds of thousands of these identical-looking objects in circulation on British roads, diverting traffic so the roads could stay forever open.

We have learnt to take the uninterrupted use of our roads as read, wrongly imagining them to belong to anyone and everyone. But in 1982 the investigative journalist Duncan Campbell revealed plans, in the event of a civil emergency, to reclassify Britain's trunk roads as 'Essential Service Routes'. Before a potential nuclear strike, the police would establish road blocks at major junctions to prevent civilian 'refugees' using them. Each of the routes was named after an animal. BAT was London to Hull via the M1 and M62, HEN was Cardiff to Hemel Hempstead via the A48, M4 and A404, FOX was Slough to the North Circular via the M4 and A4. Britain's nuclear strategy was to preserve a viable political state by bottling up the civilian population in nuclear target cities like London and Manchester, while the VIPs used the trunk roads to get to their bunkers.[12] Any hoi polloi who didn't fancy being pulverised would have to use the B-roads, which would presumably be rather busy. Motorways are always the preserve of the powerful, who graciously allow us to use them until we might need them to save our lives. And yet most of us only really notice a road when it is closed, or there is something wrong with it – which is why the roadblock has become such a powerful tool of protest, especially now the minutely synchronised routines of just-in-time capitalism render it one gigantic traffic jam away from social anarchy.

An empty motorway is such a surreal contrast from the usual swathes of traffic that it is almost mesmerising. Deserted roads, as Thomas Hardy wrote, 'bespeak a tomb-like stillness more emphatic than that of glades and pools', an 'incubus of the forlorn' created out of the contrast of 'what is with what might be'.[13] The millions of viewers who watched the television coverage of Princess Diana's funeral in September 1997 were privileged to see the road in this state, as the funeral cortège made the 77-mile journey from Westminster Abbey to Althorp, and a rolling roadblock cleared traffic for half-a-mile ahead and behind. The hearse and its police outriders moved slowly out of London along the North Circular, with the cars at a standstill on the opposite carriageway, before reaching Staples Corner and turning towards the huge, deserted sweep of the M1 curving north. But as the car made its way slowly along the motorway, it became clear that the road was empty only of cars. Thousands of people had gathered in places where it would have been unwise and indeed illegal to stand in normal times – along the grass verge, on the hard shoulder and in the middle of the central reservation. Some even spilled on to the left lane as the hearse approached, and showered flowers on to its roof. As traffic on the southbound carriageway ground to a halt, motorists parked in the fast lane then leapfrogged the barriers and walked across the motorway. Apart from a smattering of applause as the hearse passed, an uncanny silence replaced the normally torrential sound of traffic.

All daily routine was put on hold. When traffic police in London found three trailing buses on the closed route ahead of the hearse, they ordered them to keep going so as not to disrupt the procession. Instead of getting off at Golders Green, the irate passengers found themselves dumped at Scratchwood services on the M1. Naturally, once the hearse turned off at junction 15A, the motorway returned to normal and motorists went back to driving along it absent-mindedly. In our modern cars, with their delicately sprung suspensions, ergonomically designed seats and controlled micro-climates, we notice so little of the road beneath us that we might as well be floating on air; but perhaps a few Britons still remember that brief moment when the blue-grey asphalt of the M1 showed up against the yellow cornfields of early autumn, and the everyday semblance of normality was shattered.

→

We think of asphalt as a lifeless material – what Iain Sinclair calls 'the dull silvertop that acts as a prophylactic between driver and landscape'[14] – but its shape-shifting qualities are actually miraculous. At the hundred-acre Pitch Lake in Trinidad, where much of the asphalt used in Britain's early motoring roads was mined, you can see this malleability in vivid form. The lake can support the weight of a person, but footprints leave deep impressions and then quickly disappear. You can smash the lake's surface into little pieces with a hammer, but if you then lay the hammer on the surface the lake will swallow it up like slow-motion quicksand.

Asphalt has just the right level of pliability for roads; it deflects very slightly every time a vehicle passes over it. But its pliability is also its downfall. As soon as traffic drives on a road, the asphalt begins a losing battle with the vehicles pounding on top of it and the shifting earth below. Like human skin, when asphalt is young it is supple and regains shape quickly, but in middle age it recovers more slowly and starts to stiffen and sag. A road, like skin, consists of several layers: underneath the surface coating of blacktop is a multilayered assortment of sand, gravel, cement and recycled waste, about as familiar to most of us as moondust. Just as doctors can read someone's inner health from the pinkness or pallor of their epidermis, road maintenance workers can read barely visible surface ruts, a few millimetres deep, as evidence of a road's tortured interior life. A machine called a deflectograph detects infinitesimal wear and tear on a stretch of asphalt and works out the road's life expectancy, and the thickness of the layer of asphalt needed to extend its life.

In turning roads into hyper-efficient channels for cars, the road-builders and road maintainers have created a bland, corporate landscape of flat asphalt, thermoplastic white markings, factory-made aluminium signs and mechanically trimmed verges – with everything measured and standardised to the last centimetre, from the distance between chevrons to the arrows on gantry signs that are perfectly aligned in the dead centre of lanes. Even roadworks all look the same. A vehicle called the Conemaster can lay cones in straight lines at 15 mph at a rate of 40 per minute, a bit like a farmer's mechanical seed-drill. Traffic safety manuals have esoteric rules for laying out cones, from the angle and exit of the tapers to how closely the cones need to be placed together 'to give an impression of continuity and an appearance of substance'.[15] These manuals are filled with strangely riveting pictures of conal arrangements, with their raisons d'être (cars to be guided round and workers to be penned inside them) absent. They look like nominees for the Turner prize.

Underneath this veneer of uniformity, though, roads are a case study in the unevenness of historical change. As human monuments, they are uniquely durable and adaptable. Most UK roads have been around in some form since at least the Middle Ages. The British section of the Antonine Itinerary, a road book showing routes through the Roman Empire produced around AD200, bears an uncanny resemblance to today's motorway network. The northern end of the M6 is said to be haunted by the ghosts of homesick legionaries, trying to find their way back to Rome along a route through the Lune Gorge that hugs the contours of the old Roman road. On the new M6 toll motorway around Birmingham, motorists claim to have spotted Roman soldiers wading waist-deep through the tarmac as if it were water.

Many of our roads are hand-me-downs, reused routes and leftover bits of tarmac stuck together in ad hoc fashion. At the end of the Second World War, Britain had 856 military airfields, containing enough concrete to build a motorway from London to Peking,[16] and some of the runways ended up as roads. Heston Aerodrome, from where Neville Chamberlain flew to Munich and returned with his famous piece of paper, and which would probably have become London's main airport if this had managed to avert a war, had its runway recycled as part of the M4, just past Heston services, in 1965. One of the longest runways in Europe, at the Burtonwood American Airbase, became a 10,000 yard stretch of the M62, a ruler-straight line across the flat Lancashire plain. If you drive on it at night, it's easy to blank out the lane lines and gantry signs and imagine the Flying Fortress bombers taking off in procession in front of you. The history of the road isn't always hidden; it's on the surface if you know where to look.

→

This book is not a complete history of the road – a project that would be as Sisyphean as resurfacing an endless motorway. It is a study in the living memory of roads. With a few necessary diversions into the arterial road era, it deals with the period from the birth of the first motorways to our more recent attempts to live with roads in a road-sceptical age. It is an imaginative history, a study of the road as a cultural artefact as much as a concrete one. We might not think that something as banal as a road could form part of the public imagination. But roads are a rich resource for what French historians have named the 'history of mentalities', the study of how our thoughts and feelings change imperceptibly over time while seeming as natural and inevitable to us as breathing. In his 1963 book, *London 2000*, the geographer Peter Hall excitedly imagined a huge network of elevated expressways stretching all the way from the centre of London into the home counties. But he has since described our falling out of love with roads as 'one of the biggest and most sudden psychological changes … that ever occurred in the history of the twentieth century'.[17] This changing collective mentality is the main theme of this book – although the shift was not quite as sudden as Hall suggests.

Just a few decades ago, the clean-planed road served as a standard-bearer for a better life. As the photographer Martin Parr has wryly reminded us, roads were a fitting subject for tourist postcards with deadpan captions: 'The M1 near Newport Pagnell', 'The Fortes Excelsior Motor Lodge near Pontefract', 'The Underpass, Croydon', 'A40 Traffic'.[18] How sad and strange these colour-saturated images now seem: all those Ford Populars and Triumph Heralds, with the shiny newness of diecast models, dotted around those impossibly empty motorways. These weirdly haunting images are a reminder that motorways are beginning to acquire a cultural history, but of a rather unsettling kind that evades the secure meanings of the heritage industry or the easy consolations of nostalgia.

One of the most difficult areas of the past to make sense of is the recent history of the everyday. When did you first drive on a motorway? You might remember if it was in the first few years of their life, when families made special detours to visit the M1 or M6. But this kind of shared quotidian history mostly resists being sorted into watershed moments. 'Memory, being a phenomenon of emotion and magic, accommodates only those facts that suit it,' the French historian of mentalities, Pierre Nora, has written. 'It thrives on vague, telescoping reminiscences ... It is vulnerable to transferences, screen memories, censorings, and projections of all kinds.'[19] Our collective memory of the road has its own censorings and projections in the form of received wisdoms and clichés – that anti-road protests are a recent invention, for instance, or that everyone was equally excited about motorways in 1959. But there is usually some truth in the clichés, and how these clichés arise and develop is itself an important part of the cultural history of the road. Roads cause such excitement and anger when they are built, and then they just seem to meld into mundane life, vanish into unnoticed routine. But this journey from the ultramodern into the everyday is a richer and more mysterious process than programmes like *Life on Mars* make out – and in it we can find out much about our own lives, history and culture.

So this book tells a story about social and cultural change, but it is told through ideas and themes as much as chronology. The role of roads in cultural memory is not a subject that lends itself easily to a linear time scheme. Memories detour, dead-end and loop back on themselves like the most convoluted one-way system; and roads themselves are places in which the past bumps up against the present in unexpected and sometimes jarring ways. Sigmund Freud once compared memory to a 'mystic writing-pad', a children's toy rather like a primitive version of Etch A Sketch, consisting of a transparent sheet of celluloid covering a board of thick wax. When the child wrote on the sheet with a stylus, it left an impression on the wax which showed up as a black mark through the celluloid. If the celluloid was lifted up the mark disappeared, just like rubbing chalk off a blackboard, but a more permanent trace remained on the wax and was visible in a certain light. For Freud, the appearance and disappearance of these marks was like 'the flickering-up and passing-away of consciousness in the process of perception'.[20] Like the mystic writing-pad, the human brain could take in an almost unlimited amount of information, but this information often remained elusive and inaccessible.

It's a good metaphor for the durability and malleability of memory, but also for the road itself and how it gives up its secrets. A road is a bit like a mystic writing-pad, in the sense that its memories are buried just under its surface. Every day it presents itself as good as new, give or take a few traffic cones. But like Freud's wax slab it bears the petrified traces of millions of journeys – all those unacknowledged, routine lives imprinting themselves quietly on the tarmac. If Heraclitus had lived into the motorway era, I'm sure he would have said not that you can't step twice into the same river, but that you can't drive twice on the same road. People are forever leaving their marks on even the dullest strip of asphalt. I don't believe in ghosts – but I do believe like Edward Thomas that roads have 'goddesses that dwell / Far along them invisible'.[21] Beneath their glassy, unreadable surfaces, roads hide histories; motorways contain multitudes.

2

THE MOTORING WE USED TO DREAM ABOUT

The M1 ought to start with a triumphal arch. In practice, it sort of sidles out of Brent Cross shopping centre.

A.A. Gill[1]

On Tuesday 12 June 1956, in a low-key ceremony in a Lancashire field, Britain's motorway age began. Hugh Molson, a junior transport minister, pressed a button to turn a traffic light green, and a foreman fitter from Newton-le-Willows called Fred Hackett drove his bulldozer through a hedge to start shifting the soil. In an unpromising start to the biggest roadbuilding programme in British history, Hackett's digger ground to a halt a few seconds later. It had run out of petrol.

The shadow of postwar austerity hung over the first motorways, and the petrol shortage was just one symptom. Strapped for cash, the Ministry of Transport inaugurated the motorway era with an eight-and-a-quarter mile stretch to relieve one of Britain's most congested towns. It bought a strip of land just 150 feet wide, the entire width of the motorway, so the contractors, Tarmac plc, had to buy extra land on which to dump the spoil. There were other signs of make do and mend: the concrete spreaders were left over from laying instant airstrips during the war, and among the more conventional bulldozers there was the odd, recycled Sherman tank. The road was to be the first section of the M6, but everyone called it the Preston Bypass.

That Britain's motorway system began in Lancashire was largely down to one man: James Drake, the Accrington-born county surveyor and bridgemaster. Drake was the unsung Macadam of the early motorway era, a spiky character who spent countless hours chivvying Whitehall officials about the north-west's need for fast roads. The Lancashire weather remained unconvinced. Some of the heaviest rain since records began fell from the start of the build and the line of the Preston Bypass turned into a brown river of mud. If there had been eco-conscious road protesters in those days, they might have attributed it to the earth venting its anger at being violated by the diggers.

Against all odds, though, Britain's first motorway was completed only five months late. At 11.15am on 5 December 1958 – 'a day of national rejoicing', according to one newspaper headline – the Preston Bypass opened. The prime minister, Harold Macmillan, standing on a small patch of grass at the Samlesbury Interchange, assumed a shaky Scottish accent to quote from Robert Burns's 'Epigram on rough roads': 'I'm now arrived – thanks to the gods! – / Thro' pathways rough and muddy.' He was driven down the bypass in a Rolls Royce Landau at a sedate 40 mph and got out of the car after half-a-mile for a photo call in the middle of the motorway. Two hundred school children watched and cheered from a nearby bridge and Macmillan waved his hat. 'In the years to come,' he said, 'the county and country alike may look at the Preston Bypass – a fine thing in itself but a finer thing as a symbol – as a token of what is to follow.'[2]

The exultant mood was fleeting. Only forty-seven days later, the bypass was closed due to 'frost heave'. The ministry had skimped on the drainage system to save money. As soon as the motorway opened, it poured with rain for weeks and then the temperature dropped. The sodden foundations froze and, when the ground thawed, the road cracked. Only about half a per cent of the carriageway suffered, but it was enough to shut the whole of Britain's motorway system – all eight-and-a-quarter miles of it – for two weeks, while workmen patched up the tarmac. The Labour MP, Ernest Davies, said in the

Commons that this 'shamefaced closing' would not have caused such a stir if the opening of a mere eight miles of motorway had not been hailed as a superhuman achievement. 'It was blown up out of all proportion to its merits,' he said, 'and this ballyhoo boomeranged.'[3]

Despite its unglamorous name and the fact that a motorist driving at 70 mph could cover its entire length in about nine-and-a-half minutes, the Preston Bypass carried the nervous hopes of a nation. Building roads is not just a matter for surveyors, ditch diggers, blacktop layers and white-line painters. The process is so painful and protracted that roads have to be imagined as well as built, tied to a vision of the future that will bring people along with it. So a road is not really finished until the grand opening, the birthing ritual that brings it into being – and sometimes, as the Preston Bypass found to its cost, it is not quite finished even then. In the late 1950s Britain was coming out of a long period of depression, war and austerity, and the motorways were a national symbol of virility, a declaration that the country was entering the modern era. From the start, though, the building of the motorways generated a curious ambivalence, as the fear of being left behind by modernity vied with the fear of irreversible social change.

→

In 1900 the future prime minister Arthur Balfour had advocated 'great highways ... confined to the carriage of rapid motor traffic,' and the word 'motorway' was first used in parliament as early as 1924. Between the first London-Brighton car race in 1896 and the semi-nationalisation of the Trunk Roads Act of 1936, however, the total British road network grew by only 4 per cent. The head start gained by European motor roads, particularly in the fascist states, was a source of some national mortification and defensiveness. When Britain's first elevated road, the mile-long Silvertown way, was opened in east London's docklands in 1934, the transport minister Leslie Hore-Belisha declared that it was as bold an undertaking as Mussolini's plans for an Imperial Avenue in Rome but was 'the conception and the achievement of Democracy'.[4]

The 1937 Nazi propaganda film, *Schnelle Strassen* (Fast Roads), showed a group of British tourists captivated by a drive on the new autobahns. They were played by German actors, but many real-life Britons were equally enthralled. The former prime minister, David Lloyd George, came to Germany with his own ruler to measure how thick the roads were (25 cm). A 224-strong German Roads Delegation from Britain carried out a tour of inspection, in a visit arranged after the German ambassador to Britain, Joachim von Ribbentrop, was made an honorary member of the AA. Later that year the architect of the autobahns, Fritz Todt, was invited to London to inspect the traffic and be guest of honour at a special dinner at the Connaught. 'Among the personal attributes of the rulers of Germany … is a mania for speed, which has found its expression in motor roads,' wrote one dissenting civil servant. 'There seems no reason why this country, with its different traditions, should blindly copy at the behest of a delegation led by the Chairman of the Cement Manufacturer's Association.' But this official seems to have been in a minority. Two months before the *Wehrmacht* used the same road to invade Austria, the minister of transport, Victor Burgin, travelled from Munich to the Austrian border in a Mercedes Benz as a guest of the Reich, an experience he found 'delightful'.[5]

Compared with these new Pyramids of the Reich, Britain's road system seemed eternally belated, the epitome of national muddle and fudge. In 1938 the County Surveyors Society finally published a plan for a 1,000-mile network of motor roads, the blueprint for today's motorways. But it appeared in *Tit-Bits*, a magazine better known for its racy stories and pictures of women in bathing costumes, in a pull-out road map with the motorways drawn on in crayon.[6] Only after the war did the minister of transport, Alfred Barnes, display a plan of the proposed motorway network in the House of Commons tearoom. It was shaped a bit like an egg-timer, with the base running from London to Bristol (today's M4), the top from Liverpool to Hull (the M62) and Birmingham the isthmus in the middle. Since petrol was then restricted and almost all new British cars were exported, it seemed a tantalising vision of a distant future, like a grown-up version of children dreaming of sweets coming off the ration.

Throughout the 1950s, journalists and politicians of all stripes attacked the lack of roadbuilding. *Punch* had a full-page cartoon titled 'Road Race', showing the Conservative transport minister, Harold Watkinson, the first politician to spot the votes in motorways, frantically unrolling a tarmac carpet in front of a pack of snarlingly impatient motor cars. Between 1945 and 1958, the number of vehicles in Britain rose from 2.5 to 8 million and this new generation of car owners mainly consisted of skilled manual and lower-paid white-collar workers driving modest Morris Minors and Hillman Minxes – the kind of voters the Tories wanted to woo with their imagery of lower-middle-class aspiration.[7] The motorways also seemed like a painless political cure for the mounting frustration with Britain's ramshackle railways. Thomas Ifan Lloyd's 1957 book, *Twilight of the Railways – What Roads They'll Make!*, advocated closing down British Railways and turning the whole of the rail network into motorways.

In the late 1950s, there were constant reports of the Russians and Americans launching artificial satellites, dogs and monkeys into space. Christopher Cockerell's eccentric creation, the Hovercraft, was unveiled. Two months before the Preston Bypass opened, the first scheduled transatlantic jet services by BOAC and Pan-Am flew from London and Paris to New York. Both politicians and the press got caught up in this Cold War fascination with competitive speed and mobility, swept along by a visceral sense that new roads belonged to the 'motorway age', a terrestrial take on the space race.

→

This goes some way to explaining the feverish excitement that accompanied the building of the first section of the M1. Unlike the Preston Bypass, it was on the doorstep of metropolitan journalists and it seemed like the first proper motorway: a 55-mile section running from Luton to Crick. The ceremony to inaugurate the build was carefully choreographed; no more Fred Hacketts with empty petrol tanks. On 24 March 1958, Watkinson stood under a pavilion awning next to a tiny hamlet called Slip End, near Luton, and set off a klaxon. An armoured column of excavating machines then broke the skyline to the south and lumbered over the hillside towards the starting point, like primeval monsters, while another column approached from the north. On meeting each other, they lowered their buckets and started digging. The press notice claimed the M1 was the biggest piece of roadbuilding in British history. Fourteen million cubic yards of earth would need to be shifted which, 'if it were emptied on to a football pitch, would make a cone more than a mile high'.[8] The motorway builders, Laing, appointed a 'High Command' with a Newport Pagnell HQ where the walls were lined with huge maps of the route just like a war room. The military mastermind was the consulting engineer Sir Owen Williams, known affectionately in the press as 'Concrete Williams' for his design of all things concrete from beer coasters to Wembley Stadium.

The image presented to the media was of cutting-edge modernity, with helicopters hovering overhead and 'robot roadmakers' on the ground, concreting trains and excavating machines which the *Daily Telegraph* described as 'rooting and snorting in the mud', with 'flaming yellow eyes' and a 'demoniac dance'.[9] But the road was not, in fact, magically carved out of the land by machine. It was built by a brigade of 7,000 workers, whose most common piece of equipment was the RB1, or humble shovel. They came from every corner of the former empire, but mostly from Ireland. Itinerant Irish workers provided the backbone of motorway-building well into the 1970s, when a pre-Boomtown Rat Bob Geldof helped to build the first section of the M25, commanding a colossal T23 muck-shifter before he had even learnt how to drive.

There were so many Irish workers on the M1 that two Catholic priests, from Kerry and Armagh, were shipped over to hear confessions and say mass in the admin huts. Only a few weeks into the build, word spread that one of these workers had been buried alive beneath a concrete stanchion of one of the Luton overbridges – although some said it was at Tingrith, and others at Chalton. He had apparently survived and was being fed and watered via a tube.[10] Like the legend of the two riveters trapped between the hulls of Isambard Kingdom Brunel's ship, the *Great Eastern*, who made themselves known through an eerie knocking below deck, this piece of folklore reads like a compensatory myth to reassert the forgotten role of labourers in the building of the motorway, when everyone was making such a fuss about the machines.

Residents of nearby villages came with deckchairs and picnic hampers to watch the motorway slowly appearing. Since the bridges had to be built first, they mostly saw finished flyovers crossing a bare outline of a road or a mudbath leading to an open field where the road ran out. Before the road was finished, Lionel Rolt, who was writing the official history of the project for Laing, motored along it in his old, open-topped Alvis, switching carriageways to avoid obstacles and often driving on nothing more than levelled earth. An Irish navvy moved a big pile of earth for him with a bulldozer so he could pass; another cleared a path through 'the chaos of machines ahead, shooing them aside like so many cumbersome elephants'.[11] Rolt thus became the first person to drive the entire length of the new motorway.

It was meant to be finished in thirty-one months, but Watkinson gambled on cutting this by a whole year. Like the navvies on Robert Stephenson's London-Birmingham railway, built along the same route in the 1830s, the motorway workers had to cope with flooding over the Great Ouse and Nene rivers, and quicksand near Watford Gap – and all this during the monsoon summer of 1958. Unlike the railway engineers, they had to tiptoe around pylons, sewers, power lines, railways and other roads; near the junction with the Luton-Dunstable road, the old Icknield Way, a football field used by a team in the Luton and South Bedfordshire League was even allowed to poke its green corner into the road line until the last match of the season, while the navvies worked round it. Yet they still finished the motorway on time – an average of a mile every eight days and a bridge every three days. By adding up all the spurs and connecting roads, they could boast that they had built not 55 but 72 miles of motorway, even if the sums seemed a bit shaky.

Watkinson would no doubt have dismissed it as a coincidence, but speeding up the schedule for building the M1 meant that it was completed in October 1959, just in time for a general election. A Tory election poster showed a young family proudly washing their Austin A35 together, perhaps readying it for a pleasure drive on the motorway. Echoing Macmillan's famous speech in Bedford two years earlier, the party's slogans were 'You're having it good. Have it better' and 'Life's better under the Conservatives'. The motorway was a fully operational advert for affluence and social mobility. The Tory manifesto declared that the rising volume of traffic was 'a yardstick of rising prosperity' and needed to be matched by 'an intensive drive to build better and safer roads'. One critic later described the M1's southern section as 'the engineering equivalent of a Conservative Party political broadcast'.[12] No one knows how much the motorway helped, but Macmillan won the election on a landslide.

By then Watkinson had been replaced as transport minister by Ernest Marples – another grammar-school-educated, self-made outsider in a cabinet of old Etonians. A former bookie's clerk and property developer, Marples ruffled the feathers of fustier Tory MPs through his very unBritish showmanship, right down to his fondness for wearing blue suits and brown shoes. One friendly newspaper profile called him 'the star alumnus of the Opportunity State'. He was famous for his 5am starts, fanatical fitness regimes and passion for all things modern. Marples's house in Belgravia was 'as efficient a machine for living in as its owner's restless ingenuity can make it', with a high-tech intercom, air-conditioning and remote-controlled kitchen.[13] He organised exhibitions on the new motorways at the House of Commons, with full-scale models and maps with flashing lights. He was such a successful self-publicist that Watkinson's role in the building of the motorway – when *The Motor* magazine had hailed him as our 'Monty of the Roads' – was forgotten.[14] Marples became known, quite wrongly, as the man who led Britain into the motorway age.

→

Such was the media interest that the M1 had four press openings, each ending with a lavish buffet lunch at Newport Pagnell. The government's official statement boasted that 'the size of the road itself so far transcends the accustomed scale as to dwarf nature itself'. The *News Chronicle*'s reporter did 157 mph on the motorway in his Aston Martin DB4, the *Daily Herald*'s man clocked up 130 mph in an Austin Healey and the *Daily Express* correspondent cruised along in his Jaguar at a mere 105 mph. The *Daily Mirror*'s motoring writer gushed: 'I have just driven seventy-two effortless, super-safe miles – at high speed. Seventy-two miles which herald a new era in motoring.' This 'space-age highway', he went on, was 'so strange it was hard to believe that I was still in England ... The "M" stands for Motorway. It might well stand for "Magnificent".' Pathe News lauded this 'safe, fast and beautiful' road designed for 'the motoring we used to dream about', while one newspaper welcomed it with 'sentiments too deep for tears'.[15]

The day before the grand opening, thirty students from Cranfield College of Aeronautics, travelling in a convoy of eight decorated cars and four motorcycles, crashed through the motorway barrier at Brogborough and headed south. They were not there to protest against the road as their undergraduate ancestors might have done forty years hence, but to run a strip of toilet paper across it and hold their own opening ceremony. They travelled about five miles with John Michie, Laing's project manager, chasing them at 80 mph, until he managed to head off the leading car and escort them off the road as hundreds of sightseers, already amassing on the bridges, cheered. The motorway, Michie explained, was 'private property until tomorrow'.[16]

VIPs were given special passes to drive on the motorway to the opening ceremony, which took place near Luton's Pepperstock Junction, almost exactly where the bulldozers had first bit into earth nineteen months and nine days earlier. The Rolls Royce carrying the consulting engineers down to Luton 'blew up like a tea kettle' because it was not used to speeds of 60 mph. Shortly after 9am on 2 November, a cold and bright Monday morning, nearly 400 invited guests crowded on to the carriageway to hear Marples's speech, relayed by loudspeakers to all the motorway's junctions. 'This motorway starts a new era in road travel,' he cried. 'It is in keeping with the bold, exciting and scientific age in which we live.' But he added a headmaster's warning: 'On this magnificent road the speed which can easily be reached is so great that senses may be numbed and judgement warped ... So here are my two suggested mottoes: "Take it easy motorist" and "If in doubt – don't".'[17]

Police officers patrolling the access roads were told to make sure that motorists, desperate to be the first to drive on the motorway, were not queuing for entry. So a game of automotive musical chairs developed, with drivers meandering round the peripheral roads in the hope of being in the right place when the barriers went up. The AA's spotter aircraft reported traffic converging from all directions, with the Newport Pagnell approach road like 'Charing Cross at rush hour'.[18] When he watched the first cars tearing down the slip road from the Luton Spur roundabout, Marples is said to have exclaimed, 'My God, what have I started!'

Motorists drove cars well beyond their capacities. The AA was called out once every six minutes to tend to tyre blowouts and wrecked big ends on cars being driven too fast. Bedfordshire police had to deal with one car whose engine had completely dropped out on to the motorway. Many drivers did not realise that a car used up more petrol at 70 mph, and emptied their tanks. In Germany it was (and remains) an offence to run out of fuel on the autobahns; in Britain the soft-hearted police carried cans of petrol to sell to the improvident. On the M1's first weekend nearly all its overbridges were crowded with sightseers, with double-parked cars creating long traffic jams. The onlookers threw cigarette packets and toffee wrappers on to the road, in an imitation of a ticker-tape parade. Children formed a more bracing welcoming committee, dropping stones, clods of earth and bits of concrete.

The simple act of driving on the new road seemed thrillingly exotic. London Transport arranged day trips along the M1 in red buses and, a fortnight after the opening, newspapers gave front-page coverage to the Queen's first journey on the motorway, driven by Prince Philip in his green Lagonda on a weekend visit to Luton Hoo. The *Guardian* reported that 'for much of the way the Duke kept to the inside "slow" lane, cruising at about 50 miles an hour, but occasionally he pulled out to overtake lorries'. The *Daily Mirror* stated that the authorities had not been informed in advance, and that 'the royal couple were not recognised by other drivers'.[19]

But even in this initial burst of enthusiasm, there were mutterings. Thirty-six hours after its opening, a part of the M1's hard shoulder on an embankment had collapsed under the weight of a lorry. Still afflicted by an austerity mindset, the engineers had skimped on land and left the slopes too steep. Lorry drivers nicknamed the hard shoulders 'strips of death' because they were too narrow for them to pull over properly, and their trucks sank into the soft ground. Two weeks into its life, subsidence bumps appeared on the motorway, and cracks spread along the asphalt like crazy paving. Williams's heavy-looking bridges came in for some flak, one critic accusing them of 'the grunting for effect of a second-rate acrobat'. Soon the motorway was forming part of a more resilient national narrative: the ham-fisted, cheeseparing British bodge. The M1, wrote the architectural critic Reyner Banham some years later, was 'the ugliest stretch of motor road in the world'.[20]

→

If you drive on the first section of the M1 today, you can sense a slight but definite change of register, as it makes a diagonal dart across the gentle contours of the Midlands Plain with a Roman-road directness unusual in a British motorway. For all the fuss made about muck-shifting in 1959, the gradients just seem to ride out the descents and rises of the soft hills like a gentle rollercoaster. There are some bits – like the stretch through Watford Gap, the Khyber Pass of the Northamptonshire uplands – where the road is simply an endless straight line disappearing into the blue of the horizon. Or at least it would have been in 1959, when there weren't rows of lorries blocking the view. Even the motorway's curves seem a bit tight and grudging, short sweeps to link up the long straightaways.

In *Waterlog*, his account of a wild swimmer's journey around Britain, Roger Deakin describes driving home, after a revivifying tour around Scottish rivers, on the M1. 'I hated coming south,' he writes, 'and I loathed the unending straightness of the desolate, black motorways. How I had longed for a bend in the road – even just a bit of a kink – for some relief from the relentless efficiency of travelling in a continual bee-line.'[21] Deakin's dislike of the motorway's undeflecting line forms part of an enduring strain in English cultural criticism. Ever since enclosure commissioners realigned the old parish roads in the eighteenth and nineteenth centuries, running them along the new land boundaries, straight roads have been a symbol of political coercion. 'Improvement makes straight roads,' wrote William Blake in *The Marriage of Heaven and Hell*, 'but the crooked roads without improvement are roads of genius.' In his rural rides of the 1820s, William Cobbett avoided the new turnpikes because they cut straight across the land, bypassing the southern villages and yeoman farmers that he believed to be the true heart of England.

In the early years of the motor car, the poet and pioneering eco-critic Edward Thomas continued this war against the straight road, arguing that if we 'make roads outright and rapidly, for a definite purpose, they may perish as rapidly … and their ancient predecessors live on to smile at their ambition'. One of the first militant pedestrians, Thomas resented the bullying way in which the motor car was monopolising the highway and ironing out its creases, turning 'the road that sways with airy motion and bird-like curves' into 'a road cut by a skimping tailor'. Thomas's accounts of his walking trips along the Icknield Way and through the southern counties are a plea for aimless rambles along green lanes over the straight itinerary of the motor road, a search for proof that there is 'nothing at the end of any road better than may be found beside it'.[22] Thomas's prose, with its digressive mix of social observation, nature study and philosophical reflection, is the perfect complement to this diehard pedestrianism.

Thomas's contemporary, G.K. Chesterton, wrote a famous poem celebrating the 'rolling English road' that, long before 'the Roman came to Rye', went to Birmingham by way of Beachy Head. Chesterton sought to preserve what he called our 'splendid parochialisms' against 'motor-car civilization going its triumphant way, outstripping time, consuming space, seeing all and seeing nothing, roaring on at last to the capture of the solar system, only to find the sun cockney and the stars suburban'.[23] Like many liberals of his era, his distaste for the militaristic imperialism of the Boer War inspired a rural little Englandism rooted in the local and familiar, a non-jingoistic patriotism later echoed in the road protests of the 1990s. In his futuristic fantasy of 1904, *The Napoleon of Notting Hill* – set, like a better-known dystopia, in 1984 – the borough's provost refuses to let a business consortium drive an arterial road straight through the area, and raises an army to defeat their plans. The planned road bears a prescient resemblance to the Westway, the elevated motorway built through Notting Hill in the late 1960s.

Chesterton's rolling road may have been marked out by the 'rolling English drunkard', but the English road actually meanders around for fairly sober reasons. Old roads bent to avoid bogs, tree trunks and dead horses; dawdling cattle tramped out the rambling lines of drove roads; and travellers had the right to divert from rough terrain on the King's highway, even if it meant flattening crops, or 'going through the corn'. This made roads wide as well as winding. The Icknield Way is thought once to have been as much as a mile across, and on aerial photographs you often see the outline of a number of roads winding up a hill, only one of which is the Vulgate, tarmacked version.

Whatever the reasons for their winding, these roads came to seem like organic growths in the landscape compared to the utilitarian roads of the modern era. English lanes were meant to twist round corners, their views romantically obscured by age-old hedgerows or gnarled oaks. But after the First World War, in the competing interests of speed and safety, hedges were shaved, trees cut down, curves opened out and doglegs dekinked. 'The roads are anybody's and everybody's now,' lamented *The Times* in 1927. 'They are bare, open, shadeless and shameless, as shiny as steel and as hard as the rigour of commerce.' The new arterials like the Great West Road and the Kingston Bypass were often compared to the old Roman roads which, as Sellar and Yeatman explained in their comic book of received ideas about British history, *1066 and All That*, 'ran absolutely straight in all directions and all led to Rome'.[24]

In fact, the arterial roads, like Roman roads, were more direct than straight and they did make some effort to 'marry' with the landscape, a term borrowed from the design of golf courses, many of which ran alongside them. But they were certainly nothing like the rolling English road. 'Nature has told us, and artists have enforced it, that "Curved is the line of beauty",' complained the author W.H. Boulton in 1931, 'and a long straight stretch of concrete road, reaching away into the distance, is, in itself, anything but beautiful.' Three years later, in *English Journey*, J.B. Priestley dismissed the brand new East Lancashire Road between Liverpool and Manchester – a quasi-motorway planned to extend all the way to the Humber – as 'very broad, straight and uninteresting, the kind that chauffeurs love'.[25]

After the Second World War, these straight arterials were seen as symptomatic of the interwar era's reckless disregard for aesthetics in its unplanned pursuit of the modern. In his classic 1955 book, *The Making of the English Landscape*, W.G. Hoskins attacked these roads that 'plunge straight across the country, regardless of contours'. He reflected sadly on this 'England of the arterial by-pass, treeless and stinking of diesel oil, murderous with lorries', and urged his readers to 'turn away and contemplate the past before all is lost to the vandals'. As for motorways, Hoskins thought the less said the better, although he did later volunteer that the Pepperstock Junction, where Marples had unveiled the M1 in 1959, was 'a ghastly infliction on the English landscape'.[26] In the long tradition of English landscape criticism, the straight road remains a recurring motif of cold-hearted modernity. It is almost the reverse of the iconography of the American road, with its classic narrative of the road trip – which is all about escaping from the rhythms of mundane existence along the dead straight, two-lane blacktop stretching out into vanishing point.

$$\rightarrow$$

British roadbuilders were less philistine than the caricature suggested. Before the First World War, most of them followed the example of the Victorian railway engineers, who laid their lines in long straights, with short circular arcs used simply to link them up. Between the wars, though, road engineers became obsessed with working out the perfect transition curve – a mathematical method of shifting smoothly between a straight and an arc so that centripetal force builds up gradually, not suddenly like on a fairground ride. The roadbuilders swapped various mathematical formulae until, in 1937, the county surveyor of Devon, Henry Criswell, produced a set of labour-saving tables for plotting beautifully fluid lines that were so user-friendly they knocked rival systems into touch. Criswell became the undisputed king of the 'clothoid curve' – a graceful arc with a slowly increasing curvature that kept motorists permanently on their toes.

When the first section of the M1 was built, Owen Williams and his acolytes were still using the Criswell bible, a field pocket book for engineers called *Highway Spirals, Superelevation and Vertical Curves.* Each M1 site office kept a copy, along with some 'railway curves' in large wooden boxes, like giant pieces from a train set, which the engineers would play around with until they found a nice alignment. But fast roads had to be much straighter than ordinary ones: engineers calculated that motorists needed to see at least 950 feet ahead, the minimum stopping distance for a car driving at 70 mph. So Williams tried to make the M1 as straight as he could – which is why today it seems like an anomalous dry run, a brief interruption in the inexorable rise to ascendancy of the transition curve.

A small cadre of journalists unimpressed by M1 hype focused on its stultifying straightness, its unrelenting parallelism. The *News of the World*'s motoring correspondent advised his readers, 'If you have an old car, my advice is don't use it on the M1, for the monotony will break your heart.' The man from the *Observer* who, unlike his racier tabloid counterparts test-drove his own little family saloon on the M1 at a demure 50 mph, also found it dull and featureless. 'It is perilously easy to convince yourself that driving along a motorway is like riding in a train without a book,' he wrote, '– safe, comfortable, relaxing and a dreadful bore.'[27]

After the M1 opened, motorway designers began to worry that long straights might have a dangerous hypnotic effect on drivers, when combined with the drone of their engines and the drum of their tyres. They were especially worried about the high accident rate on the unbroken straights of the prewar German autobahns. One scary theory was that on an arrow-straight road the eye would be drawn to infinity but would have to refocus constantly to look at the road signs and other cars, making drivers sleepy. Owen Williams sent his engineering son, Owen T. Williams, on field trips to New York State to study Robert Moses's suburban parkways. Williams and son wanted to learn from the curved aesthetic of these roads, which could be traced back to the eighteenth-century English landscape garden, with its use of meandering paths in reaction to the geometric gardens of French palaces.

At a time when America was abandoning the parkway tradition for its unlovely interstates, Britain's motorway engineers began to bring this picturesque tradition home, creating flowing alignments that stitched themselves smoothly into the topography. Lancashire's motorway master, James Drake, believed that roads should be like 'sculpture on an exciting, grand scale, carving, moulding and adapting ... earth, rock and minerals into a finished product, which must be both functional and pleasing to the eye'.[28] But the motorway was really rescued from straight-line tedium by an unlikely saviour: the computer. Computer simulations allowed engineers to visualise the route and work out transitions without any need for railway curves in wooden boxes. The M4, designed by computer from the early 1960s onwards, is a gentle series of transition curves from London to south Wales.

But on Britain's motorways, pragmatics was always more important than aesthetics. The engineers had no carte blanche to remake the landscape. The M1 was fairly simple because it cut through fields: only five houses, and three bungalows near Luton, had to be flattened. Williams was said to have personally visited the forty landowners who opposed the motorway route and talked all but one of them round. The negotiations were still presumably more fraught than those depicted in Laing's promotional film, *Motorway*, narrated by the BBC newsreader Richard Baker, which showed some surveyors chatting to a farmer and sealing the deal moments later with a smile and a handshake. Like other roads, motorways had to take the line of least resistance – and, often, the line of least expense. The M6 was built in bits while the cashflow allowed. These sections were conceived and designed by county surveyors who, if they thought about aesthetics at all, saw the motorway as a way of promoting their own region. When the Staffordshire section of the M6 opened in 1962, the county council thought the road would serve as 'an excellent advertisement for the beauties of the county'. On the bus leading the inaugural cavalcade, a commentator with a microphone sang the praises of the 'gorgeous' route: 'And on our right, we have Trentham gravel pit.'[29]

At the end of the 1960s, Christopher Booker recalled this early period of motorway building in his book *The Neophiliacs*. Sometime in the late 1950s, he argued, Britain had suffered a kind of collective psychosis in which it became fanatically obsessed with newness. Man was seduced by an image of '"thrusting" motorways, vistas of glass and metal and concrete throbbing with a mechanical pulse and giving off an aura of inhuman excitement', swept along 'on a nyktomorphic sense of progress and modernity into a science fiction future that is nothing more than a creation of his own mind'. Nyktomorphic was Booker's own coinage, from the Greek for 'night shape', to suggest a culture unmoored from reason and reality, and consumed by fantasy projections and 'auto-suggestive illusions'. For Booker the motorways were part of a wider cultural desire to be 'with-it' and 'go-ahead' that infected everything from the mass hysteria of youth culture to politicians' emphasis on redevelopment and modernisation, their strident warnings about middle-aged complacency and stagnation.[30]

The motorways did feature heavily in a particular science-fiction future, albeit one populated by slow-moving string puppets. Gerry Anderson's 1960s TV series, *Thunderbirds*, set in 2063, often showed agent Lady Penelope travelling on the motorways in a souped-up Rolls Royce driven by her manservant, Parker. (The 1968 feature film, *Thunderbirds 6*, used the unopened M40 near High Wycombe for a live-action sequence in which Lady Penelope flies under a motorway bridge in a Tiger Moth – a manoeuvre carried out by the celebrated film stunt pilot, Joan Hughes, who was arrested for not simply taxiing under the bridge as ordered.) Beyond the world of puppets, though, Booker's phallic imagery of thrusting motorways now seems oversold.

There were too many pragmatic considerations in this crowded island – like maintaining access for farmers or skirting round bits of mining subsidence – to cut cleanly across the landscape or range a curve in an elegant circular arc from beginning to end.

Even the M1, now that we have got used to it, intrudes fairly apologetically into the landscape, a few bold lines cut short by self-effacing curves. Today it does a passable impression of a twenty-first century motorway. Owen Williams's bridges have gone, a recent victim of the widening of the motorway to four lanes. Naturally, those lumpish flyovers that everyone hated in 1959 were now regarded as part of our distinguished architectural heritage and the Ministry of Transport ruled that a photographic record be made before they were demolished. Then machines with cutters like crabs' claws came in the middle of the night to smash through the reinforced concrete, and the broken bits of bridge were swept up quickly and taken away to be recycled as hardcore for the motorway's extra lanes. The bridges that took a week to build were pulled down in a matter of hours, under cover of darkness, to minimise the disruption to traffic.

If you really want to return to the early motorway era, you need to drive north on the first section of the M1 and, at junction 17, take the two-lane slip road on to the M45. I can almost guarantee that no one will follow you up it. Unless you live near this motorway, you have probably never been on it, perhaps never even heard of it. When the first section of the M1 was built, there were no nearby motorways to connect it with, and it was thought that no A-road could cope with all the traffic from a motorway spilling on to it. So at each end, little motorway spurs were built just before the last exit, in the hope that some traffic could be tempted off before it all careered into the final junction. At the southern end of the M1, the three-mile M10 St Albans Bypass diverted traffic east. At the northern end, the eight-mile M45 Dunchurch Bypass shifted traffic halfway to Coventry.

For its first dozen years, the M45 was as busy as you would expect a road signposted for Birmingham to be. But when the northern and southern ends of the M6 linked up in the Midlands in 1972, the M45's traffic vanished overnight, and today it is Britain's quietest motorway.

A few years ago, BBC news online ran a story about plans to turn the M45 into a heritage motorway. The emergency roadside phones would be rehoused in 1950s-style blue cabinets, the police would patrol the road in vintage Ford Zephyrs and only vehicles built before 1970 would be permitted to drive on it. It was, of course, an April Fool, but it is not actually that far from the reality. With so few cars using the road, no one has bothered to update it. It is a Macmillan-era motorway preserved in amber. True, the grass-sown hard shoulders have been concreted over and the central reservation now has a crash barrier. But Williams's bridges are still there, arching over the modest two-lane blacktop, which has none of the modern impedimenta of chevrons, brown tourist signs or gantries. For a few wistful minutes you will find you are back in 1958, driving along that bewitchingly empty Preston Bypass, which was the same length as the M45, give or take a quarter-of-a-mile. This, you may think – at least until the road debouches you brusquely on to the A45 at a surface-level roundabout – is the motoring we used to dream about.

→

The M1 no longer plays such a prominent role in our national motorway mythology. The thrill it once provided now seems to belong to a remote era. Today the motorway system's most enduring symbol is the complete antithesis of the M1's undeviating line: a knotted web of eighteen elevated roads on a built-up bit of land north-east of Birmingham, called Gravelly Hill. Harold Watkinson announced plans for this interchange in October 1958, even before the Preston Bypass opened. It would be the motorway system's 'missing link', he promised, joining up all the north–south motorways to turn Birmingham into the centre of the road network – the Crewe station of the motorways. Finally opening the interchange in May 1972, the environment minister Peter Walker called it 'the most exciting day in the history of the road system in this country ... We are opening the motorway hub of Britain.'[31]

It was a rare moment of triumphalism in Britain's anxious relationship with the elevated road. Since the 1920s, roadbuilders had been talking up the virtues of 'grade separation', building flyovers to make sure separate streams of traffic never met. Modernist architects admired elevated roads as examples of the beauty of pure engineering unsullied by aesthetics. Le Corbusier's 1922 plans for his *Ville Contemporaine* envisaged the centre as a vast motorway interchange. Flying over the winding Paraná, Uruguay and Paraguay rivers in South America in 1929, he announced that the machine age would 'undo the terrible rings of the meander', before declaring himself appalled at the 'wormlike viscera' of São Paolo's streets. 'You have a crisis of circulation,' he told the city's prefect, who was rather taken aback by this unsolicited lecture. 'You can't service a diameter of 45 kilometres by making spaghetti in the labyrinth.'[32]

Britain's ambivalence about elevated roads mirrored its faint-hearted affair with modernism. In the 1920s, overhead roads began to be touted as the solution to London's traffic jams. An early motoring evangelist, Lord Montagu of Beaulieu, had a vision of roads lifted 200 feet off the ground, supported on huge piers, some of which would house apartments, earning rents to pay for the roads. Montagu believed that, unlike the ugly brickwork of the Victorian railway viaducts, overhead roads could be 'beautiful, inspiring, and suggestive of the immense, humanly directed machine we call London'. Most Londoners demurred, thinking roads on stilts not worth the loss of sunlight and air. 'Like the bewildered Trojan in the doomed city,' one newspaper leader put it, 'as we are confronted with the eighteen piers to the mile, we ask *Quam prendimus arcem*?' ['What citadel do we now occupy?'] Owen Williams, then a young engineer, proposed the opposite solution – putting the buildings on stilts, supported by steel or concrete columns, so the cars could drive under them – which seems like the definition of a desperate remedy.[33]

The idea of roads on stilts returned in the post-Second World War enthusiasm for blue-sky planning. In September 1959 the normally quite conventional landscape architect Geoffrey Jellicoe published his plans for the new town of 'Motopia', sponsored by the Glass Age Development committee of the Pilkington Glass Company. This town of 30,000 inhabitants would be built around a geometric grid of elevated roads rising 50 feet into the air, with roundabouts at each intersection, and the ground level reserved for public parks and canals. The sound and smell of the cars would, Jellicoe promised, travel upwards and be dispelled into the air. The traffic would be invisible from the ground, hidden by concrete buttresses and hedgerows. The town's residents could travel to and from work by water bus, and airport-style travelators would transport housewives between shops, located in weatherproof arcades under the roads. The motorist would drive to the roundabout nearest his home, veer down an incline leading to a mews road, park his car there and take the lift down to his house. Or he would simply land his wheeled helicopter at one of the heliports, fold in the rotors and drive straight to his front door. Unlike Le Corbusier's hypothetical *Ville Contemporaine*, Jellicoe's ambitious plans to separate 'mechanical and biological man' were designed for a real place: the Middlesex town of Staines.[34]

It is now customary to dismiss these postwar utopian schemes as unworkable or even dystopian, infected by a historical arrogance about their capacity to remake the world. But this reflex dismissal is infected by its own kind of historical arrogance, a suggestion that our forebears were stupider than us, criminally naïve about the world in thrall to the car that they were creating. In fact, many of these schemes were flawed attempts to manage cars and make life with roads bearable. With its gridplan streets and roundabout intersections, Jellicoe's town looks a bit like an elevated version of the future town of Milton Keynes – which is now similarly dismissed as the automotive dystopia of 'LA, Bucks,' but usually by people who have never been there. Motopia may have been no worse a fate for Staines than its current status as an unglamorous anytown, misread by the comic character Ali G as the Thames Valley version of an inner-city American ghetto. The future of Staines was eventually decided by its closeness to the M25 and Heathrow – which turned it into a kind of motopia by default.

When real flyovers arrived, they were not part of Glass Age masterplans, but the only practical way of extending the motorway system into west London. On 30 September 1959, a fortnight after the unveiling of Jellicoe's Motopia, the film star Jayne Mansfield opened the Chiswick Flyover – to the horror of the local Tory parliamentary candidate, who thought it a disgrace that this risqué American film star should be asked to inaugurate a major London road. Mansfield's star was on the wane and she was not the first choice, the racing drivers Stirling Moss and Donald Campbell having already made their excuses. She happened to be available in a break from filming an undistinguished comedy, *Too Hot to Handle*, at Borehamwood studios. Dressed in a figure-hugging magenta dress, she cut the ribbon with gold-plated scissors, blew kisses at the crowd and was taken up and down the road in a chauffeur-driven limousine. 'It's a sweet little fly-over,' she commented, perhaps more used to the multi-level inter-sections in America.[35]

The opening of the Chiswick Flyover did not placate those who felt that Britain was lagging hopelessly behind the rest of the world in the building of urban motorways. After a working tour of road projects in Paris and West Berlin in 1961, the Tory MP Edward du Cann returned 'with a sense of impatience if not of shame' at how many more flyovers and underpasses these cities had built. *The Times* asked: 'How far are we, in this motor packed island, from the style and planning that put Sweden twenty-six years ahead with Stock-holm's Slussem Cloverleaf or its Tegelbacken Intersection?' It looked longingly towards Düsseldorf, the 'paradise of the elevated road'.[36]

Already, though, the flyovers were losing some of their lustre as they became embroiled in political wrangling. Ernest Marples remained a major shareholder in Marples Ridgway, the company he co-founded in 1948 which was involved in much of the early motor-way building. When this company won the Hammersmith Flyover contract in 1960, the press challenged him over the conflict of interest. In a nod to the ancient road running along the chalk escarpment from the Dorset coast to the Norfolk Wash, this flyover became popularly known as the Marples Ridgeway. Marples was forced to divest himself of his shares – although probably not, as some history books have alleged, by selling them to Mrs Marples. One MP asked the minister whether he would see to it that 'before the opening ceremony the huge nameplates "Marples", which are scattered all over it, are removed in order that people can see the flyover?'[37]

In 1962 the new satirical magazine, *Private Eye*, an opponent of Dr Beeching's plans to decimate railway branch lines, suggested that the minister of transport was a power-crazed demagogue. It claimed to have intercepted a secret document detailing 'the Marples Master Plan'. The plan's aim was to run down every form of transport in Britain apart from the car. Useless motorways would be 'scattered casually around the country to fool the public that Something is Being Done', and before long the result would be chaos and gridlock. Soon 'the nation will be in Marples' hands. Then will be his hour. His secret army of traffic wardens, who have been in active training at the taxpayer's expense for the past two years, will take over all points of strategic importance. And Marples will assume supreme control of the national destiny.'[38] Even after Labour came to power in 1964, Marples remained in the public eye through the enduring 'Marples must go' graffito, painted in three-foot-high letters by a death-defying protester, presumably hanging (and writing) upside down, on an M1 overbridge near Luton. 'Marples Must Go' began as a viral car sticker campaign in the autumn of 1963, a protest not about frantic road-building but about supposedly draconian restrictions on motorists like yellow lines, parking meters and drink-driving clampdowns. After a while no one could remember why Marples had to go, but when the graffiti finally wore away a few years after his death in 1978, it had become such a landmark that there were calls for officialdom to retouch it.

By the mid-1960s, building an urban motorway had become a thankless task. As the Chiswick–Langley section of the M4 cut through Harmondsworth and Harlington, local youths stole a bull-dozer and crashed it, tore out the roadside telephones, threw stones and bits of fence on to the road and rode bicycles over the newly-laid concrete. Louis Hill, the project manager, looked back nostalgically to the building of the Hammersmith Flyover, completed in 1961, when new roads were more appreciated. (The eminent architectural critic Nikolaus Pevsner, not one for scattering praise like confetti, had called this flyover 'elegantly cantilevered'.) Hill found it sad that 'people will drive across the viaduct without giving a thought to all the headaches they had' – like the freezing winters when the concrete had to be kept warm, or the rainy days when the steel bars had to be covered up to stop them rusting. 'I made a special contraption for crashing a champagne bottle over Hammersmith when we laid the last beam,' he said. 'I haven't bothered for this one.'[39] The stories about men interred in the wetmix persisted, but took on a more sinister tinge. Underworld legend had it that buried underneath the uprights of various London flyovers were three notorious gangsters who had 'disappeared': Tommy 'Ginger' Marks, Jack 'the Hat' McVitie and Frank 'Mad Axeman' Mitchell.

→

One of the sharpest commentators on this new cityscape was a novelist living right in the middle of it. Even before these urban flyovers were built, J.G. Ballard was fascinated by the motorways, which started to be laid down near Preston just as Royal Court audiences were gasping at the sight of an ironing board on the London stage in John Osborne's play, *Look Back in Anger*. Ballard felt that the voguish writings of the angry young men were not 'responding to what was really important about society … The laying down of the M1 was much more important than anything Jimmy Porter's father-in-law thought about this or that. The motorway system had a much bigger influence on freedom and possibility.' On first arriving in postwar austerity Britain from Shanghai as a teenager, Ballard had been struck by how old and decrepit the country and its buildings seemed, a mirror image of the undernourished, haggard faces of its people. When he first looked down from the ship at Southampton docks he saw 'black perambulators like mobile coal-scuttles' which he eventually realised were English cars, pale shadows of the Packards and Cadillacs he had been used to in Shanghai.[40] Ballard saw England itself as a kind of fiction, caught up in snobbish, class-ridden illusions about its own past.

Convinced that his mother country was mired in nostalgia and kitsch, Ballard embraced anything that seemed like an intimation of modernity and of the more fluid expat society he had left behind. In 1960 he moved to Shepperton, a tranquil west London suburb on the banks of the Thames which, a few years later, began to be colonised by the peripheral landscape of the M3 and Heathrow Airport, an improvised zone of elevated intersections, transit hotels and multi-storey car parks. 'The twentieth century at last arrived,' Ballard wrote approvingly, 'and began to transform the Thames Valley into a pleasing replica of Los Angeles, with all the ambiguous but heady charms of alienation and anonymity.' He saw the elevated roads of west London as an antidote to the national obsession with preservation and pastiche, and in particular the stuccoed terraces of north London that were then being restored and gentrified by the frontier middle classes. These roads were 'concrete-motion sculptures of considerable grace and beauty ... an heroically isolated fragment of the modern city London might once have become'.[41] And no one ever thought of building a neo-Gothic flyover or a mock-Georgian underpass.

But Ballard was no kneejerk neophiliac. This new urban landscape may have made a liberating break with the past, but he also saw that it could be cold-hearted and isolating. The terrible beauty of the motorways was part of the twentieth century's marriage of rationality and horror, the capacity of technologies and bureaucratic systems to float free of their creators and destroy the capacity for human empathy. Ballard's passionate ambivalence towards roads was evident in a piece he published in the AA magazine *Drive* in 1971 about how the urban freeways were overpowering the areas around and underneath them. 'It may well be that these vast concrete intersections are the most important monuments of our urban civilization, the twentieth century's equivalent of the Pyramids,' he wrote, 'but do we want to be remembered in the same way as the slave-armies who constructed what, after all, were monuments to the dead?' For Ballard the motorway flyover was a modern manifestation of the sublime, in the literal sense of the word employed by eighteenth-century philosophers like Immanuel Kant and Edmund Burke: something that combined aesthetic awe with existential dread. In his 1973 novel, *Crash*, set in the

dense network of roads between the Westway and Heathrow, the flyovers 'overlaid one another like copulating giants, immense legs strad-
dling each other's backs'.[42]

A year after *Crash*, Ballard published another novel, *Concrete
Island*, in which all motorway lyricism is set aside. A young architect
called Robert Maitland suffers a blowout while driving down the exit
lane of the Westway, and crashes his Jaguar through the pinewood
trestles that pass for safety barriers. Since no driver is either inclined
or able to stop for him, he remains stranded for weeks in the triangle of waste ground between three elevated roads. The entire book is
set in this in-between land created in the impenetrable interstices of
the urban motorways, which fly imperiously over the people who are
trapped in their concrete shadows. (In real life, of course, these people
tend to be council-house dwellers rather than architects.) Unlike most
science-fiction writers, Ballard eschewed the use of time travel and
parallel worlds, believing that these distancing devices defused the
genre's capacity for political and cultural critique. His novels are typically set in a present that is both instantly recognisable and a portent
of things to come. Since auguries of the future date quickly, it feels
strange today to read these apocalyptic scenarios played out around
the humdrum west London flyovers, which now blend almost invisibly
into their urban setting behind a forty-year coat of grime and petrol
fumes. Perhaps that is why, when David Cronenberg filmed *Crash* in
the mid-1990s, he relocated it from Shepherd's Bush to Toronto.

→

Ballard's torn feelings about the motorway were really just a reflection of popular attitudes at the time. Indeed it is possible to read
the changing shape of the motorway interchange as a history, in concrete, of our growing disenchantment with these roads. Britain's first
big motorway interchange, linking the M4 and M5 at Almondsbury
in Gloucestershire, was a 'four-level stack'. This meant it had four
levels of traffic crossing at its central point, these curving slip roads
rising unapologetically into the air and making the shape of a Maltese
cross from above. Watching it being completed in 1966, the transport

minister Barbara Castle declared, 'These are the cathedrals of the modern world.'[43] Britain's next big interchange was at Worsley near Manchester, an elongated tangle of flyovers and tunnels linking the M61, M62 and other roads. At one point where several of the roads ran parallel, it was seventeen lanes across – earning it an entry in the *Guinness Book of Records* as the widest road in the UK. When opened in 1970 it was surrounded by churned mud ruts and embankments topped with excavated peat and colliery waste. It looked like a bit of Los Angeles had landed on the moon. The authorities were so worried about motorists losing their way that they erected 'find your way back' signs on the roads emerging from it. It was officially known as the Worsley Braided Interchange, but the men who built it nicknamed it 'Spaghetti Junction'.

Luckily for Worsley, this name was already bagged. On 1 June 1965, Roy Smith, a reporter for the *Birmingham Evening Mail*, had written about the exhibition of plans for the Gravelly Hill Interchange, describing it as 'like a cross between a plate of spaghetti and an unsuccessful attempt at a Staffordshire knot'. The front-page headline read simply, 'Spaghetti Junction'.[44] At the time, spaghetti and the motorway junction seemed equally alien to the British sensibility. Only eight years earlier a spoof BBC *Panorama* documentary had convinced millions of viewers that spaghetti grew on trees in Switzerland, and picking up the long, sauce-sodden strings with a fork remained a challenge to the British notion of table manners. But the main thrust of the metaphor was probably that spaghetti just arranges itself as a series of random loops and coils on a plate – and, despite the fact that Le Corbusier had once imagined elevated roads as clean lines cutting through contorted medieval street patterns, that is how haphazard and unplanned the new interchanges now seemed.

In fact, Gravelly Hill was meticulously planned, and its convoluted design reflected its long and difficult gestation. For a complex junction it was amazingly frugal with land, just thirty acres compared to Almondsbury's one hundred. There were tortuous discussions about demolitions, including a spirited 'save our fish' campaign that helped rehouse a quarter-of-a-million fish removed from a nearby pool. Each

section of road was of slightly different width, built to its own specific requirements to save space, so some of the road decks looked
more like spaghettini than spaghetti. Its chief engineer, Roy Foot, was
particularly irked about one concession to the pre-motorway age:
the concrete columns had to be arranged so that the canal towpaths
under the road had room enough for horses to pull barges.

Despite this arduous birth, Gravelly Hill generated a certain
amount of giddy excitement, even if it didn't quite match the febrile
reaction to the M1 in 1959. By May 1970 the junction was complete
enough for curious members of the public to be found on it. By September 1971 motorists were driving on it prematurely and illegally,
and children were caught walking along it on the way to school. Two
months before the grand opening, in a late example of motorway-
spotting, a Burton-on-Trent coach firm, Viking Motors, ran trips
there for 65p return. A spokesman for the West Midlands Tourist
Board reasoned, 'Four thousand years ago people would probably
have gone to see the Pyramids for the same reason.' The shiny new
Gravelly Hill Interchange also featured as a scenic backdrop in the
film musical *Take Me High*, in which Cliff Richard plays a merchant
banker mistakenly transferred to Birmingham rather than Paris, who
goes to live on a canal barge in Gas Street Basin. In a non-speaking
scene with a moody instrumental of Moog synthesisers and wah-wah
guitar playing in the background, Cliff whooshes along the canals in a
mini-hovercraft, admiring the new junction. Arriving in Birmingham
for the premiere, the film's star went rather off-message by criticising
the city's one-way system.[45]

'Check your petrol, oil, water and tyres, chaps,' advised the *Daily
Mirror* below an aerial shot of the junction in May 1972. 'And don't
forget your compass. This is Britain's biggest version of a new-fan-
gled invention ... It stands, or rather writhes, outside Birmingham ...
if you dare, you will be able to penetrate it for the first time the week
after next.'[46] There were dark warnings in the newspapers that choosing the wrong lane could send you on a 20-mile detour. Motorists
worried that they would drive round the junction in perpetuity, unable
to find their way out. The comedian Ken Dodd called it the eighth

wonder of the world, because 'you get on and wonder how to get off'.

In fact, not being able to get off Spaghetti Junction is almost impossible – however lost you are, and unless you insist on driving round and round the Salford Circus Roundabout, it will spew you out on to another bit of road soon enough, even if it's not the one you want to be on. Far from being the nation's motorway hub, all it does is connect the M6 with the Aston Expressway and lots of other local roads. When it opened it did finally link up the M6 on both sides of the city, but that would have happened anyway and the building of this complicated junction simply delayed it. If you are driving through Spaghetti Junction on the motorway, all you have to do is keep going in a straight line.

Reyner Banham, who had just got back from admiring the massive LA freeway intersections, did his best to puncture the myth. Spaghetti Junction, he argued, was 'a suburban folly', and all the PR about motorway hubs was just a ministerial joke, or perhaps 'the real joker is the Spirit of Brum Rampant, pulling a great local con job, the first successful civic ripoff at the expense of the M-way programme'. Birmingham's surveyor, Herbert Manzoni, had masterminded redevelopment in the 1960s, including an inner ring road reaching right into the city centre, and Banham believed that the junction's ulterior motive was to link the M6 with Manzoni's ring-road system – since the motorway could otherwise ('O rage and despair in the Chamber of Commerce!') have bypassed Birmingham completely.

Banham worked out a 'tourist route' coming from both directions on the M6 for those motorists who wanted to 'dig the kinaesthetic scene' at this 'agreeable little suburban megastructure'. By looping the loop round the Salford Circus Roundabout, which hoovers up all the local roads and feeds them into the junction, you could do a full sightseeing tour.[47] As Banham noted, it is really Spaghetti Junction's parochialism, its desire to link up with all the Birmingham roads, that makes its flyovers loop back on themselves so confusingly. Birmingham city council certainly saw the junction as an opportunity for local boosterism. Once it had opened, they sought government approval (refused) for an annual grand prix on the city's expressways, which would be cordoned off for the occasion in the style of the Italian Mille Miglia.

The hype surrounding Spaghetti Junction soon began to backfire. *Monty Python's Flying Circus* probably had the junction in mind when, in an episode filmed a few days before it opened, they imagined an eighteen-level motorway interchange built by characters from Milton's *Paradise Lost*. In July 1972 a local newspaper held a competition to rename the interchange and readers' suggestions included 'Jungle Junction' and 'Bowels of Satan'. Worried it was projecting the wrong image, the authorities tried to suppress the vernacular name. An official decreed that 'the term "spaghetti" should be strictly discouraged. It was the use of this nickname that helped to give rise to many fears about the junction before it was opened, which have since proved groundless.'[48] Soon the junction's bogus claim to be the nation's transport hub was cruelly inverted. The best thing about Birmingham, people joked, was that you could get out of it quickly.

But Birmingham's biggest image problem was that it kept hymning the praises of its road system long after urban motorways had ceased to have any utopian associations. As late as 1981, Telly Savalas was employed to present a half-hour promotional film, *Telly Savalas Looks at Birmingham*, which was shown nationally as a supporting feature in cinemas. 'Birmingham's road systems are revolutionary,' intoned the American actor better known for playing Kojak. 'The inner ring road. Queensway. A four-mile circuit of dual carriageways, tunnels and overpasses, linking up with the main arteries of the city and the Aston Expressway ... You feel as if you've been projected into the 21st century ... Yes, it's my kind of town.'

In truth, the spaghettification of the motorway intersection had less to do with revolutionary visions of the future than the more mundane problem of land politics. If you check out the bird's eye view of the Almondsbury Interchange on Google Earth, the vast acreage of land it has been permitted to consume means that it looks beautifully symmetrical, almost as though it has been drawn by a Spirograph, Denys Fisher's geometric child's toy for creating mathematical curves that was launched in the year it opened. By comparison, the later interchanges at Worsley and Gravelly Hill seem tortuously human-made and messy but still impressively monumental, like a piece of land art by Robert Smithson. Even before Spaghetti Junction opened, though, it was clear that the age of these convoluted free-flowing junctions was over, killed off by the prohibitive costs and land-hungriness of their generous loops.

The result has been the proliferation of that eternal bane of the motorway junction, the three-level roundabout interchange – essentially, just a fancier version of a roundabout where there are two flyovers so you don't need to enter the circle if you're going straight on. Yorkshire's Lofthouse Interchange, for example, was hailed as 'the new Piccadilly Circus of the north' when it was being planned in the 1960s. As the crossing point of the M1 and M62 it has a bigger claim than Gravelly Hill to be the nation's motorway hub. But to save on space and cost, instead of a free-flowing interchange they built an enormous roundabout. When the M62 finally arrived at the junction in 1976, there wasn't enough room for the cars and it started clogging up in the rush hour. You can't rebuild a motorway interchange from scratch without creating gridlock, so fixing the Lofthouse Interchange descended into a saga of Icelandic proportions. Today it is a mess of tacked-on tunnels and slip roads. But there is no accounting for taste, and the most unlikely bits of road can find themselves rehabilitated. 'Seen from the air, the ribbons of curving carriageway seem to interlace with the pleasing intricacy of an Elizabethan knot garden,' enthused the improbable figure of Clive Aslet, the conservationist and *Country Life* editor, about the Gravelly Hill Interchange.[49]

→

If you walk under the Gravelly Hill Interchange today, you may struggle to find any pleasure in the intricacy. You may indeed struggle to walk under it at all, since much of it is fenced off with signs warning 'No unauthorised people on site' or unpassable pylons crackling with electricity and notices saying 'Danger of Death: Keep Off'. At Salford Junction – the waterway in the bowels of Spaghetti Junction where three canals meet up in the industrial revolution's version of a motorway interchange – there is a footpath, an apparent invitation for humans to perambulate. But the pedestrian bridges climb so high over the canals that you are just a few metres from the M6 overhead, and the juggernauts drumming over the expansion joints sound like violent thunder cracks.

You can meander under the junction for hours and see some strange human remains – a pair of ripped hi-vi trousers, a Loohire chemical toilet turned on its side, a cuddly toy probably thrown from a car – but no actual human being. In the mid-1990s there was a story that the council had created a gravel beach here, with artificial sunlight provided by overhead pylons, and hardy locals bathing in the canals 'in a surreal version of Romans at play beneath the Pont du Gard'.[50] There is some sand and gravel there today, but no suggestion that it has been put there on purpose. Perhaps it was all a Brummagem joke designed to lure unsuspecting tourists into this unpeopled wasteland.

Considering that about one-and-a-quarter billion vehicles have so far driven over it, the junction is bearing up well. The pillars are brown with fumes and blistered by rain, and you could put your fist inside some of the cracks. But the 250,000 tonnes of Gravelly Hill concrete still look crushingly solid and immovable. The American environmental author, Michael Pollan, has written thus about concrete: 'There's no turning back, no melting it down to try again, as plastic or metal permits, no cutting it to fit, like wood. Here in a handful of cold gray slop is the irreversible arrow of time, history's objective correlative.'[51]

The Romans invented it, the French worked out how to reinforce it in the late nineteenth century and concrete remains the most heavily used substance in the world apart from water. But in Britain concrete has become an all-purpose metaphor for the planning disasters of the 1960s – not just the flyovers but the whole, related inner-city landscape of pedestrian subways and tower blocks. Many of the subways have since been replaced by footbridges, and the ceremonial dynamiting of high-rises has been a common sight in inner-city areas since the Thatcher era, with local authorities even placing adverts in newspapers, arranging seats for onlookers and inviting celebrities along to detonate the charge. Such theatrical demolitions seek to consign these buildings to the dustbin of history, along with a tradition of 'socialist' planning with which they are indelibly associated. The tower blocks had very obvious defects, from faulty lifts to mould on the walls, and one of them (Ronan Point) even collapsed spectacularly after a gas explosion. But the flyovers were, at least technically, a success. They did not crack up and were easy and safe to use. So they have remained, as a stigmatic image embodying the delusions of that era.

Concrete's reputation is now set in stone: everyone knows it is ugly, unkempt and unEnglish. Opponents of new roads and houses talk of the folly of 'concreting over' the countryside, even though hardly any British roads or houses are made mainly of concrete. As the signature material of the 1960s, it serves as the scapegoat for more complex and intractable social failures. The view from underneath a motorway flyover, with its takeaway cartons and syringes on the ground and its spraycan graffiti defacing the stanchions, is a sharp answer to those excitable images of virgin motorways in the late 1950s, opened by bouncy politicians on bright autumn mornings. Perhaps sometime in the future, as the musician and polymath Brian Eno has speculated, 'stained concrete and dirty steel will look rather quaint and friendly and welcoming, like exposed brick does now'.[52] But underneath Spaghetti Junction, this future seems some way off.

3

HATFIELD AND THE NORTH

The whole road system of Great Britain ... is, without excep-tion, the most awkward and absurd institution on the face of the earth.

Chambers's Edinburgh Journal, 1845[1]

Wandering impatiently through the self-indulgent shock art at the Royal Academy's Sensation exhibition in the autumn of 1997, I came across something so weird and beautiful that I nearly gasped. It was a work by a young British artist, Jonathan Parsons, called *Carcass*. Parsons had painstakingly cut out all the major roads from a road map of Britain, rearranged these slivers of blue, green and red paper into his own 3D map, and hung it upside down in a softly-lit glass case. It was as though all the country's skin and muscle had been stripped away and what remained was this skeleton of the road system, which was so dense that our knobbly island shape was immediately recog-nisable, even upside down. I wondered at first if *Carcass* was some oblique endorsement of the anti-roads movement that was then in the ascendant, but it seemed too subtle and understated to be agitprop. They looked so tenuous and fragile, those thin shreds of paper linking us all together.

A road map, it would be fair to say, is not normally a source of aesthetic delight. The problem is that it is neither one thing nor the other. Some maps are glorious abstractions – like Harry Beck's famous London Underground map, which shows only the various routes and the relative positions of the stations along horizontal, vertical and diagonal lines, a beautifully uncluttered cartogram with roughly equidistant points, and a very non-literal relationship to street-level geography. Other maps, like the classic 1:25,000 OS *Explorer* maps with orange covers, are beautiful because they abstract as little as possible, so their worlds are waiting to be explored in whatever way you want. Every type of road, from the dotted maroon lines of footpaths to the thick azure marine of motorways, has its own visual symbol and elegant typeface. Each line of tarmac is carefully slotted into the contours of the surrounding landscape, its gradients, embankments and cuttings tenderly delineated. No road has bragging rights over any other.

The road atlas, though, is neither a complete abstraction nor an attempt to document the landscape meticulously. It presumes to be an approximation of reality, when in fact it is reworking the land for its own purposes, replacing the country with its own distorted version. Villages become black squares, built-up areas brown splodges, forests a mass of green, and the Little Chef and IKEA logos are the boss of them all. Worst of all, the roads are a chaotic mess. Everyone knows that a city *A-Z* is a piece of propaganda for the road system, because roads are shown on a much bigger scale than any other feature of the landscape. But at least with an *A-Z* there is a certain logic to the street layout because cities are semi-planned, so neat squares and concentric crescents flow pleasingly into streets and avenues. On a road atlas, the roads go all over the place, to wherever the towns are, and the whole thing is a frenzied muddle of multi-coloured lines. Even before the inevitable moment when they come loose from their spiral bindings and the page corners curl up, road atlases are uninviting objects, forever associated with the mild panic of being lost on the road in the stale-aired claustrophobia of a car.

If you formed your view of Britain's geography from a road atlas, you would think that tarmac had taken over every corner of the land.

Robert Macfarlane begins his book about searching for Britain's 'wild places' with some reflections on our most common type of map, the road atlas. 'Pick one up,' he writes, 'and you see the meshwork of motorways and roads which covers the surface of the country. From such a map, it can appear that the landscape has become so thickly webbed by roads that asphalt and petrol are its new primary elements.'[2] But as Macfarlane discovers, this impression that maps create, that roads are brutal colonisers of open country, is misleading. The trunk roads on atlases are drawn so thickly that if they were to scale they would be hundreds of yards wide. Railways, meanwhile, are left as spidery black lines – even though double-track railways can take up as much space as trunk roads, and railway junctions and marshalling yards consume vast tranches of land. Roads, including the verges, make up less than 2 per cent of all the land in Britain, and most of these are local streets. If we viewed Britain from the air, we would see that dark satanic asphalt has not yet destroyed our green and pleasant land. The country's patchwork-quilt field patterns are far more conspicuous from above than motorways. For most of the time we do not have this Olympian perspective on roads, however, so we rely on the fragments of meaning we pick up at ground level. Our reading of the road depends on the flawed language of the road map and its real-life accessory, the road sign.

Another artist I discovered at the same time as Parsons was Julian Opie, who seemed fascinated by the tiny piece of the world we see through a car windscreen. He had done a series of roadscape paintings called *Imagine You Are Driving*, all subtle variations on the same grey road with white lines receding into the distance, surrounded by blue sky and green verges. The sharp outlines and block colours seemed to be lifted from an arcade racing game, as well as anticipating the aesthetics of satnav – that modern rival to the map that threatens to render roads even more unreal and dreamlike. Opie also did blurry, photo-realist pictures of the M40 at night that looked like action paintings: black voids illuminated only by the blinking taillights, cat's eyes and central-reservation lights curving round.

Opie is now best known for the schematic band portraits on the album cover of *The Best of Blur*. Each band member was reduced to his symbolic essence – two dots for eyes, two short lines for eyebrows, two dots for nostrils, two lines for the mouth and underlip – but the result was the opposite of caricature. Everyone was immediately recognisable from the flop of a fringe or the curve of an eyebrow. As the art critic Tom Lubbock noted, they were 'portraits in the style of road signs, as if people who devised hairpin bend warnings had been asked to turn their language of fat, black lines to the fine particularities of individual likeness'.[3] Just to reinforce the point, Opie went on to do a series of animal sculptures mounted on poles that resembled road signs in their styling and colouring – although they did not direct anyone anywhere.

Some people find Opie's work bland and unemotional, but I disagree. His roadscape and roadsign art made me look at the road anew and realise that its generic language was not simply dull and meaningless. Road country, after all, can be a bewildering place to navigate. The recent BBC documentary series, *Britain from Above*, showed this beautifully with the help of the GPS traces left by vehicles fitted with satnavs. Computer simulations mapped on to aerial photographs traced the patterns made by myriad journeys, satellite trails darting around like hyperactive glow-worms to produce mind-numbingly complex patterns. Like Parsons's dismembered map in a glass case, these patterns hinted at the strange beauty of our hidden collective life but also the sense that we live on a crowded, busy little island and that the road system could at any moment implode into anarchy. So perhaps in this confusing world there is value in blankness and simplicity, in reducing human interaction to a sort of visual Esperanto that can be recognised by everyone. A world condensed into the blankness of a road sign or the bare lines of a road map would be soulless and alienating in one way, but it could be rather enchanting as well – a world without the isolated anxieties of individual consciousness or the messiness of real life, where everyone and everything could be instantly understood.

→

At the beginning of the motor car era, road maps were romantic objects. The motoring pioneer, Lord Montagu, wrote in *Car Illustrated*:

> Before a journey the study of a map suggests all kinds of delights ... Thus we of the wheels think before beginning our tours ... For it is a plan of the earth laid out on paper, a diminutive reality, though miles are but inches. And the motorist who has a soul will dote on his maps, cherish them, and thus keep fresh in mind past pleasures and the hope of future delights.

Montagu compared poring over a road map to reading a musical score, sensing in the gradients and corners 'a stimulating discord or a soothing harmony, the place for a great crescendo or a passage melodiously lingering between piano and pianissimo'.[4]

British road maps were unusually faithful to topography compared to, say, American motoring maps, which showed the roads and not much else. The American west was only settled just before the arrival of the motor car, and the new national highway system was meant to integrate the disparate states. The bold-line aesthetic of US road maps helped this process along by inviting travel across the country, stressing clarity rather than topographical accuracy. British road maps were different, having evolved from the Ordnance Survey's famous attention to parochial detail. They were used by cyclists or rich pleasure motorists who wanted to explore the countryside. Bartholomew's 1907 *Contour Motoring Map of the British Isles* included an inset map identifying 'industrial areas to avoid'.[5]

After the First World War, motoring was no longer just a rich man's hobby and the system for guiding motorists became more functional. The Road Board had begun numbering the network in early 1914, just before war broke out, but it was simply trying to identify the main roads that needed grants to maintain them. When the new Director-General for Roads, Henry Maybury, restarted this work at the Ministry of Transport in 1920, he realised that numbers could also be added to maps and signs to help motorists find their way. So he ditched the original plan of having separate road numbers for each county, and began looking for a system to cover the whole country.

The obvious precedent was the French system of National or 'N' roads first established by Napoleon, radiating from Paris to the frontiers like the spokes of a wheel and numbered in a clockwise direction. The French system was patchy until the 1900s, when André Michelin, founder of the tyre company, argued that more systematic numbering would instil a sense of national unity and promote tourism. Michelin, who obviously had a vested interest in encouraging travel by road, claimed to have received a letter from a (presumably imaginary) 'Lord Jimmy' who insisted that, if France adopted Michelin's numbering system, Britons would flock there for their holidays. In an advertisement in the magazine *Le Plein Air*, Michelin asked:

> Why do rich foreign tourists hesitate to visit our country that they love and admire? Because it is very difficult for them to get their bearings on our roads that are so poorly marked. It would be different if they were numbered. France would then see the development of automobile tourism take off, and she would become *Switzerland*, rich and prosperous, as a result of motoring.[6]

Having convinced his own countrymen, Michelin turned his attention to Britain. He wrote four papers on road numbering for the Ministry of Transport – one of which suggested that 'the first numbers would be given to the roads leaving London in a northerly direction and then turning from left to right in the sense of the hands of a watch'.[7] With Michelin's helpful nudge, the British adopted a French-style radial system, with London its hub. So the A1 ran north toward Edinburgh, the A2 south-east to Dover, the A3 south-west to Portsmouth, and so on. Edinburgh was its own mini-hub for the A7, A8 and A9. These spokes created 'cones' within them, like the triangular slices of a giant pie. Each cone took its number from the A-road on its anticlockwise edge, and all roads within that cone started with that number. The closer to the centre of the pie the road started, the lower the second number was: the A10 ran from London to King's Lynn, for instance, and the A19 from Doncaster to just north of Newcastle. By 1923 the ministry had completed this epic categorising task and classified every A- and B-road in the country.

→

All taxonomies, in their compulsive desire to name and order things, betray the beliefs of their makers. Whenever people have imagined Britain's roads as a system, they have generally had an idea of the nation in their heads. Late medieval historians like Henry of Hunting-don and Geoffrey of Monmouth claimed that the 'royal roads' of Watling Street, Foss Way, the Icknield Way and Ermine Street were built by Belinus, a king who supposedly reigned in the fourth century BC, and who once led an army to the Italian peninsula and invaded Rome. Victorian scholars believed that the tracks that follow our southern chalk scarps, like the South Downs Way and the Great Ridgeway, were used by neolithic and bronze age people to trade and visit sacred sites. Current thinking is that these roads are unlikely to predate the Romans, and the Victorians were carried along by wishful thinking that the ancient Britons who built Stonehenge were also capable of devising a prehistoric motorway system.[8] Like John Cleese in *Monty Python's Life of Brian* wondering what the Romans have ever done for us, both the medievals and the Victorians seem to have unconsciously reclaimed Roman roads for partisan purposes.

The most audacious attempt to impose a retrospective pattern on our road network was made by a sixty-six-year-old Herefordshire businessman called Alfred Watkins. On 30 June 1921, he was driving along a road in Blackwardine, a small village near Leominster, when he stopped his car to look at a map. Suddenly he had a vision of a series of straight alignments of human-made landmarks and natural features 'like a chain of fairy lights'.[9] Watkins had discovered Black-wardine Ley, the first known leyline. His 1925 book, *The Old Straight Track*, argued that prehistoric trackways were built straight, using objects such as standing stones, tree clumps and hillside mounds as sighting points. He believed these leys to be routes for traders carrying salt, pottery and flint across a roadless wilderness, and that a learned caste of surveyors-cum-soothsayers worked out the routes – the staff-carrying chalk figure, the Long Man of Wilmington, being one of these 'ley men'. Watkins's theories followed his heart. He was a dedicated preservationist, deep patriot and anti-modern who had already published a broadside against decimalisation in 1919 titled *Must We Trade in Tenths?* He was as keen as any medieval historian to deny the Romans credit for inaugurating our road system. His book inspired an amateur army of leyline hunters and 'straight track clubs', sharing theories and arguing over what constituted a straight line.

It is striking that Watkins developed his theories at precisely the point that a modern form of geomancy, the road numbering system, was coming into being. Of course, this was devised by clear-headed, literal-minded civil servants who would have had little time for Watkins's romanticised communion with the past. But theirs was also an attempt to impose an invented order on a jumbled, ad hoc series of roads. If Watkins was searching for deep England, they were guided by the unwavering orthodoxy that London and Edinburgh were the centres of the known universe. Their road numbers spread out from the English and Scottish capitals like ripples on a pond, with higher, less important numbers the further they went. Inconveniently for the civil servants, though, all life and traffic did not revolve around London and Edinburgh. So this left a dilemma about numbering roads, like the A57 from Liverpool to Lincoln, that leaked across the cones. The sticking-plaster solution was to allocate a number based on the furthest anticlockwise cone the road entered, on the principle that roads proceed around the country clockwise. But do roads really go round the country in this ordered, well-mannered way? And surely the start of a road is also the end of it, depending on where you are coming from?

In any case, it was unclear why all the numbers had to link up with every other number like a sudoku puzzle. The Ministry of Transport seemed to think that this would make navigating easier. But no motorist has ever driven along Britain's roads by numbers. As long as each road has a number that is not duplicated by another nearby road, it doesn't matter where it begins or ends or whether the whole system makes any sense. In Northern Ireland, where they assign A and B numbers randomly, motorists seem no more (nor less) confused.

The road numberers thought they were being clinical and dispassionate. Officially, no road was 'better' than any other: what mattered was how it fitted into a system, based on the importance of the various roads as through routes and not on how wide or well-built they were. In reality the system created a brutal and self-fulfilling hierarchy. The length of a road's number was inversely proportional to its importance, so B-roads always had three or four digits to mark their lowly status. The vast majority of roads were not given a number at all, disappearing into a void of uncategorisability. If they were lucky they became C-roads, the minor roads numbered clandestinely by local authorities which were supposed never to appear on maps and signs (but sometimes did by mistake).

Classifications work best when they are fairly static, like the Linnaean system for flora and fauna, or the Dewey decimal system. The modern-day Linnaeuses at the Ministry of Transport did not realise that the road system is an evolving entity, and that the messiness of the real world would soon begin to intrude. As the roads developed, the numbering system had to be tweaked until its already shaky internal logic crumbled. Even if the Ministry had wanted to start all over again there was too much inertia in the system – too many sunken costs embedded in everything from road signs to paperwork – to go back to the drawing board. Often the numberers simply flouted the rules, through ignorance or cussedness.

The system may have lacked logic, but giving numbers to roads that had barely changed since the car arrived was a clever piece of kidology. As the historian David Jeremiah writes, it was as if 'with a stroke of the pen, Britain had acquired a modernised road system'.[10] The numbers created a sense of the roads as a self-contained country, a world with its own inner life. Road numbering was a shared language that soon became unarguable and inevitable. A road with a number could recede further into the unnoticed landscape of everyday life. Road maps also served as propaganda for the numbered roads. Red, once used to denote the most dangerous roads, became the default colour for the A-roads, which were drawn thicker to make them stand out. Road maps now omitted details like contours and spot heights. A bare white landmass replaced the green and brown shadings of topography. Britons became far more attached to road numbers than the French, whose system they had stolen. The route was now more than simply a matter of the destination; the road's number was as significant as the place at the end of it. On a road map composed of lines, letters and digits, the rest of the world was simply wiped away.

→

But a road is messier than a map – and even as Britain's road maps were being simplified, her roads were suffering from sign anarchy. Up until the 1950s roadside verges were like plantations of cast-iron saplings, a snafu of signs in countless shapes and styles, erected over many years by everyone from the AA to cycling clubs. The signs were also dangerously wordy, part of a national design tradition that is literate rather than visual. The architectural critic Ian Nairn complained that the 'British disease' of putting everything into words in road signs had turned 'the whole landscape into a legal document'.[11] The arrival of the motorways made sorting this out a matter of urgency – and the man for the job was Richard (known as 'Jock') Kinneir, a lecturer at Chelsea College of Art. Before the war he had studied at the same college under Graham Sutherland and Henry Moore, but after the war he gave up any artistic ambitions and became a designer instead, working for the new Central Office of Information and the Design Research Unit. He described himself, with an atypical flourish, as a 'visual engineer'.

In the mid-1950s Kinneir was building his own house at Ham in south-west London, and got talking to a neighbour, David Allford, while they were waiting for the Green Line bus to Hyde Park Corner. Allford was a young architect who had just won the contract to design Gatwick Airport, and after this bus-stop conversation he commissioned Kinneir to design its famous yellow-on-black direction signs, which became the BAA standard. Colin Anderson, chairman of the P&O shipping line, heard about Gatwick and asked Kinneir to sort out his company's chaotic baggage labelling system, which was per-plexing porters and creating lost luggage mountains. When Anderson was made chairman of the Advisory Committee on Traffic Signs for Motorways, he appointed Kinneir as his chief designer.

Kinneir and the committee drew on some sporadic research about reading road signs, mostly carried out in California. It suggested that a driver took four seconds to absorb the contents of a road sign, during which time a car travelling at 70 mph would have travelled 400 feet; and that the maximum safe angle that drivers could divert their gaze sideways to look at a sign was 15 degrees. As British motorways would mostly have three-lane carriageways and hard shoulders, the sign might be as much as 50 feet left of the driver's path – which meant she would have to finish reading it at least 200 feet before reaching it. So a motorway sign needed to be readable at 600 feet, and the lettering would have to be huge: at least 12 inches tall.

The first solution Kinneir proposed – abandoning the little panels within which place names were enclosed on the current British road signs to make better use of space – was uncontroversial. But his second – ditching block capitals in favour of a mixed-case, sanserif font – wasn't. The decline of the capital letter since the Victorian era, when humble nouns were often capitalised, reflected the gradual waning of social deference, and a sense that casing letters was a hier-archical impediment to natural human interaction. As the modern-ist architect Adolf Loos put it in 1920, 'one cannot speak a capital letter'.[12] Sanserif, the stripped-down font with no decorative cross-strokes at the top and bottom of letters, also had plebeian connota-tions because it was first used in low-church chapels and expensive shops where the rich customers liked the sales people to be aware of their inferior status. Edward Johnston's immaculate sanserif typeface had been employed on the London Underground since 1913 but sans was mainly associated with avant-garde cultural movements like the Bauhaus. In mid-1950s Britain, abandoning capitals and serifs was still a subversive act: when Oxfordshire's county surveyor tried out some mixed-case sanserif signs, he was publicly ticked off by the Min-istry of Transport and told to remove them at once.

Donnish in appearance and modest in demeanour, Kinneir was an unlikely member of the avant-garde, a very English modernist. He believed pragmatically that the tops and tails of lower-case letters, combined with a clean sanserif, would be easier to read at speed, but he also thought that the capital's natural authority would have more impact if it was used sparingly at the start of words. 'We've moved on from the Victorian concept of empire,' he argued. 'Notices in capitals are symptomatic of authoritarian government ... The Romans used capitals. They're appropriate to that way of thought.'[13]

Kinneir rejected the mixed-case sanserif on continental signs, like the German DIN (*Deutsche Industrie Normen*) used on the autobahns, as too cold. Instead he came up with a gentler version of the 1890s German font, *Akzidenz Grotesk* ('jobbing sanserif'), and named it 'Transport'. It was softer and quirkier than continental lettering, with more rounded 'o's, curved stalks on the 'a's and loops on the 'l's and 't's, and the curves segueing into each other almost like joined-up handwriting. On the early motorway signs, this curved aesthetic infected the tiniest details – from the rounded edges of the arrows to the wonky vertical direction line (now defunct) designed to stand out against the straight edges of the sign itself. Kinneir's team also fastened on a gentle colour scheme: zinc-white lettering against an ultramarine/azure-blue background, like cirrus clouds drifting across summer skies.

Road signs at the time were primitive stencils, perhaps touched up a bit with a paint brush. But Kinneir's assistant, a young South African émigrée called Margaret Calvert who had been his student at Chelsea College of Art, prepared the mock-ups with all the attention to detail of a Dutch master. First she traced the letters and numbers on to rectangular tiles; then pasted them on to drawing boards with cow gum; then cut the letter shapes out carefully with a knife and pulled off the surround; then rolled the blue paint on and, once it had dried, peeled off the letterform ('so satisfying') to reveal the finished sign. Testing the fonts and letter spacing involved 'a lot of squinting' in the studio.[14] They tried out the signs in an underground car park in Knightsbridge and in Hyde Park, propping them up against trees and walking towards them slowly, to the bemusement of onlookers. The Anderson committee then piloted the signs at RAF Hendon, all piled into one car with the former racing driver Lord Waleran at the wheel, driving as fast as he could along the runways. Finally they trialled them on the unopened stretches of the Preston Bypass and M1, driving at 90 mph in powerful police cars.

Kinneir's provisional designs provoked heated exchanges among Britain's typographers – particularly over the lower-case letters, which needed more space than capitals and which many thought would make the signs so big that they would dominate their surroundings. One landscape architect complained that they were 'crudely coloured and overpoweringly large' and 'give an impression of having been designed for lunatic drivers'.[15] Kinneir's fiercest opponents were David Kindersley, a distinguished stonecutter and typographer, and his friend Brooke Crutchley, the printer at Cambridge University Press. They had already collaborated in the late 1940s over the design of a font for Cambridge street signs, after the council had mooted a narrowly spaced sanserif – a foretaste of the future. Together they designed a seriffed capital font, Kindersley, which ended up being adopted not only in Cambridge but throughout the country, and is still used on many street signs today. That controversy only reached the letters page of the *Cambridge Evening News*, but the motorway signing storm found its way on to the BBC's *Tonight* programme, which staged a debate between Kindersley and Kinneir under the benevolent chairmanship of Cliff Michelmore.

Kindersley designed his own rival motorway font, in seriffed capitals. For a sample he took the direction sign for the Park Street Roundabout at the end of the M10 in St Albans, the one also used by the Anderson committee because it marked an entry into the motorway system from the south. Kindersley's sign was half the size of Kinneir's. He did some mock-ups and managed to persuade the government's Road Research Laboratory to test them. At the end of 1960, a group of volunteers assembled at RAF Benson in Oxfordshire. They were seated on a raised platform, about fifteen of them at a time, each armed with a push button connected to a moving chart recorder. A Vauxhall Wyvern, with a series of signs strapped to its roof, was driven towards them at speed. Each volunteer pressed the button as soon as he could read the sign. Kindersley's font turned out be more readable than Kinneir's, but only by statistically insignificant margins. Somewhat anticlimactically, the laboratory concluded that the different designs were all as good as each other and so 'it seems reasonable to make the choice on aesthetic grounds'.[16]

Committee member Noel Carrington – a designer and typographer now mainly famous for founding the Puffin picture book series for children – later voiced his suspicion that, while they spent two years arguing over lettering, 'the backroom boys of Road Research had it mostly sewn up beforehand'. Inertia also played its part in the decision. By the time the committee wound itself up in December 1960, the provisional signs had been used for a year on the M1, and for eighteen months on the Preston Bypass, and they seemed to perform well enough. Kinneir later recalled the ecstatic moment when he realised that the signs really worked. One evening, after a motorway committee meeting in the north, Lord Waleran offered him a lift back to London in his Jaguar. As Waleran put his foot down to pass the other cars and drove down the M1 at 95 mph, Kinneir was 'delighted to see the signs were legible when one was doing that speed at night'.[17]

→

Kinneir and Calvert soon moved on to tackle other roads, under another committee chaired by Sir Walter Worboys – a task every bit as urgent as on the motorways. In 1961 the typographer Herbert Spencer had driven from Marble Arch to Heathrow Airport, and photographed all the signs along the way. He discovered 'a jumbled jungle of words in a vast range of styles ... a remarkable demonstration of literary and graphic inventiveness in a field where discipline and restraint would be both more appropriate and considerably less dangerous'. This bombardment of prose, he complained, 'provides any driver reckless enough to heed it with more words than some novels'.[18]

Kinneir and Calvert's non-motorway signs had a meatier font but were essentially the motorway design in different colours: black letters with a white background for minor roads, white or yellow letters with green background for primary routes. This mid-shade of green, chosen to blend in with the flora and named 'Slough Green' because the Road Research Laboratory in this town concocted it, was a compromise between the bright green preferred by Kinneir and the dark green suggested by the Festival of Britain architect and Anderson committee member Hugh Casson – 'like the colour of old dinner jackets', he mused. The signs were piloted on a stretch of the A34 at Hall Green, Birmingham, in July 1963. At the launching ceremony, Ernest Marples said, 'I am anxious through this demonstration to get the frank opinions of motorists. We who have gone to a great deal of trouble over these signs may have got into a bit of a groove about them. Fresh minds may well help us.'[19] As with the motorway signs, this gesture at consultation was disingenuous. Once the road signs were up, they were unlikely to be changed unless they were a disaster.

Far from being that, these signs initiated an inexorable shift to lower-case lettering in British public life. London bus blinds joined the bandwagon in 1961, British railway station signs caved in by 1962 and the Habitat store pioneered the all-lower-case logo in 1964. As Crutchley later complained, the motorway signs also accelerated the rise of sanserif to typographical ascendancy. Soon it dominated every area of design and had even, he noted ruefully, 'found its way into our prayer books'. Although he predicted an eventual serif revival, he feared the motorway signs would remain forever, 'brash reminders of an aesthetically impoverished age'.[20] Now that all-lower-case sanserif is the font of choice for firms that want to seem trendily informal, it is hard to get inside the head of these fierce controversies. The signing war was a winner-takes-all game, at the end of which Kindersley and Crutchley's failure was complete. They had spent years pushing their views, made a thorough nuisance of themselves and failed to make even the mildest modification to the signs. There was, though, one tiny concession to those who thought Kinneir's signs too large. Their ugly backs were painted dark grey-green – the old dinner-jacket colour that Hugh Casson liked – to make them less conspicuous.

Much more was going on in these arguments about fonts than the

question of finding one's way around Britain's roads. All the protagonists were typographers, of course, and they really did get animated
about stroke widths and letter spacing, believing passionately that
alphabets were the lingua franca of all civilised communication. But
in the history of type, arcane arguments about legibility are often
about other, buried issues. The Anderson committee sat in the years
between the Suez crisis of 1956 and the Macmillan government's first
discussions about joining the Common Market in 1961. In his grip-
ping history of font design, *Type*, Simon Loxley argues that the end of
empire encouraged Britain to underplay its cultural differences with
mainland Europe.[21] There is no evidence that the motorway sign committee was under orders to adopt Europhile typefaces, but Europe
certainly seemed nearer and less alien than ever before, and pan-Euro-
peanism was being touted as a general antidote to national decline.
Opponents of the new signs probably hated them for similar reasons,
fearing an erosion of British identity by continental modernism – and,
more pointedly, with the war a recent memory, by the clinical competence of Germanic sanserifs. *The Times* worried that these 'coldly
efficient strips of metal' were crowding out the old British signposts,
which 'faintly resembled a hat stand and pointed vague, lofty fingers
down leafy lanes'.[22]

The sanserifists thought that road signs should fit the minimalist
aesthetic of the motorways themselves, and that legibility and beauty
were natural bedfellows. But Kindersley and Crutchley thought that
stylish serifs would alleviate the severity of the new roads. They preferred the sweet disorder of English tradition to the unemotional uniformity of European modernism – the dogma that the same lettering
should be used whether it was guiding passengers around an airport
or motorists along a motorway. But while Kindersley, as a stonecutter
by trade, had a natural empathy with traditional Roman capitals, he
was no Luddite. After licking his wounds over the motorway signs
defeat, he began working on a system that could automatically calculate the spaces between letters to ensure maximum readability. He
wanted to do away with the letterpress tradition of setting letters on
rectangular blocks, which the Kinneir signs had used. With the help

of the University of Cambridge's computer laboratory, he invented the Optical Letter Spacer machine, which located the letter's optical centre so it could have its own bespoke spacing rather than simply an off-the-peg rectangle. For all its computer wizardry, its basic principle belonged to the small craft workshop: each letter's uniqueness should be lovingly appreciated.

Most of all, Kindersley and Crutchley saw the motorway as a modern intrusion into the natural landscape. Their main objection to Kinneir's signs was that they were so huge they could be seen off the motorway. When Crutchley expressed 'horror at the size of the structures that would be needed ... as big as a council house or a two-decker bus', his choice of examples perhaps betrayed the residual anxieties of his class. In other respects he was before his time, this preservationist attitude being more widely voiced from the late 1960s onwards. A few years after the signing row, Crutchley became a vocal member of the campaign to stop the M11 skirting Grantchester, home to Byron's Pool and Rupert Brooke's Old Vicarage. 'Is it conceivable,' he wrote longingly in 1980, 'that Britain will ever again know an age when decent design comes as naturally as it did, say, in the days of Good Queen Anne?'[23]

Today it no longer matters whether Kindersley's serifs were a missed opportunity or a minor historical footnote. Readability does not occur in a cultural vacuum. As Loxley argues, the history of type is largely about the failure to factor out human eccentricity, habit and custom from the 'scientific' question of legibility. Jock Kinneir's signs now just seem beautifully obvious, the house style of the motorway, swiftly clocked without the need for a second glance. But success for a designer is cruel if it is measured in this way: by the extent to which one's work is ignored. When the BBC's *Culture Show* and the Design Museum ran a campaign in 2006 to find our national 'Design Icon', Kinneir's signs made a longlist of twenty-five selected by experts but failed to make the shortlist of ten voted by viewers, beaten to the cut by Grand Theft Auto and Tomb Raider. The eventual winner was Concorde, a crook-nosed, heavily subsidised plane used only by the jetset and now extinct. 'I think it's about glamour,' the *Culture Show*'s executive producer said. 'Seeing Concorde was like spotting a very famous person outside a restaurant.'[24] No one would ever describe motorway signs like this, and the search for 'icons' itself reflects a stress on fashion and nostalgia over everyday utility in the discussion of design. Kinneir's signs are certainly not 'iconic' – one of the most overused and misused words of our times. He has no blue plaque to commemorate him, no entry in the *Dictionary of National Biography*, and hardly anyone who drives the motorways has heard of him. But then, to adapt Wren's epitaph: if you seek a monument, look left.

$\rightarrow$

Even leaving aside the vexed question of lettering, the pedantry that went into designing the motorway signs was quite heroic. Anderson's committee spent days debating how the signs should be illuminated, how far direction signs should be situated from the slip roads, how many place names should be on a sign and how to abbreviate long names. 'Birmingham' appeared on almost every sign on the first section of the M1: would the provincial pride of Britain's second city be wounded, the committee worried, if its name was constantly shortened? In the end they ruled that truncation should be a last resort and a town's distinctive syllables should always be retained – hence 'Birm'ham', 'N'hampton', 'L'ton Buzzard'.[25]

Precisely because a road sign is part of the ubiquitous paraphernalia of daily life, its acts of naming can resonate with gnomic meaning – perhaps in a muted version of the belief in word-magic and the power of incantation that was prevalent in primitive and preliterate societies. Many northerners will identify with Jan Struther's Mrs Miniver, who always felt 'a stab of excitement' when she saw the sign at the top of London's Finchley Road for 'the North';[26] or with the esoteric 1970s prog-rock band who were so moved by the sign on the A1 for 'Hatfield and the North' that they named themselves after it. (Alas, some tin-eared official has now amended this to the less mellifluous 'The North, Hatfield'.) The north has no official status, so its appearance on a road sign seems somehow incongruous, as though this emotively cultural concept has been given a sort of legal recognition.

In fact, signs for 'the North' on Britain's roads have always been a matter of pragmatism, not poetry. When signs were first erected on the M1, the nebulous destination 'the North' seems to have been partly chosen to soothe the provincial egos of places like Doncaster and Sheffield, which were miffed that Leeds was being touted as the catch-all name to represent northbound.[27] (The choice of the 'control city', the name used as the forward destination on signs, was a sensitive issue because it was a free advert for a town and an implicit invitation to go there.) On road signs, though, the north recedes infinitely in the act of searching for it. If you travel up the M1, signs for 'the North' lead you all the way into Yorkshire; and on the A1, 'the North' appears right up until the last junction before Edinburgh. The definite article and capital letter have fooled us into thinking that this roadsign north is a place or even a state of mind, when it is really just a compass point.

There are, of course, signs for 'the South' on the M1 going down to London, and even the odd sign for 'the West' (but not, oddly, 'the East') on the M4, but the signs for 'the North' seem to carry a special resonance. The big north–south motorways, the M1 and M6, were built first in order to shorten the furthest distances on our long, thin island. We forget how far the north and south once were from each other. Before the motorways arrived it could take a whole, exhausting day's drive of ten or eleven hours to get from London to Carlisle. The first period of motorway building was a good time for the north, and the provinces generally. The symbolic north of the early 1960s – of Harold Wilson, new wave cinema, the Beatles, Granada TV and massive redevelopment schemes in the inner cities – stood for the degentrification of national life, the modernising meritocracy that would sweep away the old grousemoor establishment. The north in this period, in the historian Raphael Samuel's words, was 'definitely Mod, and on the side of radical change'.[28]

There was another important factor in this new symbolic geography. The first motorways were known by names rather than numbers – partly because the Ministry of Transport could not decide on the numbering system until the last minute. Right up until its first section opened, the M1 was the London–Birmingham or London–Yorkshire motorway, even though it stopped short of Birmingham and did not make it to Yorkshire for another eight years. Even after the motorways were opened, names survived alongside the numbers. When work began on the M62 in 1966, the county surveyors, James Drake and Stuart Maynard Lovell, tossed a coin on the Pennine border near Windy Hill to decide whether the motorway would be known as the Lancashire–Yorkshire or the Yorkshire–Lancashire Motorway. (Drake, who was used to getting his own way, won the toss and the former name prevailed.) Naming motorways as intercity or cross-county highways added to this sense that they were realigning the relationship between places. The psychological and actual compression of distances served as a dynamo of invisible social change. 1960s jazz and beat music owed a lot to the motorways, which transformed gigging by extending the range of journeys. Up-and-coming northern bands like the Beatles particularly welcomed the M1 because it made it easier for them to reach the audiences and recording studios in the south.

The road system was evolving rapidly, miniaturising the country. Seaside holidays were no longer limited to the 200-odd resorts with a railway station – the M5, for instance, played a key part in introducing mass tourism to Devon and Cornwall. The middle classes did particularly well out of motorways, which hugely extended their radii for commuting and weekend cottaging. As soon as the motorway opened, estate agents began advertising houses in Newport Pagnell as lying in 'M1 country'. Enterprising gentrifiers would buy up small farmhouses – the mechanisation of farming left plenty available – and then make a getaway down the M4 each weekend to the Cotswolds and Cornwall, or up the M1 to the Derbyshire moors and Yorkshire dales. By 1973, there were 200,000 second homes in Britain, many of them supported by mortgage tax relief and government renovation grants.

In 1962 Ernest Marples had announced plans to complete a thousand miles of motorway in the next ten years. This suspiciously round number contained more than a hint of targetology, but the target was met on time in 1972, a rate of building of more than a mile a week.

When the missing 'Midlands link' of the M6 opened that May, motorists could get the full benefit of this thousand miles. Manchester was now about three-and-a-half hours from London, and Glasgow about seven hours. Reyner Banham wrote that 'the much-maligned motorway system is finally beginning to deliver its ancient, almost-forgotten promises'. If you lived in fashionable north London but unfashionably craved haggis, he pointed out, 'Lockerbie in Dumfriesshire is the nearest source of any haggis worth eating ... I can now be in Lockerbie High Street within six-and-a-half hours.'[29]

While Banham may have been unusual in his eagerness to make a thirteen-hour round trip to procure haggis, many shared the sense of the motorways as a single, breathing entity. Newspaper editors sent journalists to drive the 304 miles from London to the Scottish borders and report back excitedly on this epic journey, made without meeting a traffic light or roundabout. The Midlands link included Spaghetti Junction and one newspaper headline read, 'I'll take the Spaghetti road and I'll be in Scotland afore ye.' Just before the late May bank holiday, newspapers reminded their readers that 215 miles of motorway had been built since the previous spring and that thousands of motorists would be 'setting off in the car to navigate the twists and turns of Spaghetti Junction' and 'Spaghetting away from it all'.[30]

→

Just as the thousand-mile motorway became a reality, though, the optimism about it began to dissolve. One symptom, or side-effect, of this disillusionment was a growing attack on the self-confident universalism of Jock Kinneir's signs. After the 1967 Welsh Language Act, which gave equal status to Welsh, the road sign became the symbol for a wider battle about making Wales bilingual. In the summer of 1969, members of the Welsh Language Society began defacing English-language road signs or uprooting them and throwing them into rivers. In court, they asked to be considered prisoners of conscience and sang 'Paint the world green', in a reference to the painting over of English names on signs. Their campaign began in the charged atmosphere surrounding the investiture at Caernarvon Castle in July, when there were even fears that a Celtic martyr with a bomb strapped to his waist might hurl himself at the new Prince of Wales. The chairman of the Welsh Language Society, Dafydd Iwan – a folk singer whose satirical record about the prince, 'Carlo', became a hit single in the principality – said: 'Our campaign aims to invest the Welsh language rather than an alien prince.' In January 1970, 600 supporters marched through Cardiff to protest against Iwan's imprisonment for refusing to pay a £56 fine for defacing signs. The Welsh Language Society focused on what it called the 'furniture of life' like road signs as the first step towards rescuing an endangered culture. When George Thomas, the minister for Wales and ardent defender of the union, warned that non-Welsh speaking drivers might crash their cars if they were confused by bilingual signs, the response of the road-sign militants was uncompromising: 'Let 'em.'[31]

In 1972 the government agreed to a progressive transition to bilingual signs. This was a smart move because it helped to defuse a much wider conflict which was spreading into the occupation of television studios and the harassing of non-Welsh purchasers of holiday homes. Thus began a so-called 'pedants' revolt' as the road signs committee spent several years deciding the correct Welsh name for places and whether the English or Welsh name should appear first on the sign. The story had a sequel in 1973, when an Edinburgh merchant banker, Iain Noble, bought 22,000 acres on the Isle of Skye. Noble was a Scottish nationalist determined to preserve Gaelic culture, even to the extent of advertising for Gaelic-speaking shepherds. He believed that language was 'a weather vane to a country's sense of pride and identity' and that to suppress it was 'spiritual genocide'.[32] When Inverness county council tried to buy some land off him for a new road, he agreed on one condition: the sign on it would include both the English and Gaelic names for Skye's capital, Portree. The council, previously a staunch defender of the Ordnance Survey spellings, accepted the bilingual sign on a trial basis. Once this precedent had been set, Gaelic signs spread gradually throughout the Highlands.

The Kinneir road signs belonged to a hopeful era of postwar reconstruction when the universalising impulses of social democracy and modernist design were at their height. The art historian Joe Kerr has called these signs 'the corporate identity of the welfare state'.[33] Their aim was simply to offer clear and legible directions to everyone. If nations are, in the historian Benedict Anderson's famous phrase, 'imagined communities' – countries of the mind, gossamer confections of flags, anthems and invented traditions which persuade us that people whom we will never meet are like us – then the Kinneir signs played a small but significant part in this imagining. Everywhere from Exeter to Perth, from Folkestone to Port Talbot, was now ruled by the logic of the blue sign. But after 1973, road signs were expected to fight symbolic battles that extended far beyond the road. Campaigners for Gaelic and Welsh road signs did so in the name of defending their ancient heritage, but they were also harnessing a new mood of regional partisanship and identity politics – one that the motorway signs committee, steeped in the paternalistic traditions of the Design Research Unit and the Festival of Britain, would have found quite alien.

People were also falling out of love with motorways, a mood symbolised by the 1973–74 oil crisis, when the OPEC countries dramatically raised oil prices after the Yom Kippur War. This knocked Europe and America into a massive recession and brought an abrupt end to the postwar era of economic growth – what the French call 'les trente glorieuses', the thirty glorious years. 'The history of the twenty years after 1973,' wrote the historian Eric Hobsbawm, 'is that of a world which lost its bearings.'[34] After the oil crisis, Britain's motorists were also in danger of losing their bearings. Ever since single-brand service stations arrived in Britain in the late 1950s, firms like Shell, Esso and National Benzole had sold maps at cost price, in order to encourage drivers to stop at their petrol stations. These petrol company road maps, used by almost all motorists, had tried to assert symbolic national sovereignty over a commodity caught up in Britain's murky colonial legacy. But after 1973 the public prestige of the petrol companies – who now had much less say over prices at the pumps but were widely thought to be colluding with the oil-producing states – went into terminal decline. The image of the smiling petrol-pump attendant, filling up a car on the cover of a road map, seemed instantly old hat. The self-service petrol station, another cost-saving device rolled out after the oil crisis, and made possible by the new type of pump nozzle with an automated cut-off, made buying fuel an impersonal affair. The petrol companies stopped subsidising their branded maps and soon the only people buying them were hitch-hikers travelling light, and even they preferred to get free maps from car-hire offices and Little Chefs.

In the year of the oil crisis Collins pioneered a new type of map that mirrored this attitude: the A3 softbacked atlas with spiral binding, also known as a 'floppy'. It seemed purposefully drained of automotive romance. Unlike the petrol company maps, which conjured up atavistic images of interwar motoring with their pastoral scenes of green lanes, floppies had cover images of motorway junctions or the view of a petrol station from a car dashboard. When the M1 opened, the junctions had been given bucolic-sounding names like Waterdale, Breakspears and Friars Wash. But the motorway system was soon too complex for names and the Ministry of Transport started numbering motorway junctions in the late 1960s. These numbers now found their way on to the floppies. With its pages of mileage charts, restricted junctions and journey times, the floppy reduced each trip to pure mathematics, its eyes trained solely on the number of the next junction.

The floppy's job was to guide you through this alphanumeric arbitrariness, for the motorways had almost destroyed any residual rationale in the road numbering system. True, England and Wales were roughly quartered by the M1, M2, M3 and M4 coming out of London – but there the similarity to the A-road pie-slices ended, because major motorways like the M5 and M6 did not go anywhere near the capital. The logic of the numbering system disintegrated further as A-roads alongside the motorways were gradually 'de-trunked' and renumbered, probably to persuade motorists to use the motorways instead. After the M40 was finished in 1991, one of the longest A-roads in the country was broken up overnight when a bit of the A34 between Oxford and Birmingham was cruelly downgraded to the A3400. Lots of old A-roads now have these renumbered bits, stranded from the trunk road system like asphalt versions of oxbow lakes. They do not quite have the pathos of the untarred roads that Edward Thomas eulogised, 'wiped out as if writ in water' when the new motoring roads passed them by,[35] for these renumbered A-roads are still needed to soak up a few cars from the crowded motorways. But their unceremonious demotion is another snub to the 1922 road numberers – another sign that the road system is a living thing, an endless work-in-progress that can't be pinned down and classified like a butterfly in a glass case.

$$\rightarrow$$

Road numbering still retains an enticing sense of partial order. The circular pie is still there, the numbers roughly fit into their cones, and most new roads are classified according to some vague approximation of the original 1922 rules. People still valiantly search for meaning in the numbering system. On the online discussion forum of SABRE, the Society for All British Road Enthusiasts, the 1400-odd Sabristi often debate about where the M25 starts and whether it is correctly numbered, or why the motorway from Carlisle to Glasgow is called both the M74 and the A74(M). In road-numbering lore, the absence of pattern – the discovery that there are so many exceptions to rules that the rules might as well not exist – only seems to revivify the search for inner mysteries. Road buffs talk in reverential tones about 'David Craig Numbers' – the elegant theory, named after the man who proposed it, that three digit numbers derive from the roads they connect. Despite a number of teasing examples, like the M621 which links the M62 to the M1 through Leeds, everyone knows the theory is wrong, but they carry on looking for evidence in any case.

Road-numbering lore seems to satisfy what the biologist Lewis Wolpert calls our inbuilt 'belief engine'.[36] As part of our evolutionary adaptation, he claims, humans are programmed to find order in chaos, to confuse correlation with causation. Roads appeal to this desire for pattern and symmetry because they make up a satisfyingly complex system in which every part is ultimately if tortuously connected to every other part. Road-number connoisseurs seem to be guided in their search for meaning by a love of the idiosyncratic – the forgotten C-road, the short, stumpy motorway left over from some grand project that never got built, the road with a number that seems to follow no rules – over the bland, easily navigable trunk routes approved by the Highways Agency. Their motivations seem far removed from the mechanistic list-making and ticking-off of trainspotters; they have more in common with birdwatchers, whose tribal subcultures place a similarly high value on seeking out the unusual and exotic.

In many ways, though, road-numbering lore reads like a more knowing, ironic version of leyline hunting, which has enjoyed a strange, post-Watkins afterlife. After the Second World War, the leyline clubs disbanded and leys were largely forgotten, many landmarks that Watkins identified having been removed when roads were widened. A more serious problem was that leyline theory was complete rubbish, easily refuted by statistical analyses of the high likelihood of finding straight lines between random sets of points. But leylines returned to prominence in 1969 with John Michell's cult book, *The View over Atlantis*. Michell was an old Etonian, ex-estate agent and Notting Hill friend of the Rolling Stones, whose ideas about Glastonbury inspired the creation of the annual festival there. He set about redrawing leylines for the dawning Age of Aquarius, imagining them as a forgotten system for manipulating energy flows, a form of spiritual engineering dating back to ancient times.

Watkins's *The Old Straight Track*, out of print for years, was reissued in 1970 and a new generation of leyline enthusiasts, influenced by the alternative lifestyles of the age, was born. Some compared leys to Aboriginal dreaming tracks or the dragon lines in Chinese feng shui; others believed they were a secret system of motorways for UFOs, flight paths directing extraterrestrials around the planet through magnetic currents; still others thought they were conduits for spirits of the dead who liked to travel in straight lines. Alfred Watkins would have given short shrift to this new-age, crystal-dangling guesswork. His leylines were not energy fields; they were prototypes of those stubbornly human artefacts, roads. In the countercultural reworking of leyline philosophy, though, the significance of roads tends to be underplayed. According to Michell, Watkins was not in his car looking at a map on that fateful day in June 1921, but on a high hilltop meditating on the view, so that 'in one moment of transcendental perception' he 'entered a magic world of prehistoric Britain, a world whose very existence had been forgotten'.[37] It may be that modern leyline thought mistrusts roads as a manifestation of over-rationalised, over-engineered modernity – the questioning of which lies at the heart of the counterculture. Michell went on to run the Anti-Metrication Board (shades of Watkins's disdain for decimals), write books about numerology and astro-archaeology, and edit the *Cereologist*, a journal about crop circles.

But in the work of the novelist and psychogeographer Iain Sinclair, the most original and inventive contemporary exponent of leylines, roads have made a comeback as purveyors of runic meaning. His books explore the mythology of ancient force fields as a way of symbolically countering a modern, corporate culture of loft-style apartments, retail parks and Millennium Domes. Roads feature ambivalently in this anarchist-leftist take on the leyline, perhaps because they are both ancient *and* modern. They may colonise common land and steam-roller over local eccentricity, but roads can still be repositories of hidden histories, 'peripatetic museums'. For Sinclair, the M25 and its environs are a 'grim necklace' that chokes the life out of London, but also a haunted hinterland that hoovers up occult sites like abandoned asylums, ex-military bases and overgrown graveyards. His favourite road, the A13, which runs from London's Docklands through the Essex badlands, is 'a semi-celestial highway, a Blakean transit to a higher mythology'. And he points out that the inventor of the leyline, Alfred Watkins, first got to know the Herefordshire roads and countryside as a regional sales rep for his family's brewing business. 'If he were still in the game,' Sinclair speculates, 'he'd be jockeying a Ford Mondeo around the motorway system, stumbling on the karma of the M25, speculating on London's orbital road as a prayer wheel, a dream-generator on which the psychic health of the city depended.'[38]

→

For those still unmoved by leylines or road-numbering lore, there is a device that seems like a perfect solution to the descent of the British road system into today's senseless disorder of unrelated letters and numbers. Like all technologies, in-car navigation likes to imagine itself as startlingly innovative, but it is really a number of older inventions cobbled together. It is also a return to the oldest means of wayfinding on the roads, the itinerary. The earliest road atlases were strip maps covering set routes and the 'auto photo guides' produced in the early days of motoring were books showing pictures of landmarks with arrows drawn on and instructions like 'turn west' or 'turn north' – like satnav in analogue form.

One of the earliest in-car navigation systems was the Jones Live-Map, patented by an American engineer in 1909. It was a turntable with a pointer on which the driver placed paper disks for individual routes. Using a variation on the old nautical method of dead reckoning, it measured distance and direction through a cable connected to the front wheels and moved the pointer to the relevant instructions printed on the paper disk. 'This miracle of technology,' boasted the advert, 'displays for the motorist every road, every corner, every crossing, every landmark, every puzzling fork and crossroad in the whole world.'[39] The Chadwick Road Guide of 1910 was a similar device that even promised to warn the driver about rough roads and speed traps. On early boneshaker cars and bumpy roads, with no opportunity for mid-course corrections, these machines must have been next to useless.

The earliest computerised in-car navigation was developed in Japan, which has an even more impenetrable road system than Britain's, with many city streets unnamed. In 1981 Honda introduced the 'Electro Gyrocator' as an option for the Accord. Using a gyroscope and odometer, it worked out the car's position and displayed it as a moving white dot on a tiny cathode-ray tube monitor, over which the driver would slot a transparent map of each area. Its relationship to the modern satnav is rather like that of the primeval computer game, Pong, to the sumptuous virtual world of Grand Theft Auto. The Electro Gyrocator was not much better than the paper disks and pointers of the early motoring era. Like them it was a solid-state system that could not respond to the changing narrative of the drive, so if you went wrong the errors soon stacked up and, unlike a broken watch, it would not even be right some of the time.

Meanwhile, the EU was plying the European car industry with huge subsidies to develop in-car navigational projects with classical-sounding names like Demeter (Digital Electronic Mapping of European Territory) and Ariadne (Application of a Real-time Aid for Driving and Navigation). The EU was willing to fund these projects because the dream of greater European unity had long been founded on the vision of a pan-continental road network. After the war, the United Nations Economic Commission for Europe fleshed out plans for a system of continental 'superhighways', built to standard specs. By the mid-1960s, twenty-one European countries had agreed to create an E-road network stretching from Scotland to the Turkish-Iranian frontier and from Portugal to the Iron Curtain. In mainland Europe these routes were often signposted, and the idea of transcontinental roads was perhaps not such a big leap for people who could already cross the continent from the great European railway stations. But most British drivers had little notion (and almost certainly still don't) that the M4 forms part of the E30 running from Cork to Moscow, or that the M62 is also the E20 from Shannon to St Petersburg. For the Eurocrats near the heart of this network, in-car navigation had the potential to turn these virtual routes into actual journeys, by guiding motorists along unfamiliar roads and past baffling signs. To be of real use for such long, complex journeys, however, they knew that it would be necessary to develop a real-time system with a live digital map in the car.

But the first company to map Britain's roads digitally did so without the aid of any government subsidy. It was a tiny firm, Next-Base, which grew out of a circle of friends who met as teenagers, programming some of the earliest home PCs at a school holiday computer camp in Northampton. In 1988, working from a friend's spare bedroom in the Surrey stockbroker suburb of Esher, they created the AutoRoute journey planner, a complete digital road map of Britain.

Three years later, about 100,000 copies were in circulation, many of them pirated. AutoRoute could work out any journey and calculate the time it would take and distance travelled. But it was only a desktop version – you had to do all this on your PC and then print out the instructions and take them to your car. Its main selling point was working out mileage, so it appealed to hauliers and sales reps who wanted to save on petrol, and the BBC and Customs and Excise who used it to check up on their employees' expenses claims.

If digital maps were to have a wider impact, there had to be some way of combining them with knowing where you were on the road at each point. Fortunately, this technology already existed: a variation on the sailor's time-honoured method of navigation, with its origins in the space race. The US Defense Department had developed GPS (global positioning by satellite) in response to the Soviet launch of Sputnik in 1957. In traditional navigation, you calculate your position by observing the sun and stars: since speed, time and distance are related values, you can work out one of them if you know the other two. GPS worked on the same principle, except it used satellites instead of stars and the GPS receivers did the algebraic calculations automatically. By 1964 the American navy had a system up and running called Transit, with five satellites orbiting the earth, which was only enough to give each spot on the earth a 'fix' about every hour-and-a-half. At best, it was accurate to within 500 metres, good enough to interest pilots and yacht owners, but no use on roads. Then, in the early 1980s, the Pentagon began developing the Navstar Global Positioning System. When the Russians shot down a Korean passenger airliner in 1983 after it accidentally drifted into their airspace, creating a tense standoff between the US and USSR, President Reagan decided to help prevent such incidents in future by making Navstar freely available for non-military use. By 1988 Navstar was a workable system of eighteen satellites orbiting 11,000 nautical miles above the earth, ensuring that at least three satellites would be accessible anywhere in the world – giving enough detail to pinpoint a vehicle's location on a road.

Meanwhile, a Silicon Valley company called Trimble Navigation had teamed up with Pioneer Electronics of Japan to develop the commercial use of satnav – showing a touching faith in the generosity of the Pentagon, who could have stopped transmitting the satellite signal any time and sunk their investment. In 1989 they developed AVIC-1, a satnav system that mapped the entire road system of Japan. The *Independent*'s technology correspondent dismissed it as 'one of the silliest new products in years'. Compared to an atlas costing a fraction of its £1,250 price, he noted, it was difficult to see in sunlight, dangerous to consult when driving and annoying for people who wanted to check where they were going instead of where they were.[40] Proof of its gimmickry lay in the fact that it came with an integral in-car karaoke system, complete with hands-free microphone. During the first Gulf War of 1991, though, American troops used portable GPS receivers to find their way across the shifting sands of the roadless Iraqi desert – and the daily media updates on the war, with soldiers pointing at moving satellite images, put satnav in a global shop window.

Soon afterwards BMW began putting satnavs in its top-of-the-range models, and these cars first arrived in Britain at the 1996 Motor Show in Birmingham. The promo for BMW's Philips CarIn system showed a businessman navigating his way from central London to Watford – beyond which it was 'here be dragons', because the digital maps did not yet reach beyond the M25. Another snag was that Navstar emerged at the end of the Cold War and the Pentagon did not want to lay on a free navigational service for the Russians. So while the Americans made the signal available to everyone, they introduced random errors of up to 100 metres. Until Bill Clinton unscrambled the signal in 2000 after lobbying from the motor industry, satnavs had to rely partly on compass readings and wheel sensors. This meant that early systems were a bit slow on the uptake, telling you about a turning just after you had passed it, like the unhelpful passenger-seat mapreader who gives you instructions in the past tense ('We should have turned left there').

The cultural critic Donna Haraway has invented a term to describe modern technologies that combine human and machine-like qualities: 'cyborgs', short for cybernetic organisms. Cyborgs exert an uneasy fascination on us because they challenge our long-held belief that all humans are unique and unreproducible. In the case of satnav, this uneasiness centres on the voice prompts that say 'take the first left' or 'at the roundabout take the second exit'. Most speech synthesisers use female voices because they are easier to distinguish from engine noise and road rumble – and British satnavs have rather clipped, bell-like, head-girlish voices, provided by the same actresses who do railway station announcements and audio book readings. Two of the early satnav voices were Susan Skipper, who appeared as Nigel Havers's posh girlfriend in the 1980s sitcom *Don't Wait Up*; and Eve Karpf, who voice-dubbed the famous line in the Ferrero Rocher commercial ('Monsieur, with these Rocher, you're really spoiling us').

By coincidence, satnav emerged around the same time that socio-biologists and evolutionary psychologists were explaining sexual dif-ferences as evolutionary adaptations – and one of their favourite case studies was gender differences in mapreading skills. This research argued that men were hardwired to solve spatial problems because their ancestors were hunter-gatherers who travelled further distances than women. For the diehard, post-feminist sociobiologists, a male driver relying on a woman to give directions was 'the equivalent of taking off his shirt and revealing a sunken chest, sure to dampen the ardor of any prospective mate'.[41]

It is true that some men did seem to recoil from being given digital instructions, and read the satnav woman's pregnant pauses, or her curt phrases like 'make a legal U-turn' and 'recalculating the route', as stubborn or bossy. 'You know how it is when you're relying on some chick to map-read and they go all silent and sulky?' asked the future mayor of London, Boris Johnson, in his *GQ* motoring column in 1999, reviewing an early Lexus satnav system. Johnson was eventu-ally won over by the satnav woman because her voice was 'so cool, so low, so scrotum-tighteningly thoughtful ... strait-laced but sensuous, firm but tender, like an NHS nurse brusquely fluffing your pillows and then leaning over to take your temperature'. The motoring journalist

James May dismissed his female satnav as a 'digital harridan', while the author Simon Winchester confessed to a sadistic pleasure in ignoring the instructions and contemplating 'the little vixen fuming away in her tin box deep in the car's bowels, forced to be voiceless while I go about my automotive business merrily unchallenged'.[42]

Of course, they were all reading too much into it. Satnav is just a dumb computer, obeying its algorithms. Some of these algorithms are fairly nuanced, computing not just distance and direction but what mapmakers call the semantics of the road: information like traffic lights, speed limits and even real-time data like jams. But they still scratch their heads over the non-standard geometries of the road, the places where it is messily unmathematical, like merges or closely spaced turns. If you are driving out of a car park, your satnav may start 'recalculating the route' before you have begun the journey – or turn into that most dangerous of navigators, the one who thinks a disastrous guess is better than admitting ignorance.

All the satnav has to go on is its map, and every satnav map is based on data provided by one of just two companies: America's Navteq and Belgium's Tele Atlas. These companies have a number of regional offices in each country, and each office has 'field data capture teams' whose job is to drive very slowly around the roads to update the maps – a practice called 'ground-truthing'. Ground-truthers work in pairs, taking it in turns to do the driving while the other person taps on or talks to a laptop connected to a GPS device. These road detectives corroborate street names, count the numbers of roundabout exits, mark out dead ends and one-way streets, and decide which bits of the road count as 'points of interest', from petrol stations to speed cameras. Like real private eyes, they supplement this intrepid tyrework with less glamorous hours in the office. Here they fast-forward through hours of CCTV footage, noting every road sign; cadge addresses and speed-limit listings from local councils and utility companies; scroll through databases of road construction contracts to get advance notice of new roads; and zoom in on Google Earth to look for road markings and bits of tyre rubber left on the road at intersections, to work out turn restrictions.

Even more than an ordinary map, a digital map reworks and distorts the world. Drawing a digital road map is not just a matter of computerising a road atlas; the software needs to understand how the roads connect up at junctions. So it relies on topology, the science of how objects intersect with each other. It shoehorns the road network into two categories: nodes (road intersections) identified by their latitude and longitude; and vectors (straight lines) representing the roads that connect the points. It is often said that there are no straight lines in nature, but on a digital road map there is nothing but. Bendy roads just become lots of little vectors strung together. A digital map also has the power to edit the world for you, to reduce it to pre-picked points of interest. One of the first people to grasp this was Rupert Murdoch, who in 1991 added ETAK, an up-and-coming Silicon Valley digital map company, to his media portfolio. Murdoch realised that digital maps would be the new *Yellow Pages*, and that companies would pay to have their petrol stations or roadside cafés mentioned.

Since even before the arrival of the car, people have worried that maps sever us from real places, render the world untouchable, reduce it to a bare outline of Cartesian lines and intersections. Radical thinkers from Guy Debord to Rebecca Solnit have argued that getting lost can be a subversive act, releasing us from the pedantry of modern map coordinates and the itineraries of the powerful, and reconnecting us with common places. Satnav feeds into this long-held fear that cold-blooded modernity is defeating vernacular knowledge, that roads no longer lead to real places but around and through them. You can sense it in all those newspaper headlines, brimming with *schadenfreude*, about motorists guided by their satnavs to the edges of cliffs or deposited in village ponds: *My satnav said to drive down a river ... so I did. Three bridges within a mile hit 62 times by curse of satnav. Pensioners in satnav mystery tour. Satnav takes bus to wrong country. Satnav errors sent 999 ambulance wrong way as girl lay bleeding. Satnav thinks quiet village is a motorway.* Some of these stories may even be true, but they probably have more to do with subconscious fears about technology than the normal life of satnav.

In fact, given that they rely on a system operated by just a few members of the US Air Force at Schriever Military Base in Colorado, which somehow reaches 11,000 miles into space and then back down to our own little patch of asphalt, it is remarkable how often our satnavs are able to give us the right call about the next roundabout. One reason for this success is that, despite the Orwellian echoes of 'ground-truthing', satnav's very complexity gives it something of the collective consciousness of an internet wiki. Navteq and Tele Atlas allow haulage and pizza delivery firms to add data in return for special deals, and anyone can use their websites to suggest updates. There would be far more cars deposited in village ponds were it not for the public-spirited reporting of missing roads by this unpaid army of road geeks.

→

Satnav clearly suits an era which has given up on understanding the roads as a coherent, logical system – an era in which map reading may be going the way of obsolete skills like calligraphy and roof-thatching. In one RAC survey, 65 per cent of British drivers under thirty-five did not know that a main A-road was normally shown in red on a map, 29 per cent mistook the M40 for the River Avon and 20 per cent never used a map at all.[43] The road system is no longer known by its epic cross-country routes ('the London–Yorkshire Motorway') but its pinchpoints like the Hogarth Roundabout or the Hanger Lane Gyratory, mentioned daily on traffic reports as vortices from which none can escape. The motorways that once carried hopes of uniting the nation now evoke images of eternal circularity, encapsulated in those mythical tales of foreign tourists (or confused pensioners, or naïve northerners) who drive round the M25 for days in the mistaken belief that it is the M1. It is now simply taken as read that the road system is a maze. In classical mythology, finding your way through a maze was a tortuous initiation rite; in the medieval era, mazes were built at the gates of fortified towns or carved on the floors of churches to ward off human adversaries and evil spirits, and to be 'lost' was an existential as well as geographical condition – it meant to be destroyed, spiritually damned, overcome by a sense of futility. Driving on Britain's roads today can make you feel similarly like a helpless non-initiate, dismissed as unworthy of the revelation of some hidden mystery.

So satnav offers you a Faustian bargain. Like Ariadne's thread it will guide you through the labyrinth, but you will forget everything it tells you so that you will need to rely on it indefinitely. Tap in a few numbers and letters and your satnav guesses where you want to go. After a few seconds' thought ('60 ... 70,000 roads analysed') it works out the route and that head-girlish voice begins to dispense its unruffled expertise. It will even rotate the map for you so you are always travelling up screen, an ever-blinking arrow pointing the way ahead. Its jerky rally-driving simulator might make a cursory reference to side streets and landmarks, but once you are on the motorway it is just a blue ribbon floating in space and all that matters is the road ahead, cut off from a world that never needs to be encountered or contemplated until the little chequered flag marks your arrival at your destination. You are here: a little island of knowledge in a limitless ocean of confusion and ignorance. Perhaps that is why satnavs are called things like 'road angel' or 'time traveller', projecting themselves not as a culmination of the Enlightenment project of scientific cartography, but as magicians and soothsayers, guiding you through the maze by psychic intuition. Early maps of uncharted territories were works of the imagination, with drawings of monsters, dragons and pygmies substituting for topographical detail. Satnav is a similarly seductive mixture of science and mystery, perfectly attuned to anyone unlucky enough to find themselves in the maddening twists and turns of that awkward, absurd institution, the British road system.

4

PLEASE DON'T BE RUDE ON THE ROAD

Last week I had a row on the road ... with a fellow in a carriage, who was impudent to my horse ... I wheeled round, rode up to the window, and asked him what he meant. He grinned, and said some foolery, which produced him an immediate slap in the face, to his utter discomfiture. Much blasphemy ensued, and some menace, which I stopped by dismounting and opening the carriage door, and intimating an intention of mending the road with his immediate remains, if he did not hold his tongue. He held it.

Lord Byron to Thomas Moore, 1817[1]

On 5 June 1994, the *Sunday Times* reported that an elder in a London Synagogue had been convicted of assault after an incident in Hendon when he leapt from his Mercedes and punched a Buddhist monk sitting at the wheel of his Nissan Micra. The exact cause of the dispute remained unclear, but was presumably not theological. The article used a new phrase to describe this strange behaviour, calling it 'a problem that police, motoring organisations and psychologists say is sweeping the country'. The convicted man was said to have been suffering from 'road rage'.[2]

The term had first appeared as an isolated reference in a local

Florida newspaper, the *St Petersburg Times*, six years earlier, probably as a corruption of "roid rage', an American phrase used to describe violent behaviour by steroid users. Road rage, a catch-all term that seemed to cover everything from honking one's horn to attacking another driver with a blunt instrument, now quickly gained pseudo-scientific respectability. Drivers cited it in court cases as a medical explanation for their behaviour. Frazzled motorists were offered massages at 'road rage bays' in M6 service stations. The RAC proposed that 'rage counselling' rehabilitation programmes be set up as a sentencing option for those convicted of driving offences. And one of the UK's largest insurers persuaded 52,000 motorists to insure against being a victim of road rage – although a year later, no claims against this policy had been made.[3]

Was road rage really overtaking the country like a contagion? The oldest cliché about manners, on the road and anywhere else, is that they are getting worse. Even in the earliest days of motoring, when the car was seen as a plaything of the rich, anti-car activists evoked the name of Jehu, the Biblical general and king of Israel ('like the driving of Jehu the son of Nimshi, for he driveth furiously'), to describe these aristocratic road hogs. 'The etiquette and courtesy of the road appear to be things of the past, and the days when motorists were one large clan ... seem to be fading away,' complained one journalist in 1919, blaming ex-soldiers who had been taught to drive during the war. As the road began to fill up with middle-class motorists and working-class chauffeurs, *The Times* lamented that 'the rule of the road is the rule of the *mens iniqua* ... Every one is on edge with the hatred that is born of rivalry or fear.' In the 1930s, the working-class city dwellers who enjoyed the popular pastime of hiking thought the middle-class drivers they met on country roads were quite deranged. In *A Charter for Ramblers*, the philosopher C.E.M. Joad compared the horn-honking motorists on a busy main road, whose cars 'break wind irritably in one another's faces', to 'a pack of fiends released from the nethermost pit'. In 1941 the Royal Society for the Prevention of Accidents blamed the strains of wartime, and the subconscious desire to live dangerously, for the 'marked deterioration in road behaviour of all road users'. And in the mid-1960s, when the number of road deaths reached a peak which has not been equalled since, the BBC presenter Gerald Priestland attacked the 'psychotic driving' seen in English cities, while a *Daily Mirror* leader railed against 'maniacs at the wheel'.[4]

But road rage was something different. This time the anger did not seem simply to be emanating from what cultural theorists like to call 'the other' – in this case, the nameless maniacs and psychotics in other cars. It was seen as an unpremeditated, temporary madness, a red mist descending on the most unlikely people – people like us. Such as the well-heeled Chelsea woman who grabbed another woman's hair and banged her head on the bonnet of a car when she tried to call for help on her mobile. Or the previously blameless bus driver who was forced to brake suddenly by a Saab driver and then chased him for five miles through the streets of Bristol, while the bus's passengers were flung from their seats and screamed in terror. Or the architect who was wrestled to the ground by other motorists after he kicked and punched an elderly man dying from cancer who had dented his beloved Ford Sierra Cosworth. Or the businessman who pursued a woman who overtook him on the inside lane, ambushed her car on a slip road and then beat her head on the blacktop until she lay unconscious. Of course, the fact that these stories were seen as particularly shocking also spoke to our class prejudices: why should an architect, businessman or Chelseaite be any less likely to feel rage, after all, or indeed be any better behaved than the rest of us? But these stories also suggested that the road was a kind of parallel universe where anyone was capable of undergoing a terrifying psychological transformation. Road rage did not just afflict the maniacs and psychotics; it was the dark heart of our inner selves.

Road rage was partly a media invention and, like all moral panics, it crystallised the anxieties of an era, acting as a kind of stress ball to absorb a much wider sense of fear and resentment about driving on our congested, polluted, decrepit roads. But these fears and resentments seemed real enough. The novelist Martin Amis called road rage 'the sewage trench – the Cloaca Maxima – of car culture'. The road rager, he argued, 'kills in the name of his Range Rover or his twin-cam turbocharged Nissan 200 SX', without realising that 'the culture he kills for is itself already dead ... the Road Rager ... is also a ghoul and a zombie: Nosferatu behind a wheel'.[5] For Amis, the modern car was a projection of status and bravado, a mobile personal space within which motorists could feel both embattled and emboldened. But many road-rage incidents seemed to be precisely that: a rage inspired not by the car but by being on the road itself. They stemmed from anger at being cut up, having one's territory on the asphalt invaded by others who acted as if they owned the road – all this in a political climate where roads were free and unlimited to use in principle, but ever more crowded and competitive in practice.

In 1994, just as the newspapers were discovering road rage, I passed my driving test and haltingly began my own career on the roads. Up until that moment I had spent very little time on roads even as a passenger, and so the behaviour of that exotic species, the motorist, was as fascinating to me as the creatures on a South Sea island might have been to an evolutionary biologist. This species mostly assumed that it was invisible – particularly at traffic lights where it would sing along gustily to its stereo or pick its nose, forgetting that it could be seen in my rear-view mirror. But when it wanted to communicate its unhappiness to another member of the species, it seemed suddenly consumed by frustration that it could not be immediately noticed and understood. It had all kinds of ways of expressing displeasure that were more melodramatic than for any other genus of naked ape. It looked like a human being, but behind a windscreen its gesticulations seemed more animated, its face more expressive, its curses more vociferous, its death stares more terrifying.

Being on the road appeared to transform the purportedly phlegmatic British into wildly gesturing southern Europeans. A driver would pass me and do the unmistakable 'wanker' sign with his shaking, unclenched fist; or he would cup his hand and draw it down from his forehead (I eventually worked out that this meant 'dickhead'). Precisely because encounters with other motorists were near-anonymous and temporary but involved the questioning of one's character and judgement, they assumed an intensity that was quite disproportionate to their actual importance. Nowhere outside silent films did people's body language seem quite so histrionic.

The road rage panic of the mid-1990s raised an interesting question about roads. Is the road its own self-governing territory within which we relate to each other quite differently from elsewhere? Or is our behaviour on the roads a distilled, more intense version of the workings of society as a whole? 'All you need to know about American society can be gleaned from an anthropology of its driving behaviour,' claimed the French cultural theorist Jean Baudrillard in his book *America*. 'Drive ten thousand miles across America and you will know more about the country than all the institutes of sociology and political science put together.'[6] Would the same be true of Britain if you drove from Penzance to Thurso? Driving on the roads is a strange activity: it is too subconscious to contain elements of a formal ritual, but it is not quite second nature either. Nor is it simply a matter of avoiding crashing into other vehicles. The road is a social space, with its own protocol and pecking orders. Roads engender the kind of infinitesimal tribal gradations that Freud called the 'narcissism of minor differences' – our propensity to project negative feelings on to people like us, while overstating the little details that differentiate us from them.[7] How else to explain the opprobrium heaped on lorry drivers, caravan owners, middle-lane hoggers, Sunday drivers? Everyone on the road is a folk sociologist doing fieldwork on the tarmac – and the first rule of sociology is that, wherever two or more people are gathered together, invidious comparisons will be drawn.

$$\rightarrow$$

In its opening manifesto of 1937, the eclectic social research organisation, Mass-Observation, announced that among other subjects it planned to study the 'shouts and gestures of motorists'.[8] This particular research project never materialised – sadly, for these shouts and gestures sound like precisely the sort of emotional outburst amid the routine of daily life that Mass-Observation so perceptively interpreted as a direct line to the nation's collective unconscious. In order to find a way of living with each other on the road, road users have had to develop some peculiar rules and customs, many of them unwritten. And in the 1930s, these rules and customs were beginning to be formalised after several decades of nervous improvisation.

Well into the motor-car era, many upper-class motorists felt they were entitled to drive on whichever side of the road they liked, rather like the old French tradition of drivers giving way to those of higher social rank. In 1904 the Tory MP for Romford, Louis Sinclair, charged with disregarding the rule of the road in Regent Street, tried to claim driving on the wrong side as a parliamentary privilege. But as the roads filled up with cars, this right of the high-born to ignore traffic codes came under strain and the rule of the road had to be formalised. After the First World War, when many soldier-drivers in France had got used to the continental rule, there was a campaign to change to right-side driving. In 1919 Lord Montagu called for an international right-side rule to be agreed at the Versailles peace conference. One reason this never happened is that many of Britain's roads were covered with tramrails, all operating on the left, and the authorities seem to have balked at the expense of reversing the order of their running.

In the mid-1920s white lines began to be painted down the middle of the road to segregate traffic, first at dangerous bends and then on open stretches like the Great West Road. Central government funded this national campaign of white-line painting and the man with the white-line roller, a familiar figure in cartoons, became a symbol of increasing state control over local life. The countryside writer Sidney Jones wrote in 1936 that village life was being transformed as 'gaily painted petrol devices have displaced the old parish pumps' and 'white lines on the roads point to an outer world beyond'.[9]

But the legal status of the white line remained unclear. In 1935 the young racing driver, Lord de Clifford, was charged with feloniously killing a twenty-six-year-old man by 'driving a motor car recklessly at the Kingston Bypass'. De Clifford had been on the wrong side of the road, although he claimed he had only swerved to avoid hitting the dead man's car. De Clifford's case gripped the nation and he became the last man to be tried by God and his peers in the House of Lords. The trial was one of the social events of the year, with admission by ticket only. De Clifford's barrister argued that the mere fact that a motorist was on the wrong side of the road was no evidence of negligence, and his client had no case to answer. De Clifford's peers took a few minutes to pronounce him not guilty.

The case highlighted a fundamental tension between policing the roads through formal laws and relying on informal, gentlemanly codes of behaviour. AA handbooks in the interwar years were prefaced with a call for good manners which advised that 'it's the little things that count. Every unimportant moment we concede to fellow travellers is an investment in the Bank of Good Nature, returning interest a hundredfold ... Courtesy begets Courtesy.' Road manners incorporated not just driving etiquette but a whole moral outlook – everything from not dropping litter to not over-revving one's engine. The prime minister, Stanley Baldwin, opening the Kingston Bypass in 1927, argued that there should be 'an unwritten code that to defile any of these great roads, either by ugly surroundings, by hoggish behaviour along them, or by upsetting or spilling litter on them, should be a bar to a man from entering any decent club or any decent home circle'.[10] The Road Fellowship League, formed in the same year, aimed to create a freemasonry of the road, cultivating good will among motorists. Members of the 'Order of the Road', founded at the Savoy a year later, styled themselves the 'aristocrats of the road' and were entitled to display a badge on their windscreens which proved that they had driven at least 10,000 miles in the last three years with no convictions (speeding, naturally, excepted). By 1932 the Order had a membership of over 2000 – excluding the thirty-five who been obliged to resign for not meeting its high standards.

The Order's chairman, racing driver Lord Cottenham, used his *Daily Express* column and BBC radio talks to promote his own idea of road manners. Cottenham blamed most road flare-ups on 'the Genus Road Hog', who was usually a lower-class chauffeur or one of the recently moneyed:

> Where the Rolls Royce, the Daimler, or the Sunbeam in days gone
> by might have been occupied by those to whom the well-being of
> their tenants and their servants was as important as the upbring-
> ing of their own children, today, those cars are occupied far too
> often by the war profiteer or the *nouveau riche*, to whom, after
> the manner of their kind, the maintenance of their 'dignity' and
> the satisfying of their appetites alike are gods.

Cottenham believed that most motorists, cyclists and pedestrians
were basically decent people and they simply had to learn to communicate their intentions clearly to each other, since 'every one is
a road user unless bedridden'.[11] Colonel Mervyn O'Gorman of the
RAC similarly blamed most accidents on poor communication, especially the eccentric hand signals proffered by motorists – a situation
aggravated by the fact that established signals like 'I'm slowing down'
(patting the air downwards) and 'pass me' (anti-clockwise wave of the
right forearm) were quite similar, and the fact that in the newer saloon
cars drivers often did not like to wind their windows down in the
rain. O'Gorman approved of the new car indicators or 'trafficators' –
semaphore arms, white-painted hands and flashing amber 'ears' that
flipped out and back with much grinding of cogs.

'O.G.', as he liked to be known, advised tolerance for motorists who broke the speed limit and he opposed the introduction of a
driving test, believing that the most important quality in a driver was
'a road sense for which a man could not be examined' and that one
of the best drivers he knew was 'so deaf that he could not hear a gun
fired close to him'. He also urged controls on impulsive pedestrians,
arguing that they should be forced to cross at right angles at marked
places, and that shopgazing should be curbed to prevent them spilling out on to the road. O'Gorman told the 1929 Royal Commission
on Transport that 'the whole trouble was that there was no canon
of custom' among road users. He set about creating this canon of
custom himself, becoming the chief architect of the Highway Code,
first published in 1931. It was simply that: a code for the considerate,
with little basis in law. The transport minister, Herbert Morrison,

said it worked on the basis that 'it is just as ungentlemanly to be discourteous or to play the fool on the king's highway as it would be for a man to push his wife off her chair at the Sunday tea table and grab two pieces of cake'. In the O'Gorman spirit, its ethics of mutual responsibility extended to pedestrians, who were told not to 'make a sudden dash into the carriageway' and to avoid standing about in groups at blind corners.[12] Every type of road user could be welcomed into the highway fellowship, by simply following its special codes and courtesies.

In their 1935 book, *You Have Been Warned*, the *Punch* cartoonist Fougasse and his co-author Donald McCullough (later to become the avuncular chairman of the BBC's Brains Trust) called the Highway Code 'the Road-User's Statute of Liberty and Magna Carta of the Road'. A runaway bestseller, this book was a comic anthropology of the eccentric behaviour of road users. Fougasse's cartoon of a driver stretching out his right arm, for instance, was translated as 'I am going to turn to my right', 'I am going to shake the ash off my cigarette', and 'the house over there with the green door is where our cook's mother lives'. The book had a semi-official sanction, being published with funds from the National Safety First Association. Scarier safety propaganda was regarded as rather shouty and unEnglish, the kind of in-your-face activity with which the Nazis, who pioneered the national road safety campaign, were associated. Propaganda that focused on the potential for accidents, advised one psychologist, would 'only produce a dangerous fear in the nervous and timid and would be no deterrent to the exhibitionist'.[13]

In 1937 the home secretary, John Simon, consolidated this restrained approach by initiating an experimental car patrol scheme. These 800 'courtesy cops' were not, he said, 'a travelling OGPU' (the forerunner of the KGB). Their job was to stamp out the idiotic practices – such as drivers using the crown of the road or cyclists riding two abreast – that 'rank with the sneezing of the Duchess's baby in *Alice in Wonderland* – the offenders "only do it to annoy because they know it teases".' The cops had megaphones fitted to their cars, and the sound of them politely asking errant drivers to pull over for a quiet word could be heard as much as a quarter-of-a-mile away. The courtesy cops even featured in the first ever reality TV show. On a Sunday afternoon in February 1939, the fledgling BBC television service filmed motorists escaping to the country along the North Circular. The cameraman took shots of bad driving, a police superintendent gave a running commentary ('a typical example of dangerous cutting in') and a squad of courtesy cops gave the motorist a ticking off – except that they were not allowed to show motorists without their permission, so often they filmed members of the film crew driving badly and the cops telling them off instead.[14]

The courtesy cop was part of an interwar image makeover for the British policeman. The middle classes had traditionally regarded the bobby with suspicion but, after his mediating role in the 1926 General Strike, they began to celebrate him as a pillar of the social order and a soother of potential class conflict. The historian Ross McKibbin argues that in these years the middle classes also came to identify themselves through a code of niceness and good manners which set them off from the uncivil working classes. This code was implicitly anti-socialist, for it was the Labour party and the working class 'which dragged "politics" into everything, which took everything so "seriously", which politicised human relationships by emphasizing conflict instead of good humour'. The rudeness of the proles was evident in their political uppitiness or 'bolshiness' – and the language used to encourage road manners was strikingly similar to the language used to deter striking workers. In both cases, middle-class commentators urged the country to pull together in a display of good humour and mutual courtesy, avoiding 'sectional antagonism'.[15]

Underneath this appeal lay an uncomfortable truth: many members of the respectable middle classes were incompetent drivers who were to blame for fatal road accidents. Rather than turning them into criminals through punitive legislation, British traffic law relied on appeals to their sense of fair play. It was always better, went the mantra of the time, to cultivate good habits than propose bad bills. So the courtesy cops did not prosecute motorists; they offered friendly advice to the careless. *The Times* blamed accidents on what it called 'motorious carbarians' – the few bad apples hidden among the vast majority of gentlemanly drivers, who could be trusted to break the law sensibly. Motoring correspondents railed against excessive regulation in the 1930s in a way that eerily echoes today's campaigns against speed cameras and road humps. 'Regulation after regulation pours from the Ministry of Transport in a never-ending flood,' complained the *Daily Mirror* in 1934, about such despotic innovations as the 30 mph speed limit, pedestrian crossings and 'compulsory whirligigs' (roundabouts). But 'courtesy and good manners may be cultivated easily enough by everyone'.[16]

After the Second World War, the government continued to rely on campaigns based on gentle warnings and exhortations: 'Be a Better Driver', 'Mind How you Go', 'Good Driving Pays'. 'How nice it would be if people showed a little more courtesy ... a little more patience', urged a 1960 public information film cartoon called 'Don't be rude on the road', showing a preternaturally polite motorist doffing his cap and waving on some pedestrians at a zebra crossing. The idea of an aristocratic club of well-mannered motorists survived well into the age of postwar mass motoring. In the early 1960s ABC TV, the ITV weekend franchise for the north and Midlands, ran a series to spread 'the ideals of the Silver Wheel', a new road safety organisation based on Christian motoring. Silver Wheelers pledged to improve manners on the road by personal example, their mottos being 'do unto others as I would that they should do unto me' and 'never retaliate'.[17]

→

The new motorways required a different kind of driving, involving short bursts of treacherous weaving and long periods of not doing very much. The government announced that the Preston Bypass would be a 'guinea-pig' motorway, and it appointed the Lancashire constabulary to file a series of monthly reports on the behaviour of motorists on the new road. In the ten months after it opened, the police observed 59 motorists driving, crossing or stopping on the central reservation; 74 driving in the wrong direction; 12 reversing on the motorway; 47 stopping on the hard shoulder when not in distress;

and 41 parking on the carriageway itself. Among those caught on the motorway when they shouldn't have been, there were a total of 40 pedestrians, 13 pedal cyclists, 2 farm tractors and 184 learner drivers.

These miscreants offered various excuses for their behaviour. The learner drivers and their minders claimed not to have seen or understood the 'start of motorway' signs. The motorists reversing or going the wrong way had mistakenly driven on to the motorway and, terrified at the prospect of driving at speed in this alien landscape, had tried to get off it as quickly and dangerously as possible. Those parked on the hard shoulder or the road itself were reading maps, resting or having a meal. Two drivers parked in the inside lane turned out to be travelling together and had stopped to repair one of their cars. While waiting for the engine to cool, they had decided to kill two birds with one stone and were eating their sandwiches.[18]

Clearly, some public education was required. But no one was quite sure whether to rely on the traditional call to good manners or come up with a new system based on clearer rules. Introducing the new Motorway Code, an addendum to the Highway Code, in the Commons in July 1959 the junior transport minister Richard Nugent said archly that it must be brief enough to be readable but comprehensive enough to cover every important point – 'like the lady's skirt, long enough to cover the subject, but short enough to be interesting'. Nugent used the old argument that drivers should adopt the same standards of behaviour on the motorway as they had in their daily lives, since 'when most of us get behind the wheel of a motor car, 5,000 or 10,000 years slip off our shoulders and we almost go back to the Stone Age again – no quarter given, the weakest to the wall, every man for himself'. But he also acknowledged that greater clarity, not just better manners, was now needed on fast roads. Those driver signals that did not indicate a definite intention, such as the 'I am ready to be overtaken' hand sign, would be scrapped. The shadow transport minister, George Strauss, agreed that if he had accepted all the invitations he had received to pass lorries in the last ten years, he would have been killed, on average, once a month. Oddly, he then went on to plead for the custom to be retained on an unofficial basis, as a courtesy.[19]

The police handed out free copies of the Motorway Code to motorists entering the Preston Bypass and, when the M1 opened, a fleet of lorries ran up and down it carrying excerpts from the code emblazoned on their sides. The AA published its own booklet with advice such as 'do not walk on the carriageways' and 'if you miss your exit, continue along the carriageway until the next exit', with a cartoon character called Mr Clogghead who ignored these rules. 'The M1 has been designed to speed the flow of Britain's traffic,' advised one RAC official sternly, 'and not for wayside picnics or "crown-of-the-road" dawdling.'[20]

The grand prix racing driver Tony Brooks wrote an article for the *Observer* after driving north along the M1 in his Aston Martin, noting the behaviour of other drivers. 'At first,' he wrote, 'everything was wrong: an L-driver teetering along uncertainly in the middle of the road, a van broadside on and reversing on a feedoff, many cars sitting complacently astride the lane lines.' But Brooks was impressed by the skills of more experienced drivers, praising lorry drivers in particular. A common theme in press articles was that motorway commuters were better behaved than the weekenders who 'turned the road into a sightseers' traffic jamboree'. 'Comparing yesterday's "Sunday drivers" with today's fine example of lane discipline,' said an RAC spokesman on the Monday after the M1 opened, 'was like watching a squad of raw recruits trying to compete with a crack Guards regiment.' The motorway was seen as 'no place for ditherers' – or women drivers. 'If families use the motorway on weekend outings father must take a firm hand,' warned one chief inspector of police. 'Any distractions from the back seat by his wife could be very dangerous.' Ernest Marples thought that the motorways had brought out a 'lunatic fringe' of drivers, but that their behaviour had soon calmed down. Using a pre-breathalyser analogy, he argued that 'it was like someone who started drinking wine and became tipsy at first, but after three months had got used to it'.[21]

In return for the liberation of speed, motorists had to put up with greater surveillance and constant nagging about their behaviour. Motorway drivers knew straightaway that they had entered an alien country, its borders marked by that 'start of motorway' sign of a road going under an overbridge, which looked more like a tuning fork or a robot with outstretched arms. Something about the approaches to these new roads, observed one author, put the nervous driver 'irresistibly in mind of the alarming mysteries of an airport', with their intimidating signs about using the nearside verge in an emergency, thundering admonitions to make 'no U-turns' and scary symbols like exclamation marks on a blood-red background or telephone boxes with SOS signs. The police dispensed with their sedate black Wolseleys and patrolled the motorways in gleaming white Ford Zephyr station wagons. They were like the cars in the American cop show *Highway Patrol*, claimed one excited journalist, with POLICE written on their bonnets in foot-high letters, flashing beacons and buglers' horns. 'With all these transatlantic trimmings,' he wrote, 'it is almost a shock to find that they are driven by large, quiet, helpful, unarmed men from the Hertfordshire County Constabulary.'[22] The highway patrol lurked on police observation platforms next to the motorways, with exits tapered to the hard shoulder so they could pursue wrongdoers – although many motorists mistook these raised areas for picnic spots. Police officers used the PA system fitted to patrol cars to bark advice, or followed drivers off motorways and gave them a telling off.

But the motorway was still a much freer, easier place than we would recognise. U-turning was a common transgression in the days before crash barriers, when the median strip was a traversable stretch of grass and gravel. In one public information film, a driver overshoots his exit and, unwilling to drive eight miles to the next slip road because he is already late, turns round on the central reservation. His wife is so upset by his behaviour ('I think you're mad and we shall be killed!') that she tries to get out of the car, surely compounding the problem.[23] In fact, the police were the worst offenders at doing U-turns, and motorists simply followed their bad example.

Jazz bands and beat groups, touring the clubs in their Commer vans and Dormobiles, were especially prone to off-message motorway behaviour. George Melly recalled that he was driving along the M1 to a gig with Mick Mulligan's band when a large front section of their rusty old van fell off. They stopped the van and, amidst much laughter, ran across the carriageway to retrieve it, even finding the time to record this jolly jape on super eight film. The Beatles were driving back to Liverpool on the same motorway when a stray pebble ricocheted up and cracked the windscreen. Their roadie, Mal Evans, simply stopped on the carriageway, put his hat inside out on his fist, punched the whole windscreen out, and drove on, in freezing fog, all the way home.[24]

The hot topic of the safety campaigns was lane indiscipline – a dangerous problem on fast roads with three lanes. The problem was compounded by the fact that many old cars did not have wing mirrors or indicators, and some drivers still used hand signals. Marples complained that lane-straddling on the motorways was 'an appalling spectacle' with drivers 'going all over the road', and he thought that Britons had much to learn from the exemplary lane etiquette of Americans. Reyner Banham also marvelled at 'the watchful tolerance and almost impeccable lane discipline of Angeleno drivers', which were still more impressive because LA freeways were not divided like 'the kindergarten rule of the road' on British motorways, with their slow, middle and fast lanes. The freeways typically had five lanes of equal status, but most drivers managed to weave between them safely with the perfect mix of self-interest and civic duty. For Banham, the self-governing community of the freeway was an American paradox, an expression of 'tolerant good sense and feeling for the common weal that is quite remarkable in a landscape more noted for extreme and intolerant individualism'. The freeway was a unique public place with its own special subculture. While driving down the exit lane of an LA freeway, Banham spotted a young woman in the passenger seat of a car pull down the sun-visor and use the mirror to adjust her hair. He concluded that, for Angelenos, driving down the off-ramp of the freeway was 'like coming in from outdoors', and they treated the mile or two of ground-level streets they encountered after that just like the front drives of their houses. The freeway system had become 'a single comprehensible place, a coherent state of mind, a complete way of life'.[25]

Banham went on to air some of these ideas in a 1972 BBC film called *Reyner Banham Loves Los Angeles*, and its title rather gives the game away. He was such a deep admirer of American car culture that his account of exemplary LA driving may have contained an element of what the historian E.P. Thompson, in another context, calls 'inverted Podsnappery', after Mr Podsnap in Charles Dickens's *Our Mutual Friend* who believes that 'no other country is so favoured as this country'.[26] Britons often compare their own road culture negatively with its European and American equivalents, not always with firm evidence. Banham did not make clear exactly how LA drivers communicated with each other so telepathically, and any evidence of their supposedly superior etiquette is now lost to history.

Just as on the LA freeways, the lane system on British motorways meant that motorists travelling quickly in the same direction had to negotiate over their roughly equal rights to the same bit of road. One way they learnt to communicate was through the automotive equivalent of a wink: the flashing light. Anthropologists know that even a simple gesture like a wink can have many different meanings – a greeting, a come-on, a conspiratorial signal or an involuntary twitch – depending on its context. In his classic 1968 sociological study, *The Lorry Driver*, Peter Hollowell found that over the years hauliers had developed a similarly rich sign language using flashing lights. They would wink their tail-lights to encourage drivers behind to overtake, or warn them not to; double-flash their sidelights to let oncoming hauliers know of an accident or, when accompanied with a thumbs down or the wave of a log sheet, a police patrol; or exchange single flashes to indicate 'your length is clear' and 'thanks'. Sometimes the flashed light was simply a greeting, a way of acknowledging the lorry-driver fellowship or alleviating loneliness on the road.[27] Two identical-looking flashes could have entirely opposite meanings but – just as most people learn to decipher the different nuances of a wink – lorry drivers seemed to know what they meant.

In the early 1960s other drivers picked up on this code and British cars began to have flasher switches fitted as standard, although they were frowned upon by the authorities. The official line for the more anonymous motorway era was that motorists should not rely on each other for help or information. Ernest Marples counselled motorists to 'treat everyone else on the road as if he was a fool' – a piece of advice perhaps open to misinterpretation. A junior minister of transport, Lord Chesham, worried about this 'growing unofficial practice on the roads ... the flashing of headlamps to indicate this, that, and the other'.[28] Actually, flashing lights lost much of their richness in the move from lorry to car, tending to mean only 'after you' or, in the motorway's overtaking lane, 'get out of my way'. The intuitive, wordless communion that Banham claimed to have witnessed on the LA freeways remained elusive.

$$\rightarrow$$

If only it were simply a matter of drivers communicating with each other clearly – of somehow defeating the semi-opaqueness of the windscreen and the poverty of motorists' sign language to attain a pure meeting of minds. But all attempt at human communication is inherently imperfect and infected by our social differences and prejudices. The French cultural critic Luc Boltanski once wrote that 'the race to appropriate road space is largely reducible to class conflict not perceived as such'.[29] Different vehicles have always jostled for space and social status on British roads. During the bicycle craze of the late nineteenth century, carriage drivers looked down on those who 'rode ironmongery' instead of horses. In the early days of motoring, the aristocratic motorists directed their anger at horse-drawn vehicles that refused to hug the kerb so they could pass. Up until the 1950s, when the car industry began to consolidate, the large number of small British motoring firms meant a wide variety of vehicles on the road – you could crouch down in a motorcycle sidecar or be 'well-off in a Wolseley', as the advertising slogan had it – which made the pecking order peculiarly conspicuous.

On the motorway the hierarchies of the road were less obvious, which perhaps reflected its associations with social mobility and mass consumerism. The motorway was free-market democracy in miniature, an embodiment of Karl Marx's famous comment that capitalists are 'hostile brothers', united by common interests and divided by cut-throat struggles.[30] Motorists were playing a deadly game where they had to cooperate to avoid crashing into each other, while also searching for competitive advantage. Officially, everyone had an equal right to occupy space on the motorway. But there was still a sort of invisible caste system in which certain drivers, particularly white-collar men in powerful cars, felt they had more right to the road than other, lower forms of motorway life.

Caravans, for instance, have been vilified as 'sheet-metal slugs' and 'human snails' ever since the 1930 Road Traffic Act, which abolished the 20 mph speed limit for cars but kept it for those pulling trailers. It is probably not just their slowness that rankles but their long associations with cosy domesticity, and the attendant suspicion that they do not take the matter of being on the road seriously enough. The first caravan users were the 'gentleman gypsies' of the late Victorian era and the earliest caravans were called land yachts, because they were associated with the languidly well-to-do. 'The caravan of today,' wrote the *Daily Mirror*'s Bernard Buckham in 1939, 'has softly shaded lamps, electric heaters, cushioned divans, bookshelves, cocktail cabinets, refrigerators, and all the appurtenances of the simple life as lived in surtax circles ... If I had got as far away from the vagabond life as one of these stream-lined lounges I think I should go a step further and put up at the swell hotel nearby.'[31] The caravan's ponderous, semi-bulbous shape – ironically, a product of the discovery of aerodynamic streamlining in the 1920s – reinforced these domesticated associations.

After the Second World War, caravans developed a counter-reputation for being cheap and flimsy, largely because, in an era of austerity, the manufacturers had to make do with non-restricted materials. The inventor of the classic Sprite caravan, Sam Alper –whose other significant role in road history was to found the Little Chef restaurant chain in 1958 – built his first model in 1947 out of wartime salvage, using a Spitfire's undercarriage and a roof made from an old barrage balloon. But while Alper may have deglamorised the caravan, his own adventures in it were rather dashing. He fearlessly dragged his Sprite across continents, keen to prove how well it performed over long distances on terrible roads. In 1952 he sprinted round the Mediterranean, covering 11,000 miles and twenty-five countries in just over a month – cannily, with a newspaper reporter in the passenger seat. Another great caravanning evangelist was Alper's friend, a swashbuckling, high-society dentist called Ralph Lee, who in 1958 steered his caravan through Norwegian dirt roads all the way to the Arctic Circle – and founded the Order of Bluenosed Caravanners for those who achieved the same feat.

Caravanning entered the mainstream in the 1960s, a decade of rapid motorway building and consumer affluence, when the Caravan Club's membership doubled and the Sprite Alpine, with its distinctive green waistband, became the bestselling model of all time. Caravans became a familiar sight on holiday roads like the M5 going down to the West Country, or the narrow lanes of south-west Wales and East Anglia, where caravan sites clustered on the coast. During these years caravanners earned their reputation for being a semi-clique, caught between the camaraderie of an exclusive coterie and the egalitarianism of a mass leisure activity. In the late 1960s there was a bitter skirmish in the Caravan Club about whether to admit camper van owners as members and for years there remained an uneasy relationship between the conventional 'tuggers' and the parvenu 'chuggers' – the Dormobile drivers who somehow managed to nurture a contrasting public image as hippyish free spirits. But the full-scale demonisation of the caravan began once its popularity had peaked. The recession and rising inflation of the 1970s hit caravan sales hard and in 1982 Alper's company, Caravans International, went bust. As cars became more powerful and motorway speeds crept up, and foreign holidays were increasingly affordable, caravans seemed plodding and stay-at-home.

The most extreme ends of the anti-caravan contingent attacked their right to be on the road at all. In the 1990s, when everything from speed cameras to traffic cones seemed to fuel the persecution complex of a certain breed of motorist, caravanners were caught in the crossfire. The Anti-Caravan Club, which boasted 27,000 members at its peak, demanded that these 'eyesores' be stored in already despoiled areas like power stations and sewage works, and called for a daylight curfew so they could only be driven from dusk until dawn.

In recent years the hatred of the caravan has subsided, perhaps because modern models, which have sorted out the traditional problems of under-braking and snaking, nip along quite quickly. In motorway demonology, the dawdling caravanner is in danger of being displaced by the middle-lane hogger. The RAC has even called on the police to prosecute these social pariahs who waste up to one-third of motorway capacity in peak periods, the equivalent of a 700-mile stretch from Aberdeen to Penzance.[32] Of course, whether someone in the middle lane is hogging it is a matter of opinion, and the phenomenon seems as much a consequence of congestion as a cause of it. Today's slow lane is often clogged with lorries, and modern motorways gain and lose lanes all the time (so-called 'lane gains' and 'lane drops'), so the left lane often turns into a slip road. Like the caravanner, the middle-lane hogger seems to have become the fall guy for more general frustrations about the ambiguities of motorway etiquette and driving on busy roads.

→

The tribe that spends most time on the road is at once the most reviled and romanticised of all: the lorry driver. The reasons, again, are historical. Ever since the birth of long-distance freight in the 1920s, British lorry driving has been dominated by small firms. With fierce competition and narrow margins, hauliers often worked on the fringes of legality – overloading their lorries, driving them too fast ('having a bash'), working more than their legal hours ('doing a dodgy') or trading in goods that 'fell off the back of a lorry'. Yet the lorry driver saw himself, and was often seen, as a knight of the road, with better manners, skill and roadmanship than ordinary drivers. When the motorways opened, though, the reputation of lorry drivers suffered. Many motorway accidents involved lorries, and these fast roads eroded the comradeship that had long existed between hauliers who met up in the all-night A-road transport caés. Older lorry drivers worried that their image was being tarnished by young 'motorway cowboys' working for fly-by-night firms.

In the late 1960s the embryonic anti-roads movement began to direct its anger towards lorries, as the small, trusty British truck gave way to the massive, continental-style articulated lorry. Thanks to a campaign in Harold Evans's crusading *Sunday Times*, these new mega-lorries came to be known as 'juggernauts' – a word that had been used occasionally since the 1900s to describe cars. The name was a legacy of the Raj: it meant 'Lord of the World' and referred to an idol of the Hindu god Krishna. The British wrongly used it to describe the gigantic car dragged through Indian towns in a procession each year, carrying the idol. Religious fanatics were once believed to sacrifice themselves by leaping under its wheels, and the modern, articulated juggernaut was seen similarly as an object that attracted unthinking obeisance and sacrificial victimhood.

Just as this new motorway demon emerged, however, a small Carlisle businessman began, partly by accident, to retrieve an older, more gallant image. Edward Stobart had got a taste for motorway life at the age of fourteen in 1969 when, during the summer holidays, he worked illegally for his father, Eddie, digging holes for signposts with a JCB on the most northern section of the M6. When Stobart junior started his own road haulage firm in 1976, his first stroke of business brilliance was to give his lorries an identity. He named his first five trucks after 1970s female stars – Twiggy, Tammy (Wynette), Dolly (Parton), Suzi (Quatro) and Tina (Turner) – and all subsequent lorries had women's names inscribed on their bumpers. Most hauliers then had open-sided lorries covered with rough canvas and rope, but Stobart's lorries had elegant 'curtains', plastic sheeting with 'Eddie Stobart Ltd' printed on in Post Office red and Brunswick green. Stobart drivers were taught to drive into a depot slowly and turn the vehicle so that passing motorists could read the name. In 1987 Edward put his drivers in uniform – at first green boiler suits, and then, in 1990, matching green shirts and ties. The dress code was rigorously enforced, and one Stobart driver got the sack for taking off his tie in a heatwave.

The musician and TV presenter, Jools Holland, popularised the cult of Stobart. In 1991 he and his band began spotting the lorries to relieve the boredom of being on the road, with the first band member to call out 'Stobart' claiming a pound. Holland was interviewed about his hobby in *The Times*, prompting letters from other Eddie watchers, who claimed to write down the names of the trucks like trainspotters or award points for each sighting. Some Eddie watchers sang the Hallelujah chorus from Handel's *Messiah*, substituting the words 'Eddie Stobart' throughout; others played the game 'Nobby and Stobby', totting up the number of Stobart lorries against those of his French rival, Norbert Dentressangle.

The Eddie Stobart cult rested on the firm's uncanny ability to rise above the Darwinian jostling for space on Britain's roads. The firm's consonant-heavy name sounded sturdily Anglo-Saxon and it proudly proclaimed its business as 'Express Road Haulage', not that *über*-hip, nebulous word, 'logistics'. For all its unmodishness, Eddie Stobart was aggressively on-trend, part of the changing culture of the motorway. Its well-groomed lorries and dapper drivers allowed it to move away from messy work like carrying slag and fertiliser into cleaner, more profitable goods like food, drink and packaging – so Eddie Stobart was well-placed to exploit that unstoppable end-of-century phenomenon, the rise of the supermarkets on the back of just-in-time deliveries.[33] Stobart became a very modern business phenomenon: the brand that wasn't a brand, that could accumulate its millions by remaining cool and non-corporate, like Ben & Jerry's Ice Cream or Innocent Smoothies. How some of its big customers, like Tesco and Coca-Cola, must have coveted this image.

The Stobart cult has somehow managed to override the low-level truckophobia from which most motorists suffer. Shaken by their backdraughts, blinded by the spray they spew up in the rain, tailgated by them in the middle lane, motorists naturally see juggernauts as the bullies of the road. But our relationship to lorries also sums up the strange ethereality of the modern economy, the way it controls our lives without us having more than the dimmest awareness of its workings. Many lorries give no indication of their contents, because they either have no logos or the names of obscure logistics firms on their sides. We do not imagine these vehicles to be part of our lives, delivering the organic dragon fruit we desperately need to the supermarkets or the Nintendo game we just ordered off Amazon to our letter boxes. The lorries might as well be empty for all that we care about their contents or relate them to the lifestyles they help us to sustain. Perhaps truckophobia is a form of psychological transference, a way of projecting all our anxieties and guilt about our prolific consumerism into a moan about the lorry in front.

Driving past it on the motorway, we don't realise that the lorry is not just a vehicle any more. It is a surrogate warehouse, a sort of dry-land cargo ship with computerised chill cabinets that allow the driver to monitor the load, as well as a high-tech living space, with a bed, night heater, telephone, refrigerator and cooker. Lorry drivers literally live on the road, spending nights parked in lay-bys with only their PlayStations and TVs for company, or guided along trading routes by their satnavs. So it is not surprising that there is such a chasm of incomprehension between the motorway-inhabiting lorry driver and the junction-hopping commuter. But that very parfit gentle knight, the Eddie Stobart driver, provides us with the comforting sense that this chasm can be filled, if only for a brief moment. If you wave, he (occasionally she) will salute, just like the RAC and AA patrolmen used to do when they saw drivers with the organisation's badge screwed to their radiator grilles. They abandoned this practice in 1961, the arrival of the high-speed motorways rendering it obsolete and even dangerous. But our relationship with Eddie Stobart betrays a certain nostalgia for the honour codes and chivalric orders of an earlier age. We look back to that prelapsarian era when drivers were supposedly one large clan speaking the same language, before the citizens of Babel were scattered to all parts of the road system and began speaking in tongues. Even on the vast, lonely sea of the motorway, we still find solace in the idea of community.

→

Ever since the interwar era, traffic engineers have had one way of dealing with these mutual misunderstandings, this confusion of tongues among road users: they designed layouts that segregated vehicles from each other, bossed them around with signs and lights, and made sure that everyone knew their place. Britain blazed the trail in traffic segregation, from the white centre line of the 1920s to the giveway rule at roundabouts introduced in the 1960s.

In Holland in the early 1970s, though, traffic engineers had a change of heart. It all began with a Delft engineer called Joost Váhl, the man behind the Dutch concept of the *woonerf*, or 'living yard', which aimed to turn residential roads into proper social spaces that could be shared by drivers and pedestrians, by removing road markings and barriers. Hans Monderman, the road safety investigator for the northern Dutch province of Friesland, believed this idea could be translated from residential streets to other roads. His maxim, *pace* Ernest Marples, was, 'If you treat drivers like idiots, they act as idiots.'[34] He was fond of walking backwards across busy road junctions with his arms folded, to prove that drivers would not run him over (and, fortunately, they didn't).

Monderman's first big experiment was in the village of Oudehaske, where he managed to reduce traffic speeds by removing street furniture. In 1992, in the small town of Makkinga, he got rid of every road sign, white line and traffic light, the division between pavement and road being suggested by subtle variations in the paving stones. In a postmodern joke on the road into town, a traffic sign welcomed visitors and informed them that it was '*Verkeersbordvrij*' (free of traffic signs). A decade later, Monderman moved the experiment to Drachten, a much larger town of 45,000 people. He stripped its busy Laweiplein junction of all its lights and turned it into a 'squareabout', a pedestrian square which motorists treated like a roundabout, with fountains that increased in height when the traffic got busier. The rate of serious injuries on this notoriously dangerous junction fell dramatically. There *were* a number of small accidents, but Monderman insisted that these were to be encouraged 'in order to prevent serious ones in which people get hurt'.[35]

Until then, this Dutch concept of 'shared space' had a single British spin-off: the road hump. The idea actually dates back to 1929, when Lord Cecil of the Pedestrian Association proposed a traffic bill calling for shallow trenches across the entry into villages to ensure that drivers slowed down. It was widely condemned as 'a trench war on cars', while others objected that '"young bloods" would go out on Sundays to see how many of these "depressions" they could drive over'.[36] The hump as we know it was invented by Joost Váhl in the late 1960s, and it arrived in Britain in 1974 under the cuddly nickname of the 'sleeping policeman'. After lobbying from the AA and RAC, though, humps were only allowed to be installed as an experiment, so after a year they all had to be flattened.

In the early 1980s, humps were built more widely on residential streets used as rat runs. In his first government job as a junior transport minister, Kenneth Clarke championed them, suggesting that groups of residents could club together to pay for road humps in their area. (Years later, as a Tory grandee, Clarke recanted. 'There is one every 100 yards on a street near where I live,' he said, 'and every time my bones are shaken, I curse my error.'[37]) One of the pioneering road-hump neighbourhoods was Oxford's Blackbird Leys estate, whose joyriders had earned it the nickname 'the city of screaming tyres'. By the mid-1990s, the government was allowing local authorities to put speed humps almost anywhere, and to construct different types of hump with varying levels of expense, speed-reducing efficacy and what the Department for Transport sweetly called 'discomfort performance'. Alongside the classic kerb-to-kerb roundtop humps, there were now 'thumps' (cheap ones made of thermoplastic), 'sinusoidal' humps (tender-hearted ones with a shallow gradient) and 'speed cushions' (kind to buses).

Humps were popular with local councils because they were a cheap way to cut speeds in 20 mph residential areas, Anglo-Saxon descendants of the *woonerf* called 'home zones'. Many motorists, however, saw them as concrete incarnations of the nanny state. In the early 2000s, there were noisy anti-hump campaigns, including marches by local residents and traffic go-slows. A man campaigning solely on the issue of abolishing humps was elected on to Derby council. Barnet's Conservative council began flattening its humps, leading to a standoff with the mayor of London, Ken Livingstone, who suspended some of its funding. An Oxford builder invited a television crew along to watch him dig up a road hump outside his house with a JCB because, he claimed, the noise from lorries hitting it was preventing him sleeping. The home secretary, David Blunkett, while naturally upholding the law of the land, said he had a 'great deal of sympathy' for the man.[38]

But speed humps were a simplification, even a distortion, of the Dutch concept of shared space, which stressed that roads should be 'self-explaining', indicating how road users should behave without the need for endless visual cues or coercion. This broader idea now began to find its cheerleaders in Britain, notably the architect Ben Hamilton-Baillie and the academic geographer John Adams. Adams believed that people had an inbuilt 'risk thermostat', altering their behaviour according to how risky they believed their environment to be – driving more dangerously when they were wearing seat belts, for example.

Spurred on by the Dutch example, these ideas about risk gained currency. The first British laboratory for shared space was Kensington High Street, a major radial road into London, which was denuded of most of its railings, traffic lights and road markings. The council was so worried about being liable in the event of accidents that they phased the work over three years. But according to two years of 'before and after' monitoring, the number of road casualties fell by 43 per cent.[39] The whole street also looked more civilised – a good advert for the new urbanist philosophy which re-imagined Britain's cities along the gregariously continental model of boulevards, piazzas and ramblas. The street had been cleared of junk, brightly lit with white light, and its median strip had been widened, planted with saplings and reserved for bicycle parking. If you strolled down Kensington High Street you felt rather sophisticated and urbane, as though you had wandered by accident into a little bit of Amsterdam.

By the time Monderman died in January 2008, Britain was at the leading edge of shared-space design, with more than forty projects around the country. The most memorable was at Ashford in Kent, which transformed its dour 1970s ring road into a 'quality street', with waymarking water channels and musical stepping stones. A series of art installations called 'Lost O' was dotted round the town to 'acknowledge the loss of the ring road and celebrate the Shared Space concept'.[40] They included the push button of a Puffin crossing placed way above arm's reach, some bicycles with deer antlers instead of handlebars, stencils of flocking birds laid down as yellow road markings and 'Regeneration Rebels', a series of billboards showing the councillors responsible for the shared-space scheme in heroic, Che Guevara-style poses. Unfortunately one of Lost O's centrepieces – a chaotic assemblage of recovered traffic signs in the middle of a roundabout – had to be removed after complaints from bewildered motorists.

The shared-space movement originated in cyclist- and pedestrian-friendly northern European cities and was about making urban streets more egalitarian places that could be enjoyed by all road users. It was only meant for certain types of road where everyone would be at low enough speeds, no more than 20 mph, to exchange eye contact with one another. In Holland, where Monderman carried out his experiments, people make a third of their journeys by bicycle. But in Britain, cyclists tend to be caricatured as lycra-clad louts, self-righteous eco-warriors, freeloaders (because they travel on roads without paying road tax) and serial ignorers of red lights (although many cyclists, of course, insist on living up to this stereotype). It says much about the implied social hierarchy of the British road that bicycling politicians are still marked out as environmentalist eccentrics or, worse, hypocrites – as happened when it emerged that the Conservative leader, David Cameron, cycled into Westminster from his home in Notting Hill while his briefing papers and shoes followed him in a chauffeur-driven limousine.

In Britain's very different road culture, shared space took on a life of its own. In particular it became part of a long-running campaign against traffic lights. In 1984, the libertarian Tory transport secretary, Nicholas Ridley, had announced that he wanted to get rid of half of London's traffic lights. He disliked them for the same reason he hated one-way streets and wheel clamping: they interfered with the freedom of movement of motorists. 'The private motorist … wants the independence and status of his motor car,' he had told Parliament in 1977. 'He wants the chance to live a life that gives him a new dimension of freedom – freedom to go where he wants, when he wants, and for as long as he wants.'[41] The Tories have remained the anti-traffic light party. During the run-up to the 2001 general election, they pledged to introduce a 'left on red' rule, a version of the North American 'right on red' which allows drivers stuck at traffic lights to turn right if the road is empty.

Writing in this permissive vein in the journal of the Institute of Economic Affairs, the television producer Martin Cassini asked, 'Who is the better judge of when it's safe to go – you, the driver at the time and place, or lights programmed by an absent regulator?' Cassini saw traffic lights as an imperfect cure for a human-made problem: the priority rule. In 1929, following Mervyn O'Gorman's advice, the government decreed that drivers on main roads should have priority over those on minor ones, rejecting alternative conventions like the French *priorité à droite* championed by the AA. According to Cassini, this historical wrong turn made traffic lights 'necessary' to interrupt priority so that traffic on minor roads could cross. The law of the lights was 'the law of aggression', forcing humans into 'unnatural patterns of behaviour', replacing civilised queuing with the coercive priority rule.[42] Traffic lights rationed road space inefficiently, added to pollution from engine idling, cluttered up urban streetscapes, and caused accidents by encouraging motorists to drive through junctions without paying proper attention. 'Whichever way you cut it,' Cassini wrote, 'some traffic experts have blood on their hands.' Apart from a few controls at peak times on major junctions, he believed that all the country's traffic lights should be dismantled. When Cassini outlined this position on *Newsnight*, the presenter Jeremy Paxman pulled a face and said, 'Crikey!'[43]

Cassini also planned to produce a documentary film called *In Your Car No One Can Hear You Scream!* As well as arguing against traffic lights, it aimed to show that 'middle-lane blocking halves road capacity, parking controls add to congestion, congestion charging causes gridlock on peripheral routes, and removing speed limits raises driving standards'.[44] Cassini posted a ten-minute taster for the film on YouTube, which showed lots of cars idling at traffic lights and London taxi drivers being interviewed about why the lights should be removed. Cassini argued in his commentary that motorists should be allowed to 'go on opportunity' at junctions like 'pedestrians on wheels'.[45]

Since its inconvenience to individuals is obvious and its social benefits are diffuse and debatable, traffic engineering can bring out the libertarian in us all. This notion of relying on the motorist's native common sense is in fact a thread running through the history of the British road – a Burkean conservative tradition that sees Britons as pragmatic and precedent-loving and resistant to abstract laws and rules. The conservative philosopher Michael Oakeshott used the phrase 'civil association' to describe these ideal kinds of semi-improvised understanding which emerged organically out of daily life. According to this philosophy, drivers filtering in turn will always be a better idea than a traffic light, because human society is an intricate web of mutual understandings that cannot be reduced to systems and dogma. There is also a common perception that the British are unusually open to this approach because of their good manners on the roads. In an interview with the *New Yorker* just before he was arrested in London in October 1998, General Pinochet said that England was 'the ideal place to live' because of the natural civility of its people. As an example, he pointed to their 'impeccable driving habits' compared with the rude road behaviour of Chileans.[46] (Perhaps Pinochet had in mind one of the catalysts for the 1973 Chilean coup: the resignation of General Carlos Prats, the head of the armed forces under Allende, after he shot at a woman driver in a fit of road rage.)

Anglophile ex-dictators are not the only ones to pass comment on this phenomenon – and, although it is inherently hard to verify, that does not mean the phenomenon is a myth. Drive on any British road and you will soon encounter a raft of undemonstrative kindnesses: the flashed headlights to let someone in front change lanes, the moving into the middle lane of a motorway to allow a driver in from a slip road, the raising of a hand or the winking of a tail-light to say thank you. All these careering cars manage to coexist, through some weird mix of altruism and self-preservation – and the very fact that we extend these courtesies to passing strangers makes it all the more impressive and touching. There is nothing like a high-speed road to remind you that humans are quick-thinking, adaptable and communal animals. If drivers can work out their own arrangements at such speeds, it is tempting to imagine that they do not really need all those niggling road markings and traffic lights.

But hang on – what happened to road rage? A few years ago, we were told that the driver who cut us up at a roundabout might be a lunatic who kept a machete in his car boot for just such occasions, or that the most mild-mannered people, once they were on the roads, could make Incredible Hulk-like mutations into homicidal maniacs. Now we were being told to resist all attempts to intervene in the universal rapport that existed between motorists. But even if such a rapport existed, it would still demand that motorists understood each other's intentions clearly – a far from simple matter.

In the late 1990s, the social psychologist Jack Katz discovered this when he conducted ethnographic research into motorists who became 'pissed off while driving' in Los Angeles. Katz deliberately avoided the melodramatic term 'road rage', but his view of LA drivers was still rather less cheerful than Reyner Banham's. Riding around the freeways with his subjects, he discovered that many of them were knotted balls of anger, a result largely of 'the dumbing asymmetry of communication' on the roads. Most altercations were attempts by drivers to communicate, in their inexpressive vehicles, that they were angry – their failure to do so simply making them angrier. Even when they had no way of knowing what another driver meant by a particular action, they could not switch off their hermeneutic instincts, inferring from quite minor transgressions, like tailgating or horn-honking, remarkably firm conclusions about why other motorists were setting out specifically to piss them off. Pissed-off drivers became annoyed not just at overt aggression but at motorists who seemed to be oblivious to them, like those who continued past exits with their indicators still flashing. What made drivers most annoyed was not having their own kindnesses and courtesies acknowledged.

Katz also made a note of a phenomenon he called the 'routine production of a sense of incredulity'. He was struck by how often his subjects used phrases like 'I can't *believe* that asshole!' or 'Would you look at that jerk? How can people *do* that.' It was as if the road induced a form of temporary amnesia, which meant that motorists had to learn all over again the bizarre behaviour of their fellow road users. 'Given that nothing has been done to reform the driving public since one confronted the last unpleasant incident,' Katz asked, 'why be amazed when one confronts yet another asshole?'[47]

It's a good question. Katz's research suggests that we cannot simply assume that the social codes we have learnt off-road will serve us just as well on the road. The road creates its own mentalities and delusions, its own ways of relating to others. But the anti-traffic light campaigners mainly based their arguments on analogies between roads and other places. They saw the road as simply part of civilised life, best organised by the rules we have learnt elsewhere, about queuing, turn-taking and so on. Why couldn't roads work like skating rinks or crowded pavements, they asked, where people avoid each other through eye contact and non-verbal signals, or like supermarket car parks and campsites, where motorists wave each other on cheerfully? Cassini's moment of revelation came after encountering the 'peaceful anarchy' at a Cambridge crossroads in 1999 where the lights had failed and drivers managed to police the crossing themselves, fairly and efficiently.[48] Whether such exemplary behaviour would continue in unexceptional situations is less clear.

Shared-space projects have certainly got rid of a lot of ugly road clutter, and on city streets where traffic moves slowly they have been a success. But perhaps we shouldn't assume that this means that the answer to how road users can cohabit peaceably was simple all along. The history of Britain's hotchpotch of traffic architecture and unwritten etiquette suggests that these are complex questions debated about since the birth of the motor car. Whatever those 'shouts and gestures of motorists' were that Mass-Observation identified, they suggest that the road has long been a fraught social space. Without being aware of this history, the idea of shared space, which originated with pedestrian-friendly designers like Monderman and Hamilton-Baillie, risks becoming a Trojan horse for a certain sort of personal libertarianism that is really about giving free rein to the motorist.

The shared-space movement believes in the basic civic-mindedness and intelligent self-interest in human nature – which is why it also believes that the distinction between road and non-road is artificial, and that blurring the border between road and pavement by getting rid of kerbs, traffic lights and signs may return us to a more harmonious way of living together. But a road is not just about human nature; it is also about history and culture. And it has never seemed to me that there is anything very natural about our behaviour on the roads. The more I drive in this semi-autonomous country of asphalt – with its winking lights, honked horns, arcane hierarchies and gestures as pantomimic as those of commedia dell'arte – the more the behaviour of its citizens just seems rich, baffling and strange.

5

22 YEARS IN A TRAVELODGE

*The rest areas are the place of time and truth, where life still
has two legs and two arms, while the robots of the freeway
lie still, dispirited, dead in their silence and powerlessness.*

Julio Cortázar and Carol Dunlop[1]

What happens when a road, designed for movement, becomes a
place where people put down roots and resume their normal, sedentary lives? That is the theme of Julio Cortázar's 1966 story, 'The
Southern Thruway', set on the Autoroute du Soleil between Paris
and Marseille. It begins with a horrific traffic jam forming late on a
Sunday afternoon, just past Fontainebleau, as thousands of weekenders return to Paris. People get out of their cars to stretch their legs
and an ad hoc tarmac community develops. As the jam goes on for
days, the motorists form war councils, appoint leaders and send out
scouting missions to forage for food. Trapped together in the mar-
ginal land of the roadside verge, they develop a sense of kinship that
is missing from their anonymous lives in the city. The story ends as
the jam suddenly disappears and the nameless hero speeds back to
Paris in search of the motorists with whom he has recently formed
this utopian community, wondering 'why all this hurry, why this mad
race in the night among unknown cars, where no one knew anything

about the others, where everyone looked straight ahead, only ahead'.[2]

In a case of life imitating art, Cortázar and his Canadian wife Carol Dunlop were inspired by his story to spend a month living on the Autoroute du Soleil in the summer of 1982. They stayed in a VW camper van, driving only short distances and parking each day at two of the sixty-five rest stops, sleeping overnight in the second. Resisting the temptation to slip through the roadside fences into the non-freeway world, they kept up their self-imposed exile in this inhospitable terrain – a more difficult task than it sounds. Living on the autoroute was technically illegal, because the road tolls meant that no vehicle was allowed to stay on it for more than two days. And in the days before mobile phones, they were cut off from civilisation and relied on friends to organise rescue missions, driving out to meet them with food, books and supplies at pre-agreed points and times.

Cortázar and Dunlop recount this epic journey in their lovely, mock-heroic book *Autonauts of the Cosmoroute*. Like the great explorers they keep a logbook with details of their diet and the flora and fauna of the rest stops. They soon learn to see the roadside, which most freeway people use only for refuelling and bodily functions, as a world in its own right. Sitting by the road in their lounge chairs, they discover a 'parallel highway ... the other path, which is, in any event, the same one'.[3] Like 'cosmonauts of the autoroute' they imagine themselves travelling through the undiscovered space of the road in their little VW command module.

Behind Cortázar and Dunlop's ludic and very French exploration of *la vie quotidienne* lies a serious point about the way we live our daily lives without noticing or reflecting on them. So it is fitting that they should focus on the roadside, an everyday place on which little human thought is expended. Because it is an improvised space, assembled quickly and unceremoniously, the roadside is actually a crucible of social change. It has a unique landscape, from boxy warehouses to advertising hoardings, and a distinctive habitat with its own resident wildlife, from motorway birds to hitchhikers. But most of the time it is simply ignored, a green and grey margin of scrubland and strip left to its own devices, where we stop only briefly or involuntarily.

Cortázar and Dunlop's project was at least made more interesting by the huge variety of rest stops on French autoroutes: some are fully fledged service stations, others picturesque picnic spots and others just little slivers of roadside concrete for parking and resting. On British motorways the only place to stop by the roadside other than the emergency hard shoulder is the service station, a building with its own peculiar national mythology.

→

There is some disagreement (not, admittedly, very fierce disagreement) about which was the first motorway service station in Britain. Blue Boar's Watford Gap opened as soon as they removed the cones on the M1 on 2 November 1959. But the service station wasn't finished so they made do with petrol pumps and wooden sheds requisitioned as sandwich bars. Nine months later, in August 1960, the first proper service station opened further down the M1, near a small Buckinghamshire market town famous for making Aston Martin cars, called Newport Pagnell. Newport Pagnell services was the pet project of Charles Forte, an Italo-Scot who had built up a multi-million pound catering empire from a single milk bar in Fleet Street in the 1930s. Newport Pagnell had to open two hours early, as a curious public crowded round the entrances waiting to come in. 'Quite a variety of people used the snack bar today,' *The Times* reported cheerfully. 'They included lorry drivers in oily overalls, young motor cyclists, families returning home from their holidays, mothers and babies, girls and dogs, salesmen and businessmen.' The décor was as bright and clean as Forte's milk bars, with a red and yellow check floor, off-white upholstered seating booths and a ceiling sprinkled with flush-fitting lights. Customers seemed pleased at the design, 'so much smarter than the usual transport pull-up'. The main dishes were hamburgers, hot dogs, soups and 'a varied selection of sweets'.[4]

The first service stations had the lustre of the new. Smartly dressed stewardesses greeted customers, just like on airlines. Motorists bought postcards of the service stations from vending machines, and sent them to friends with scrawled accounts of new customs on the back:

'We are having a cup of coffee on our way back along the motor-way.'[5] Many of the restaurants occupied the covered bridges over the motorways, so that patrons could practise a new form of sightseeing: watching traffic. Forton services' 65-foot-high tower, nicknamed the 'magic mushroom' by lorry drivers, had a sun terrace with views on a clear day to the Irish Sea.

Young people embraced the service stations as a more alluring alternative to the only other all-night hangout, the 24-hour launder-ette. Like the similarly voguish espresso bar, the service station filled a cultural void for British youth. It was a congenial place to while away a few hours without spending much, an open-all-hours escape from the soporific British Sunday and what the cultural critic Tosco Fyvel called the 'pall of boredom', the 'dead and shuttered look' that descended on the average British town after dark. Leather-clad bikers could stare at the teenage girls who perched on the snackbar stools 'patting beehive hairstyles and sipping shilling beakers of Cona coffee' while 'dreaming about Albert Finney, American blue jeans and holidays to Rimini'.[6]

After midnight, gigging musicians would bump into each other at the M1 service stations and exchange gossip about venues and record-ing deals. The Beatles, according to one Newport Pagnell counter-assistant, were 'very unruly' and threw bread rolls at their manager, Brian Epstein. Pink Floyd's drummer, Nick Mason, recalled the Blue Boar at Watford Gap at two o'clock on a Sunday morning looking like a Ford Transit van rally as bands made their way back from gigs, and 'crushed velvet trousers outnumbered truckers' overalls'. When Jimi Hendrix first arrived in Britain, he heard the name 'Blue Boar' so often that he thought it was a new nightclub and asked which band was playing there that night. Chris White of the Zombies called it 'the feeding trough of the mid-60s' Beat Boom'.[7]

The food at service stations was quite edible. The jazz musician Humphrey Lyttelton later wrote that 'while driving home down the M1 in its early days, I had often drooled in anticipation of the splen-did egg, sausage, beans and chips dispensed through the night at the Granada Service Area, Toddington. The team of West Indian ladies there knew just when to rescue the eggs from the sizzling hell of the griddle.' In 1966 the frozen fish company Ross opened the Terence Conran-designed Captain's Table restaurant at Leicester Forest East on the M1, with serving staff in sailor suits, décor like an ocean liner and an open balcony on to the motorway like a ship's deck. The manager wore four gold stripes on his cuffs and a pianist played Chopin on a baby Grand while patrons tucked into their flambé curry or Jamaican fish jambalaya. Service station operators like Granada, Top Rank and Mecca had backgrounds in the entertainment industry and turned their cafeterias into theme-park feeding halls inspired by Butlin's holiday camps; what one architectural historian calls 'a kind of Dallas meets Disney meets *Star Trek* fantasy dropped down in Middle England'. Mecca's Trowell services on the M1 near Sherwood Forest (or near enough) had a Robin Hood-themed Sheriff's Restaurant and Marian's Pantry, with a fibreglass greenwood, medieval banqueting hall and 3D mosaic of jousting outlaws in the foyer. Mecca promoted Trowell as 'an oasis on a concrete strip'.[8]

Motorway restaurants had one big drawback. Service station operators were allowed to apply to local authorities for alcohol licences, but Newport Pagnell's application was turned down like all the others. So Forte sold a de-alcoholised white wine called Wunderbar made from extracting alcohol from low-grade wines from the Middle Rhine, using a patented vacuum process. The wine critic, Hugh Johnson, called it 'mediocre, thirst-quenching and quite pleasant'. At a time when driving under the influence was more socially acceptable than today, a dry motorway felt like another example of mean-spirited English puritanism. A group of French tourists, reduced to nipping out to their coaches in the middle of a five-course meal at a motorway service station to drink off-licence wine from paper cups, complained that a restaurant without wine was 'like an hotel without beds'.[9]

By the mid-1960s, habit had worn a hole in the service station's glamour, and the operators were stuck with long leases, legal obligations to provide free facilities like toilets, and rules against advertising themselves on the motorway except with a generic sign for a knife and fork. Most of the service stations were losing money. Only Forte, with its long expertise in assembly-line cooking, was having much success. In 1965, a study by the Bartlett School of Architecture – commissioned by the government to find out why the service stations were struggling – concluded that they had delusions of grandeur. The novelty of motorway gazing was wearing off. All those bridge and tower restaurants were architectural follies that simply stopped customers doing what they wanted to do, which was get in and out of the building quickly. The roadside has always been bandit country and the service station, with minimal surveillance and the chance of a quick getaway, was suffering from chronic vandalism and theft. Motorists were stealing thousands of pounds worth of cutlery every year, along with less obvious things like wooden trays, toilet-roll holders and toilet seats.[10]

In the late 1960s, the service stations began to implement the policy of 'least commitment' recommended by the Bartlett study. They cut down on waiters and introduced more sliding-tray cafeterias. One of the new-era service stations was Washington-Birtley, opened on the A1(M) in 1970. It had a robotised restaurant with a range of dishes including duckling à l'orange and coq au vin. Once customers had liberated their chosen meal from the rotating vending machines, they heated it up in a microwave, aided by female assistants in miniskirts. All food was served on disposable plates and cutlery, which could be tossed into a compacter along with the leftovers. Another new service station was the M1's Scratchwood, which hid itself down long slip roads. With its subdued décor and acoustically absorbent floors, it was an 'anti-motorway service station', intended as 'a haven of tranquillity, a soothing influence on frayed nerves, and a refuge from the stresses and irritations of motorway driving'. The canny use of mirrors in the restaurant offered the visual illusion of green fields on all sides and no motorway in sight. Woolley Edge on the M1 was also invisible from the road and designed like an Alpine ski lodge with scissor trusses and a sloping timbered roof to fit its moorland setting. 'The motorist is being invited to imagine himself in a non-motorway world,' wrote the critic in the *Architectural Review* appreciatively, 'to fancy that, as he switches off, he can hear a faint tinkle of cowbells.'[11]

Anyone who used a motorway service station after about 1970 will know that this attempt at Phoenix-like reinvention was not a great success. A leitmotif of 1970s rock music was an un-rock'n'roll-like concern with the poor food at motorway cafés, from the Kinks' song 'Motorway' to Roy Harper's 'Watford Gap', which was so scathing about the food that Blue Boar sued his record label for defamation. The service station was a land of dirty carpets, plastic plants, canned music, flooded toilets, unswept floors, unemptied ashtrays, sticky tabletops, broken cups, stewed tea and congealed food slowly expiring under hot lamps. Customers responded in kind to this literal interpretation of 'least commitment'. The service station became a favourite place for rival gangs of football hooligans to meet up for a fight. In one pitched battle at the M62's Birch services at the start of the 1975–76 season, Leeds and Chelsea fans uprooted saplings and used them as weapons. The battle spread on to the overbridge and about forty windows were broken, showering glass on to the M62 and leaving terrified onlookers exposed to the motorway. By the late 1970s, the equivalent of fifty miles of graffiti was being removed from the walls of this one service station each year.[12]

It was around this time that the Hungarian émigré and restaurant critic, Egon Ronay, achieved national renown for the vigour with which he berated motorway caterers for their 'almost universal contempt for their customers' palates'. One of his reports merited a full front page in the *Daily Express* under the headline, 'Eat before you drive'. Ronay's impact lay partly in the rhetorical delights of his vocabulary of disgust. 'At least half the sausages are very poor,' he wrote in a collective review of the service stations he visited in 1977, 'unsightly, bready, burnt, skinny and shrivelled ... all fish is frozen, often thrown straight from the refrigerator into the frying pan. Practically no decent chips can be found – they are soft, soggy, often grey. The ubiquitous peas, from poor brands, are ... often found swimming in a livid green liquid.' A year later, Newport Pagnell came in for special criticism for its 'stale fish fried in old fat, gristly meat, rubbery pastry, watery carrots and shrivelled peas', not to mention its 'badly worn carpets, dirty seats, sluggish table clearing, rubbish and cigarette ends'. The same guide discovered 'inedible gravy under stale pastry' (Leicester Forest East, M1), 'revolting sausages: hard, burst, pink and shapeless' (Knutsford, M6) and 'steak pies and burgers as bad as we have experienced anywhere' (Michaelwood, M5). On a more positive note, Aust services on the M4 had progressed from 'appalling' to 'acceptable'.[13]

After Ronay's comments provoked questions in parliament, the government set up an independent inquiry into service stations, headed by Peter Prior, chairman of Bulmers cider. Prior and his committee toured Britain, often accompanying lorry drivers in their cabs, and making unannounced visits to motorway cafés. Prior himself drove 55,000 miles and ate three meals a day at service stations for five months. 'And if you think it's good fun eating motorway meals at the Government's expense,' he said, 'just ask yourself when you last had an unforgettable evening in a motorway restaurant.' The committee's report, published in 1978, came to the not very startling conclusion that motorway meals were poor and overpriced – but it also found that the operators were not guilty of daylight robbery. The real villain was the government, which was taking too big a cut of the profits. Most of the thirty-nine service areas made hardly any profit, and twelve were losing money. They were clueless rather than culpable. Many service station staff

> …were incapable of distinguishing good food from bad. Two members sampled 'steak and kidney pie' at one area which they considered to be the worst item they had tried anywhere. It tasted awful and looked awful. Later when the members disclosed their presence, the manager, in the course of a tour, indicated the pie. 'Take a look at that,' he said, with genuine pride, 'that is what Egon Ronay thought was dreadful.'[14]

But the public did not seem as outraged about the service station food as Egon Ronay. Of those customers interviewed at the service stations, 41 per cent found the food 'enjoyable' and another 45 per cent found it 'acceptable' – although the committee conceded that this might have meant 'not quite bad enough to complain about'. A similar survey of people interviewed at home was more negative, suggesting either that these people were steering clear of the service areas because they were so bad or that motorway food was worse in the memory.[15]

The columnist Bernard Levin did not dispute that most people seemed happy with the food but this only convinced him that 'the British are fed like pigs because they do not mind eating like pigs'. The worst thing about complaining about the disgusting fare, squalid setting and incompetent staff, he wrote, was that 'all around you are your fellow-customers, thinking (and sometimes saying aloud) that *you* are in the wrong, and that the cold, greasy bacon, the eggs cooked in rancid fat, and the margarine-strewn slice of stale bread, represent a Lucullan banquet which you ought to be glad to eat'. Levin insisted that there would be 'assault and battery in most of Europe, a lawsuit in the United States, and murder on a lavish scale in France, if somebody started to serve in those countries the cheap food that is found acceptable in this one'.[16] The legendary awfulness of the motorway service station was probably partly down to its sheer unavoidability as the only place to stop on long road journeys. It was where the opinion-forming elite was forced to encounter mass catering, and assumed that what it discovered there was uniquely vile. The horridness of the food and ambience became an overworked metaphor, a synecdoche for the malaise of postwar economic and moral decline – our post-imperial, post-industrial identity crisis encapsulated in a gristly Scotch egg.

$$\rightarrow$$

The roadside has long inspired this kind of jeremiad, because it feeds into resilient English narratives of nostalgia and loss. The roadside verge is a hybrid place, neither urban nor rural, in which elegists can contemplate the natural world and lament its encroachment by modern abominations. These anxieties date back to the interwar period, when the rise of the motor car and the arrival of the National Grid meant that houses and factories tended to be built along roads rather than near coalfields. Many observers saw in Britain's new roadside topography the symptoms of moral degeneration and social crisis.

The architect Clough Williams-Ellis is now best known for Portmeirion, the Italianate model village in north Wales used as the location for the 1960s TV series *The Prisoner*. In 1928, though, he became famous after writing a striking polemic, *England and the Octopus*. The 'octopus' was London, or urban culture, spreading its tentacles into the countryside through the new arterial road system. Williams-Ellis's book is written in a tone of high moral dudgeon, its chief enemy being the shallow conurbations created by ribbon development – 'the disfiguring little buildings [that] grow up and multiply like nettles along a drain, like lice upon a tape-worm'.[17]

Williams-Ellis employed a common rhetorical ploy of the time, fastening on seemingly trivial roadside phenomena – enamelled Michelin signs, bungalows with pink asbestos roofs, advertising hoardings – and grouping them together to suggest that the English landscape was being swamped by clutter and squalor. Along the unplanned roadside of the interwar years, these objects would appear unannounced like 'barbarian invaders' (Williams-Ellis's description of bungalows). Petrol pumps, which, the AA conceded, were now 'even as the lilies of the field, albeit not quite so pretty', were a particular target for moral outrage. One letter-writer to *The Times* thought their design 'so ghastly as to suggest an invasion by Martians'. After driving back from London along the A2 Kent road, the Archbishop of Canterbury pronounced himself appalled by the petrol pumps, tea kiosks and bungalows for which he 'found it impossible to find a suitable adjective' and he urged people to 'work together for the spiritual vitality of the community and to preserve what remained of our English country'.[18]

There were some ill-advised attempts at prettification, including petrol stations with thatched roofs and garages disguised as pagodas or Tudorbethan houses with names like 'Ye Olde Petrol Pumpe'. The Roads Beautifying Association, founded in 1928 with the support of the Ministry of Transport, believed fervently in the suburbanisation of road culture, envisaging long rows of flowering cherry trees and poplars planted at crossroads, arterial roads modelled on the Acacia Avenues then springing up in semi-detached suburbia. Compared to the RBA, Williams-Ellis was a modern. Inspired by Robert Moses's American parkways, he wanted to fuse the linearity of the road with the natural contours of the countryside. He thought there was 'something rather noble about the broad white concrete ribbons laid in sweeping curves and easy gradients', which should not be disguised by picturesque decoration. *England and the Octopus* wore the exasperated air of enlightened despotism, born of frustration that ordinary people – this majority who were the 'unburied dead' and 'a perpetual drag on all progress whatsoever' – could not see the everyday ugliness in front of them. England, wrote Williams-Ellis, was 'the Country of the Blind – we cannot see and we do not care'.[19]

In his 1934 travel book *English Journey*, J.B. Priestley was slightly more sanguine. The book begins with him travelling out of London in a coach along the Great West Road, and seeing the art deco roadside factories on the 'Golden Mile' through Brentford, built by American-owned companies like Firestone Tyres, Coty Cosmetics and Gillette, which had flocked to suburban London after the 1927 Tariff Act imposed heavy taxes on imports from outside the empire. Priestley notes how unEnglish this landscape looks after the jumbled streets of west London, as though he has 'suddenly rolled into California'. Compared to his fixed idea of a factory from his Bradford childhood as 'a bleak, soot-covered building with a chimney', these new buildings seem to be 'merely playing at being factories'. Their pleasing façades, behind which they make insubstantial products like toothpaste and potato crisps, are 'like a permanent exhibition ground, all glass and chromium plate and nice painted signs and coloured lights'. Throughout *English Journey*, the roadside serves in this way as a metaphor for cultural change, an augury of a future England made up of Tudor-style chain pubs, lock-up shops and redbrick villas where 'everything and everybody is being rushed down and swept into one dusty arterial road of cheap mass production and standardized living'.

At the end of the book, Priestley gets stuck in thick fog as his chauffeur drives him back to London on the Great North Road.

Unable to see out of the window, he lights his pipe and hunkers down, dismissing as 'only blinding vapour' the England outside his car and instead contemplating the country he has discovered on his journey. This England, he decides, is three different countries: the old feudal England of towns and villages, the nineteenth-century England of the great industrial cities, and the modern England 'of arterial and by-pass roads, of filling stations and factories that look like exhibition buildings' – the country he might have seen out of the car window if the fog had lifted. This England is 'essentially democratic' but 'unfortunately it is a bit too cheap ... Too much of it is simply a trumpery imitation of something not very good even in the original.'[20]

Not everyone who reflected on the roadside in the 1930s was quite so measured. In 1937, the rural writer and broadcaster John Moore recounted his flight over the Cotswolds in a hired Tiger Moth. 'One can see the tracks of the beast very clearly from the air,' he wrote. 'I could see the towns and even some of the villages nibbling their way outwards, not wisely and orderly, but as haphazard and casually as caterpillars nibbling at a leaf; I could see the mess creeping along the sides of all the roads.'[21] Moore's essay appeared in a collection titled *Britain and the Beast*, edited by Williams-Ellis, who had gathered together a group of writers and artists to protest against a growing threat to the nation. The 'beast' did not refer, as one might perhaps have expected in 1937, to the looming threat of fascism; it denoted the pink-painted bungalows and mock-Tudor semis lining the new arterial roads. Williams-Ellis described his contributors as 'a coroner's jury, conducting the inquest on a mutilated corpse'.[22]

After the Second World War, this view of the roadside as a presage of Britain's dark future was voiced even more stridently. In 1955, an angry young man called Ian Nairn drove from Southampton to Carlisle with his friend, the artist Gordon Cullen, mostly on the A34. Nairn was a self-taught architectural critic who believed that 'the roundabout down the road' ought to make you 'gasp with joy'. But he meant this journey to be 'a travel agent's trip in reverse – picking out the bad, not the good' and it is easy to see why he chose the A34, because it ran all the way up the spine of the country and, before the motorways arrived, was the main route for lorries going from South-ampton docks to Manchester. It was built-up along almost its entire length. Nairn wrote about his journey in a special issue of the *Architectural Review*, in a long essay accompanied by Cullen's sketches.

Like a latter-day Cobbett, Nairn used his non-rural ride along the A34 to reflect on the state of the nation. He found the local detail of Britain's towns and countryside blurring into a single, loveless land-scape of ugly concrete roads, hideous street furniture and identikit buildings. Nairn used a new word to describe this mess – 'subtopia', a conflation of 'suburb' and 'utopia' – which he feared was taking over the country like a 'gaseous pink marshmallow' and 'amorphous destroyer'. For Nairn, this uncaring roadside landscape of concrete and chicken wire was the symptom of a deeper malaise – a mass psy-chosis which had its roots in our fatalistic acceptance of mediocrity, 'a miasma rising from the heart of our collective self'.[23]

Ironically, Nairn was writing just as the roadside was becom-ing more carefully planned after years of unregulated sprawl. The spec-built houses that lined the interwar arterial roads – in the Stock-broker Tudor style that the cartoonist Osbert Lancaster christened 'bypass variegated' – had been stopped in their tracks by the war. The 1947 Town and Country Planning Act introduced strict controls on advertising hoardings and petrol stations and the new motor-ways were going to be quite unlike the untidy landscapes of the A34. Nairn's polemic was curiously Janus-faced, flailing alike against the unregulated interwar roadside and the regulated postwar roadside. He loathed subtopia's 'unwitting agents' like bus-stop poles and road signs that were 'treated by their authors as though they were invis-ible'. But he loathed equally the more recent attempts to design the roadside, like the 'municipal rustic' of ornamental planting in railed-off mini-gardens or roundabouts with carefully manicured lawns and flower displays.[24]

When this issue of *Architectural Review* was published as a book, *Outrage*, it was an unlikely bestseller. The Duke of Edinburgh popularised the term 'subtopia' in a speech arguing that there was 'no excuse for unattractive design'. The word became a rallying cry for cultural critics on both left and right who felt uneasy with rising affluence or increased state controls, and who could now affix this unease to an abstract noun. The poet and critic John Betjeman, who wrote a friendly review of *Outrage* in the *Spectator*, argued elsewhere that we 'have ceased to use our eyes ... Beauty is invisible to us', and evoked the bogey of 'suburban man' whose 'indifference to the look of things is catching'.[25] Like Nairn and Williams-Ellis, Betjeman felt that most people responded to the roadside with indifference because they lacked the visual sensibility to notice the ugliness.

But can ugliness really be invisible? Aesthetic judgements change from era to era. Petrol pumps and bungalows, which once excited such anger, have long since disappeared into the unnoticed background of daily life. In any case, like Catherine II of Russia riding through the Potemkin villages, the hollow façades built by her minister in the Crimea, these critics mistook the frontage of the roadside for the substance of the nation. They saw it as an invidious expansion of the town into the country, when actually it was more like an urban mirage that vanished as you went further inland. At the root of their aesthetic and moral objections lay a political outlook that was a peculiar mix of conservatism and radicalism. It combined a reactionary's fear of lower-middle-class, suburban mediocrity with a radical's anxiety about untrammelled commercialism and an undemocratic state taking over common land.

→

The problem was that no one was quite sure who owned the roadside – mainly because, most of the time, no one had any desire to use it. The collective impulses generated by the Second World War, and the requisitioning of vast tranches of land to build airfields, had brought the question of landownership to the fore. The Royal Commission on Common Land, which reported in 1958, argued that the one-and-a-half million acres of uncommitted land in England and Wales, ranging from village greens to uplands, should be open to the public. But it ignored one of the largest areas of common land – the roadside.

Before the war the road was the King's highway, free for all his majesty's subjects to use, and these rights of commonage extended to the verge. The lay-by was a space outside polite society, where lorry drivers would 'nut down' (catnap), sometimes in the company of the prostitutes who naturally gravitated towards roads. In 1965, a consultant venereologist claimed that the opening of the M6 had helped to reduce cases of VD in Bolton because these 'lorry girls' were no longer passing through the town.[26] Another disreputable roadside activity was 'lorry-hopping', also known as 'hitch-hiking', an inter-war invention sustained by the mobile workforce of the depression era and a growing army of bored commercial travellers and hauliers ready to offer them a lift in return for company.

When the motorways arrived, many thought, wrongly, that their verges were common land and, since they were only enclosed by waist-high post-and-rail fences, pedestrians could easily use them for hitchhiking, traffic-gazing and flower-picking. Gradually, though, the verges became an impenetrable no man's land and motorways turned into barriers in the landscape, as impassable as railway lines. In 1966 *Country Life* noticed 'the growing tendency for motorways to act as local boundaries – artificial rivers'. Although tunnels and bridges were built under and over the M1 for farmers whose land had been severed by the motorway, they soon began exchanging land with each other so their farms no longer straddled the road. Local hunts on the first section of the M1 – which, with its shire landscape of pasture fields and hedgerows, was classic foxhunting country – swapped land too.[27]

The hitchhikers were not so easily deterred. The government had actively encouraged hitching during the war to save petrol and allow soldiers to get back to camp, but after the war it retained its dodgy reputation: in 1960 one writer lamented the growing acceptance of this 'highwaymanish technique'.[28] The arrival of the motorways coincided with a hitchhiking boom, swelled by the huge growth in student numbers in the early 1960s. Another big group of hitchhikers in the 1960s and 1970s was made up of birdwatchers travelling to remote parts of Britain to see exotic birds, for this was the golden age of twitching. The birder Mark Cocker recalls:

Back then, if you could have got into some hypothetical control module in space where you could monitor birders' movements around Britain's road networks, the screen would have appeared as an endless chaos of random blips, each one representing young twitchers hitching back and forth across the country. There would have been occasional patterns – clusters heading towards Norfolk in May, a brief lull in July, a further rush towards Shetland in September, or Cornwall in October.[29]

The *Hitch-hikers' Manual*, published in 1979 by a young travel journalist called Simon Calder who had been thumbing lifts since the age of thirteen, provides a record of the rich hitching subculture that formed in these years. Calder included a table of different permutations of hitchhikers and the typical time it would take them to get a lift, from single women (10–15 minutes) to three men (90 minutes). Men generally did better if they travelled with women and hid behind a hedge, a common ruse that sounds like something that only happens in comedy films.

Since the motorways were the fastest way to move around, their junctions and service stations quickly became the most popular hitching places. There were long queues of hitchers at hotspots like Staples Corner at the foot of the M1, with their own (imperfectly executed) etiquette about sharing lifts or standing back so as not to spoil fellow hitchers' chances. Few drivers followed this code of conduct, though, simply picking up whomever they liked. In this competitive environment, hitchers went in for attention-grabbing gimmicks like wearing ties or dinner suits. The unscrupulous leant on crutches or wore soldiers' uniforms. While the fancy dress varied, hitching at motorway junctions added one essential accessory to the classic outstretched thumb: a cardboard sign, because drivers needed to know which direction the hitcher was going. Battle-hardened veterans even carried chalk and a piece of wood painted with blackboard paint or, better still, a sheet of white plastic and a marker pen. They also knew that adding 'please' to the place name, or words like 'hopefully' and 'eventually', worked wonders.

Calder provided strip maps of the major motorway junctions, including details of where it was illegal to stand because it was part of the motorway. In fact, the law against hitching and picking up on motorways was widely flouted – although the police, who generally regarded hitchers as feckless hippies, would fine any they caught on motorways and search them for drugs. Calder advised hitchers who were dropped off at illegal places to head through the fields to another road or, if caught by the police, to 'fabricate some sinful lie about the driver attacking you, and showing them the rip in your jeans that proves you had to jump out of the car'. Even though it yielded the highest ratio of pick-ups per passing car, the night was still a bleak time to thumb a lift and hitchers were often stuck on motorways overnight without any prospect of escape – in which case Calder recommended that 'the grassy folds and slopes of motorway junctions can be quite cosy, but you are inclined to roll into ditches'.[30]

Calder was writing just as hitching began its slow decline, which he later attributed to Thatcherism's 'I'm all right Jack' ethos, its silent destruction of the civic-minded impulse.[31] But there were probably more concrete reasons for its decline, such as the introduction of the student railcard and cheaper coach services in the 1970s and, more recently, young people going further afield on gap years. Hitching on motorways also became more difficult as barriers and 'no pedestrian' signs were erected at junctions. This created hitching voids where no one wanted to be dropped off, especially the vast interchanges like Almondsbury and Lofthouse where major motorways crossed – the black holes in the hitchhiker's galaxy.

→

The turning of the motorway verge into a *terra nulla* had another unintended consequence. The 1947 Agriculture Act had given farmers guaranteed markets, but demanded massive economies of scale from them in return. Farmers received huge grants to raze long grasses and hedgerows, so that machinery could work the land quicker. At the end of the war, England and Wales alone had nearly 800,000 miles of hedgerow, but over the next forty years they lost almost a quarter of it. Between 1960 and 1966, the early motorway era, hedgerows disappeared at a record rate of about 10,000 miles a year.[32] Vast areas of land, particularly in the Midlands and East Anglia, became American-style prairies broken up only by roads.

Conservationists began to realise that the motorway verges could serve as replacement nature reserves, particularly in the arable south where pasture was disappearing rapidly. When the M1 was finished in 1967, the conservationist Michael Way coordinated a botanical survey of the entire roadside verge between Hendon and Leeds and discovered that, just like the railways, the motorways were eco-havens. Pollen and seeds hitched a ride on car bumpers or blew along the wind tunnels created by moving traffic and roadside cuttings. In 1974 the nature writer Richard Mabey calculated that there were nearly half-a-million acres of roadside verge in Britain, an area of land bigger than the statutory nature reserves.[33] By now the UK had joined the Common Market and prairie farming was about to grow fat on European subsidies and the Common Agricultural Policy – so more hedgerows vanished and nature again retreated to the roadside verges.

In fact, the roadside verge is really the modern equivalent of the hedgerow – although it has yet to acquire its Edmund Blunden, the poet and conservationist who in 1935 misquoted King Lear's fool to foretell that 'when there are no more English hedges, and the expedient of barbed wire has carried the day everywhere, "There shall the realm of Albion / Be brought to great confusion."'[34] We normally think of verges as the motoring equivalent of a screensaver, an endless green sward interrupted by the occasional abandoned tyre or stray plastic bag. Yet as Mabey showed, it was part of an 'unofficial countryside' that was valuable almost because it was so unnoticed and unloved. The roadside was deceptively diverse, cutting through every type of landscape and geology, and including not only the grass embankments but also the balancing ponds and settling pools needed to drain the carriageway of rainwater, which often attracted wildlife. It was the dogged, unlovely nature of the roadside – from the rare fungi and algae that thrived in the drip-zone under crash barriers to the wild flowers that flourished on the poor-quality soil of the verge – that made it ecologically important. By 1971 the Department of Transport was planting a million trees and shrubs next to motorways each year – more than the Forestry Commission planted in the whole country.[35] Mostly native broad-leaved species like Alder, Ash and Oak, motorway trees were an antidote to the hated conifers of scientific forestry. Humphrey Lyttelton described driving on British roads in autumn as 'a balm to the soul' when compared with motoring between interminable rows of evergreens on the German autobahns, which he compared to 'a trip through a giant toothbrush'.[36]

This unpesticided verge also became a refuge for animals that were losing their natural breeding grounds to intensive farming. Small mammals like the field mouse and the short-tailed vole colonised the unrazed ground and attracted airborne predators. All those hitchhiking birdwatchers, in search of exotic species in Norfolk and the Hebrides, began to see much of interest while they thumbed for lifts on the verges. The kestrel, alias the 'motorway hawk', was soon hovering motionless in the air, hang-gliding on the updraughts of air created by motorway cuttings. Conservationists attached nest boxes to the backs of motorway signs and in the spring of 1973 the Young Ornithologists Club instructed its members to look out for hawks while being driven in their parents' cars, so that numbers could be estimated. The red kite, an endangered species clinging on by its claw tips in mid-Wales, found a new home around the M40. In 1989 the Royal Society for the Protection of Birds reintroduced a small number of kites to the Chilterns, and they are now found all the way along the motorway – notably at the Stokenchurch Gap, the colossal chalk cutting between Oxford and High Wycombe featured in the opening credits of the BBC sitcom *The Vicar of Dibley*.

The roadside is where nature's freebooters – wagtails and linnets scavenging for seeds on service station tarmac, crows and sparrows foraging for apple cores and crusts thrown from cars – go for a free lunch. Crows are unfazed by human company and can often be seen from busy roads, particularly (according to rook spotters like Mark Cocker and Roger Deakin) on the wooded roundabouts of the A1. A recent BBC wildlife programme awarded the crows at one M4 service station the title of 'Bird Brains of Britain' for their ingenious method of raiding the bins, using their beaks and claws to pull the black liners upwards so they could pilfer the contents at the bottom.[37] Songbirds fare less well by the roadside, because they need to hear each other sing in their courtship and nesting rituals, and the white noise of motorway traffic drowns them out. The roadside is the songbird equivalent of a sink estate, avoided by all but the least potent males.

Most other animals, though, are drawn fatally to these corridors of speed. Snakes and lizards bask on the hot asphalt in the sun. Sheep and deer lick the rock salt left by gritters. Sweet-toothed sheep are also partial to the new type of grit, coated in molasses, which is used because it is less corrosive to cars. Millions of birds are killed while picking up insects which have themselves been dashed to the ground by cars. About 30 per cent of Britain's population of barn owls die every year flying slowly and close to the ground across roads looking for prey. Swans are bamboozled by wet roads, which can look like water from above. Most of these crash landings occur in the autumn and winter, when young, L-plated swans have just left the nest. They come in to land with their feet outstretched, expecting a gentle touch-down, and their weight and wingspan make it impossible to abort the descent even if they realise their mistake at the last moment. Where roads cross rivers, the road's warm thermal mixes with the river's cold one, creating strange currents that can suck swans out of the sky. The landing doesn't normally kill them, but they often break wings or legs and are run over.

Tessa Hadley's novel *The Master Bedroom* memorably opens with a spectacular crash on the M4 in Wales just after the Brynglass Tunnel, caused by a swan falling from the sky. At first the plunging object looks like 'a bundle of dirty washing wrapped in a sheet' but then it 'threw out one long wing, dazzling white feathers ranged in rows of perfect symmetry'.[38] The woman whose car it lands on believes it to be the reincarnation of her husband's first wife, whose suicide involved a similar fall to earth. Hadley's falling swan is a symbol of the unfamiliar lurking within the everyday – aptly enough, since the sight of a swan on the motorway is both surreal and commonplace. The motorway service station operator, Welcome Break, recently dropped its long-serving logo of a flying swan, perhaps worried about these gruesome associations. On the M25, which crosses lots of water and is made of smooth, lake-like concrete, a swan on the carriageway is as common as a car crash. The worst swan blackspot is on one of the busiest parts of the whole road network, the M25 at Junction 13 where it crosses the Thames. The Highways Agency is called out two or three times a week here, on average, for swan removals.

Is it peculiarly British to fret about roadkill and to invest it with meaning? The word originated as a hard-boiled American term that reduced the many species killed on the roads to a non-guilt-inducing, uniform mass. In the US you can buy roadkill colouring books for children, and the word has taken on a more general meaning as something that is useless or redundant ('I'm just roadkill in the kitchen'). Some Australian restaurants allow patrons to bring in their own roadkill to be cooked. It is hard to imagine motorists in these countries being enlisted in their thousands to count the number of dead animals they see on roads, as the People's Trust for Endangered Species does for its annual UK roadkill survey. According to its figures, about a million mammals (including 800,000 rabbits, 50,000 squirrels, 50,000 badgers, 50,000 deer and 25,000 foxes) die on Britain's roads each year, along with 3 million pheasants and 7 million other birds.[39]

Nothing embodies the British attitude to roadkill quite like the plight of the common toad. Each spring, in a seasonal arc starting in Cornwall in late February and reaching the frozen north by April, about a million of these creatures emerge from hibernation and up to 40 per cent of them die crossing roads on their way to their spawning grounds, either from being splatted by cars or from falling down roadside drains where they suffer lingering deaths. While frogs can bound quickly across roads, toads walk or hop, taking up to ten minutes to cross, and they also find mounting kerbs tricky. So, since the early 1970s, a very British (or, more accurately, southern English) institution has evolved: the toad patrol, in which volunteers work through wet nights to carry them across roads in buckets.

But our concern for roadkill is uneven. We care more about toads, badgers and hedgehogs than the mass murder of pheasants, or the millions of butterflies and other invertebrates that die every year on car bumpers. The sentimentality may also be misplaced because the point of roadkill surveys is to extrapolate from the body count the numbers in the species as a whole, so the relative absence of squashed hedgehogs is not something to celebrate but a sign of declining numbers – although listeners to the BBC Radio 4 statistics programme *More or Less* proposed a Panglossian theory that they were getting savvier about crossing roads.[40] Roadkill encapsulates the well-meaning ethical bemusement that now runs through our relationship to nature, our efforts to pay recompense for the unnatural world we have absent-mindedly created – in this case one that can kill so many animals in the thoughtless pursuit of speed. In 2007, one breakdown company introduced a scheme called 'friendly fines for fallen fur and feather' in which new members made a contribution to an animal charity in mitigation for the animals killed on roads – a sort of roadkill offsetting. The current vogue for roadkill cuisine has its origins in the foraging movement initiated by Richard Mabey's classic 1972 book *Food For Free*, although Mabey himself said he was 'too sentimental to scrape up road-kill pheasant'.[41] The food-taboo destroyer Hugh Fearnley-Whittingstall brought it into the mainstream on one of his first television programmes, in which he prepared a ragout of roadkill.

Roadkill cuisine is perfectly in step with the values of the burgeoning slow food movement. First, thrift: a piece of roadkill is a meal going to waste, although most of the time (unless the dying animal managed to crawl over to the side of the road) it is too mangled to be edible. Second, local sourcing: roadkill is intrinsically seasonal and each region has its delicacies – the West Country its otters, the Isle of Wight and Aberdeenshire their red squirrels, Bedfordshire and Buckinghamshire their wallabies (escaped from zoos). Finally, good husbandry: a run-over badger has led a fuller life than a battery-farmed chicken. TV's 'roadkill chef', Fergus Drennan, whose signature dishes include wild squirrel stew and badger intestine sausages, even won an Ethical Cuisine award from PETA (People for the Ethical Treatment of Animals). 'If you must consume meat,' went the award citation, 'the only ethical way to do it is to scrape it off the road.'[42] But perhaps there is also an element of personal absolution in roadkill – we feel better about eating an animal if it was the car in front that killed it.

→

Undisturbed and undervalued, the ecology of the roadside has mostly benefited from benign neglect. Human settlement by the roadside has led a similarly laissez-faire, below-the-radar existence. When the first motorways arrived, there were some isolated attempts to appreciate the new vistas they opened up. Margaret Baker's 1968 handbook *Discovering M1* was the first ever 'glove-compartment guide to the motorway and the places of interest that can be seen from it', written for car passengers and 'arranged for easy assimilation at around 60 mph'.[43] It valiantly listed visual highlights like the radio aerials at Daventry, the granite rocks of Charnwood Forest and the medieval ridge-and-furrow fields near Crick. The vogue for motorway sightseeing was short-lived, but enjoyed a brief revival more recently with the motorway sights guides written by Mike Jackson, a director of location shots for *Antiques Roadshow*, who got the idea for them while driving round the country with its presenter, Michael Aspel. Jackson then spent months travelling up and down the motorways, writing about landmarks like the Penrith factory where they make the dough balls for Domino's pizzas and the globular salt barn on the M5 in Worcestershire known locally as the 'Christmas pudding'. But Jackson only got round to covering the M4, M5 and M6 and seems to have no plans to do any others. Despite his laudable efforts, the roadside remains the most commonly viewed and least contemplated landscape in Britain.

We tend to think of landscapes as natural phenomena, with some inherent quality that exists outside our understanding and ownership of them, even though almost all of the British landscape has been altered in some way by humans. When it first crossed over to English in the early seventeenth century, the Dutch word *landschap* or 'landscape' was a technical term for a painting of inland scenery. Later it came to mean the view itself, particularly one that could be taken in at a single glance. But in both cases it was an insistently cultural idea, a human reading of the natural world. Because they are rarely seen statically, roadscapes undermine our Ruskinian ideal of landscape as a view seen at once from a privileged vantage point by a single viewer. (Jackson's books go heavy on the safety warnings: 'Drivers: do not use while travelling.') Our culture has learnt to interpret landscapes in a particular way – to read water meadows as picturesque, mountains as rugged or fenland as inscrutable. But we haven't been taught to read roadscapes, because they seem too mundane and too fleetingly viewed to form part of any imagined ideal. In order to make sense of them, we need to re-educate our eyes.

Look out of the car window: what do you see? Big sheds. Big sheds are those huge, windowless boxes you can hardly fail to notice on motorway journeys. For most of their history, they have been left off maps, ignored by the general public, invisible in their ubiquity. The grandfather of the big shed, the 600-acre Slough Trading Estate, was established as long ago as 1920 on a dumpground for old military vehicles. When George Orwell wrote that 'the germs of the future England' could be found along 'the arterial roads',[44] he meant places like Slough, home to new light industries which enabled it to escape the great depression. When the Trading Estate was founded, its main advantage was its good railway links, but as the new industry of road haulage emerged, its greater good fortune was to abut right on to the old London–Bath Road, now the A4. So the Trading Estate became the engine room of the interwar consumer revolution, the maker of Dulux paint, Horlicks, Mars Bars and Maltesers. John Betjeman famously wished some friendly bombs would fall on Slough, and the Council for the Preservation of Rural England complained that the Trading Estate could be seen from Windsor Castle and 'like a great white scar standing out prominently from the landscape, [it] reminded some of them of the Hindenburg line'.[45] Slough continues to occupy a unique place in British culture. The BBC sitcom *The Office* was set in a paper merchants on the Trading Estate and the A4's Brunel Roundabout appeared in its opening credits. In some ways, the national disdain reserved for places like Slough is a mirror of the way we imagine the roadside, this place which is at the leading edge of economic change but also somehow marginalised and 'boring'.

Most people probably imagine today's big sheds to be a product of the deregulated planning regime of the Thatcher era that let a thousand out-of-town B&Qs and Novotels bloom. In fact, they were pioneered by a socialist retail society and championed by a minister who, less than a decade later, would be demonised by the tabloids as a leader of the 'loony left'. In the late 1960s the Co-op hatched a plan to build huge regional warehouses that would increase its bulk purchasing power. Anthony Wedgwood Benn, as the minister of technology was then known, awarded the company a £150,000 innovation grant, in return for which it agreed to share its knowhow with the industry. So in 1970 the Co-op built its first distribution centre at Birtley in County Durham. Birtley wasn't just huge; it was automated, with high-bay racking systems reached by robotic cranes commanded by a massive ICI computer, allowing the dispatch of goods to the shops at a then phenomenal rate of 5,000 boxes an hour.

The big shed revolution really began in 1972 with the completion of the M6 and the linking up of the first thousand miles of motorway. LSSBs (large single-storey buildings) sprang up quickly on low-lying land near motorway intersections. The innovation of the Thatcher era that confirmed the big shed's hegemony was just-in-time, a system first used by Toyota in Japan in the 1950s, which delivers goods only when needed so they are not sitting on a shelf depreciating in value. By centralising their warehouse stock and keeping goods moving, firms could release cash flow, perhaps even sell things before they had to pay for them. 'Logistics' was this new art of moving stuff around, and the system's beating heart was the big shed.

'Like strips of shredded truck tyre,' wrote the architectural critic, Martin Pawley, 'you can find Shedland anywhere there is a motorway.' Pawley, the natural heir to Reyner Banham as a champion of motorway culture, believed that the British wrongly put their architectural energies into protecting historic buildings in cities because the country's intelligentsia generally lived and worked in the older, more scenic parts of London. The lack of attention given to the big shed in its boom years of the 1980s was an effect of Thatcherism's strange combination of free-market radicalism and cultural nostalgia – which manifested itself architecturally in lots of new builds in heritage styles, from neo-Georgian public buildings to private houses with coaching lamps and leaded lights. But while proposals for a small extension to the National Gallery in Trafalgar Square were endlessly debated after Prince Charles dismissed the original design as a 'monstrous carbuncle', millions of square footage of shedspace were being built quickly and near-invisibly all over the country. Architectural historians of the future would marvel at this skewing of priorities, Pawley argued, and realise that the most generous patron of architecture in this period was the logistics industry.[46]

Even more than the housing market, logistics depended on 'location location location', and the property hotspot was right at the heart of the trunk road system. When the M69 from Leicester to Coventry opened in 1977, it linked up with the M1 and M6 to create a 'golden triangle' in the Midlands with some of the best transport links in Britain. From here, lorries could reach 92 per cent of the UK population and return on the same day. In the middle of the golden triangle is Europe's largest distribution park, Magna Park, founded in 1988 by the property arms of Asda and the Church of England, and covering 500 acres on an abandoned RAF airfield. Companies migrating to Magna Park channelled their goods through there to an extreme degree. Toyota's Magna Park warehouse, for instance, was only 50 miles away from its manufacturing plant at Burnaston near Derby. But instead of parts being shipped straight there, they were sent from Derby to its giant European distribution centre in Belgium and then on to Magna Park – a journey of 583 miles – just so the stock could be maintained at the minimum level.

Most of us might think this an odd way to run a business, but that just shows how little we know about the invisible workings of this big shed economy. Giving nothing away on the outside, big sheds just look like dumping grounds for goods, but they are far more dynamic than that. Their cavernous insides are library-quiet apart from the low hum of computers and robotic machinery, but goods move at such a rate that they can arrive and leave within a few hours. Big sheds are the hubs for the unseen networks that sustain our daily routines.

In the late 1990s, faced with rising land prices, the big shed moved outside the golden triangle into other parts of the country. Big sheds that might seem to metropolitan types to be in the middle of nowhere – Stoke, Doncaster, Skelmersdale, Andover – are actually in the centre of everywhere, the nodes of invisible trading routes. So omnipresent are the big sheds becoming that a government quango called Community Resilience UK has plans, in the event of a natural disaster or mass terrorist attack, to requisition them as emergency mass mortuaries.

In 1933 Stephen Spender wrote about the new electricity pylons that were colonising the country as 'those pillars / Bare like nude giant girls that have no secret', whose 'quick perspective of the future' dwarfed 'our emerald country by its trek'.[47] As far as I know, no contemporary poet has rhapsodised thus about big sheds. But they have a similarly monumental quality, just arriving imposingly on the landscape without explanation or apology. Anthony Gormley, one of the few people to squeeze any aesthetic interest out of the Daventry International Rail Freight Terminal, has called megasheds 'the most permanent unconscious memorial to the age of mobility' and said they are 'as much a part of our history as the rural barn'.[48] Built quickly from prefab materials, big sheds are as transient and recyclable as garden sheds. The steel walls and roof panels can be melted down or used for scrap, the concrete floors recycled as hardcore for roads. Some are built by 'clad racking', which means plonking all the equipment on site and covering it with a plastic membrane, instead of walls. If only houses – still clinging to the antiquated technology of bricks and mortar – could be built so quickly and cheaply.

While big sheds transform the roadside silently and invisibly, people get agitated about smaller, more visible intrusions. In recent years, farmers' attempts to sell advertising space in the fields next to motorways – by mounting hoardings on tractor trailers, which get round the rules about roadside advertising because they are 'temporary' structures – have excited the sort of anger that petrol pumps produced in the interwar era. Charles Madge of Mass-Observation wrote in the 1930s that advertising hoardings had a 'queer poetry' that read like a collage of the 'social unconscious'.[49] Today's trailer ads have a similar knack of tapping into our cultural obsessions, whether it be by cultivating our persecution complexes ('Trafficlawyer4U.com: we defend the motorist!'), our bodily insecurities ('Smile: with dental implants') or our credit crunch anxieties ('Wecanwriteitoff.com: debt destruction!').

There were similar complaints a few years ago when the service station operators bent the rules that forbade them from advertising their branded outlets on motorway signs, by forming new companies called 'Roadchef Costa Coffee', 'Welcome Break KFC' and 'Moto Marks and Spencer'. These names duly went up on the signs. Whatever one thinks about these visual intrusions – and personally I admire their chutzpah – they seem trifling when compared to the much bigger, unnoticed changes occurring in our roadscape. They encapsulate all that we think we know about the shouty self-promotion of our economy, and none of what we don't know about the undemonstrative stuff that happens under (and on) the surface of our daily lives. The future of the economy still rests in places like Slough, where three million Mars Bars leave its trading estate each day, piled up in lorries heading for the nearby M4, M40 and M25. Many of them end up at the roadside: according to Mike Jackson, one service station operator 'sells enough Mars Bars each year to carpet 34 miles of motorway three-lane carriageways'. As Jackson also points out, this big shed universe will be even less visible when the trees planted by motorways reach maturity and block the view.[50] Going, going: enjoy your distant prospect of the Amazon warehouse near Milton Keynes while it lasts.

→

Shedland is fairly abstract and intangible, a country glimpsed briefly and subconsciously in the corners of our eyes. Our main encounter with the roadside remains the service station – an institution that, since Egon Ronay's damning verdict on it, has had an unlikely afterlife. And it's really in the service station, where we are captive customers and horrified onlookers, that we can most clearly see the changing nature of the roadside since the start of the motorway era. For the service station remains almost as unloved as in the 1970s – but it is also a perfect example of the human capacity for carving cultural meaning out of the most unpromising raw material.

In the Smiths' song 'Is it Really So Strange?', Morrissey sings about a man chasing his lover up and down the M1 and losing his bag at Newport Pagnell. Explaining the song's inspiration, he said he found 'that mood of a Northern person going to London and then returning home very poignant. You can't describe how you feel when you go from South to North, stopping at the service stations. It hits a deafening note.' The DJ John Peel once described bumping into Morrissey at another service station on the A1(M) near Newcastle (presumably Washington-Birtley, long since stripped of its vending machines and mini-skirted hostesses): 'To my astonishment, he announced that this was his favourite motorway service station! I think that was taking pickiness a bit too far because never in my life – and I'm a man who likes to make lists – have I felt a need to make a list of my favourite motorway service stations.'[51] But Morrissey's love of service stations is not so surprising. Like the out-of-season seaside resorts and rainy northern towns he also chronicles in his songs, they mine a rich seam of English ordinariness and gone-to-seed glamour.

Service stations have unexpectedly acquired a history, their own form of quasi-nostalgia, embedded in a whole range of filmic and literary references. In the 1967 film *Charlie Bubbles*, Albert Finney and Liza Minnelli stop at a deserted Newport Pagnell on a night drive to Manchester. One of Morrissey's heroines, Shelagh Delaney, wrote the screenplay and the Smiths used a still of the film for the sleeve of their 1984 single, 'William, It Was Really Nothing'. Willy Russell probably had this homage in mind when he wrote *The Wrong Boy*, a novel about a depressive nineteen-year-old from Oldham who unburdens his heart to his hero, Morrissey, in a series of letters written from service stations and roadside stops. Writing in the café at Birch services, he finds it comforting that Morrissey might have sat at the same table while on tour with the Smiths. 'I wonder what your thoughts were as you sat in this shrine of self-service gratification,' he muses, 'with its granary bar and its battered cod and its breadcrumbed haddock beached on a hotplate, far far from the rolling sea.'[52]

Newport Pagnell remains the locus classicus, the *Ur*-service station. Only the name of Watford Gap rivals it for bathetic resonance. If you turn into it off the M1 today, you will find that no trace of the original 1960s building, with its plastic-bright, multi-coloured fascia, remains. The new Newport Pagnell, built in the 1980s, is a halfway house between the confident, glass-sided modernism of the first service stations and the modern bungalow villages of the most recent ones, with their redbrick walls and mansarded roofs. A bland silver box with a curved, cantilevered roof over the entrances, it resembles nothing so much as a provincial airport.

The bridge over the motorway is now deserted and most of the windows, through which sightseers used to watch the 1960s traffic, are frosted up. This uninhabited walkway separates a northbound and southbound side with an identical-looking KFC, Coffee Primo and W.H. Smith's. Entering and leaving the service station absent-mindedly, you probably would not notice the two Newport Pagnells, virtual mirror images of each other. If you explored the site's perimeter, where only motorists exercising their dogs venture, you could walk under a barrier saying 'authorised vehicles only' and soon find yourself in a network of lakes, now a wetland centre, created out of gravel pits dug to build the motorway; or in a housing estate smelling of privet that leads into Newport Pagnell, the inoffensive town whose name the service station stole. But of course it's very unlikely you will get that far: a third of all service station patrons only stop to use the toilet. The service station might as well be a tarmac island in the middle of nowhere. Each Welcome Break service station features a huge blown-up photograph specific to the place by its entrance, but Newport Pagnell has a picture of an Aston Martin – not much of a clue, especially since car production ended in the town in 2007. The shop will sell you a copy of *Buckinghamshire Life and Chilterns* and a street map of nearby Milton Keynes, but otherwise there is no inkling that you are anywhere but the hyper-generic roadside.

→

Just as it did with the rest of the roadside, Thatcherism transformed the service station into a non-specific corporate space, a universal style borrowed from shopping malls and airports. One of the Thatcher government's first privatisation schemes in 1979 was selling the motorway service area freeholds and allowing private franchises to invest in the sites. The infamous cafeterias gave way to 'food courts' – open-plan spaces with communal seating surrounded by different counters for McDonald's, Burger King and Kentucky Fried Chicken. The Thatcher reforms also made it easier for service stations to branch out into other areas. So the 1980s became the age of the chain motel.

This was a fortunate development for John Blyde and Peter Hutchinson of the Bedfordshire timber frame manufacturers, Potton, who at the time were becoming very frustrated with their main business of building houses. Potton had been a pioneer in prefab housing in the 1970s, supplying local councils in new towns like Milton Keynes and Basildon. But the Thatcher government had killed off council housing and new planning guidelines for private houses insisted on a fussy, traditional style which did not suit Potton's prefab methods. So they hit on a new type of prefab building: the American-style budget hotel. They built a prototype on a golf course owned by the company and invited the major hotel chains for a viewing.

This hotel was a simple two-storey building with a small reception area and corridors serving forty identical rooms. Each room was a timber-framed 'pod', pre-fitted with an en suite bathroom, lights, furniture, a television and pictures on the wall. When the room was ready for its first guest it was wrapped in tarpaulin, transported to the site and winched into position. This giant Legoland of box rooms was then clad with a traditional brick veneer, a tiled roof and perhaps a half-timbered upper floor. The whole process, from finding a site to taking in the first guests, took less than four months.[53]

Forte bought the concept off Potton, reasoning that the business travellers with modest expense accounts unleashed by the Thatcherite economic revolution now wanted something better than a poky B&B with a bathroom down the corridor. The first 'Little Chef Lodge' opened in 1985 at Barton-under-Needwood on the A38 in Staffordshire.

It made a virtue of its no-frills service: you paid at check-in and there was nothing in the rooms that might require extra payment, not even a telephone. Room service was a tea-making kit. The reception was unmanned in the mornings, so you let yourself out and foraged for your own breakfast, preferably at the neighbouring Little Chef. The hotel was soon rebranded a 'Travelodge'. By the end of the 1980s, Potton had built nearly 200 of them. In their wake came a prefab army of Travel Inns and Welcome Lodges, two-storey snap-togethers lining the roadside, differing only in their levels of automation, from self-cleaning bathrooms to breakfast served from a coin-operated dispenser.

The budget hotel embodied the spirit of the roadside: uninspired, anonymous, informal, open to everyone. Charles Forte fought all his life against the snobbish attitude of the high-end hotel industry towards this classless ethos. Although he also owned some of the world's swankiest hotels, when he got embroiled in a long battle to take over the Savoy in the 1980s its board derided him as 'no more than a man who runs motorway cafés and ice-cream parlours'. This may explain why Forte and Margaret Thatcher, both lower-middle-class high achievers with a deep suspicion of upper-class hauteur, hit it off. When Thatcher opened Forte's South Mimms service station on the M25, the weekend before her landslide victory in the 1987 election, she declared 'how much I love the style of Lord Forte' while he called her 'this wonderful woman that God sent from heaven'.[54]

But the true champion of the motorway café was Thatcher's successor, John Major. In the early days of his premiership, on his way to a conference in Scarborough, he stopped off at a Doncaster Happy Eater, ordered a fry-up and, following a prime ministerial tradition set by Harold Wilson, called for the HP sauce. Happy Eater was a roadside chain with a reputation best summed up by the probably apocryphal story of the customer who asked for an omelette and was told he couldn't have one because 'they haven't sent us any'. The newspapers got wind of the story that Major had stopped in one – indeed, had a habit of doing so – and he seemed happy with the association. A couple of years later, a television profile of Major filmed him through the window of a Happy Eater, with a Mozart piano concerto playing in the background.

Major's fondness for Happy Eaters is now filed under the same fun-poking folder as his other major contribution to road culture: his introduction in 1992 of a Cones Hotline, which allowed motorists to ring up and demand that these annoying plastic bollards be removed from roads. In 1995, when the government disbanded the hotline, it admitted that out of the 17,700 calls it had received, only five had led to the removal of cones – although, in fairness, many of the callers were practical jokers ringing up to order Cornettos.[55] Like the Cones Hotline, Major's liking for what he quaintly called 'wayside inns' came to symbolise his lacklustre premiership and its fatal association with Pooterish trivia. But we forget that, in the brief honeymoon period after he came to power, it signalled that he was a heroically ordinary chap, someone with whom you would happily share your bottle of brown sauce. Margaret Thatcher might have been willing to cut ribbons at South Mimms, but she would not have been seen dead in a Happy Eater.

Major turned the roadside café into a test case for his flagship Citizen's Charter. He gave a memorable speech at the 1992 Tory Party conference, complaining about the lack of service stations on the M11. 'Take the bureaucratic controls,' he thundered, 'which means Whitehall decides whether you have the chance to stop off the motorway. Every parent knows what I mean. Next services 54 miles – when your children can't make 10 … *They've* got to go, so *those rules* have got to go.'[56] Under Major's reforms, derided as the 'Happy Eater's charter', private developers could build service stations without government interference. But nothing much changed: local councils rarely gave planning permission, and the cost of building a site the size of a small village in the middle of nowhere discouraged all but the biggest operators. The Happy Eaters disappeared, along with Mr Major, in 1997 – their new owner, Granada, converting them into the more glamorous and successful Little Chefs. The big chains did the same corporate makeover on the service stations, getting rid of the grot and turning them into quasi-airports: clean, efficient and expensive. Out went the litter, dirty floors and flooded toilets and in came baby-changing facilities, dog feeding stations and 'washroom hygiene monitors', who checked the toilets every hour.

The anthropologist, Marc Augé, refers to these sites such as airports, chain hotels and service stations, created by the speed and mobility of modern life, as 'non-places'. For Augé, the non-place is a self-contained society with its own anaesthetised micro-environment. Its role is to turn us into generic customers, relieving us of responsibility and identity. Airports have globally standardised signs and icons that invite us to surrender all power to the people who check us in, take our baggage and usher us through security. Likewise, the whole point of a service station is to offer a smooth, undemanding break in the endless flow of the motorway. No need for human interaction: you can do all your conversing with the sliding doors and hand dryers. Marketing people call it the 'distress purchase' and coach drivers the 'comfort stop'. People turn in because they have to change drivers, buy petrol or relieve themselves. No one – Morrissey excepted, perhaps – would go out of their way to visit a service station.

→

And yet we do seem unusually fascinated by the people who linger in these non-places that the rest of us use only fleetingly and distractedly. In September 2007 every British newspaper carried a story about the septuagenarian couple, David and Jean Davidson, who had been living in a Travelodge for twenty-two years. On closer inspection, the story turned out to be more complicated. It began in 1985, when the Davidsons became the first couple to stay in the inaugural Travelodge at Burton-under-Needwood, en route to visit an elderly and infirm aunt in Staffordshire. They began staying there for three or four nights a week until the aunt died four months later. The Davidsons enjoyed the experience and the following year began spending weekends at the Newark Travelodge on the A1, staying there on and off over the next ten years. In July 1997, on the day it opened, the pair moved permanently into Room One of the Grantham Travelodge at the Moto services on the A1(M). They liked the fact that there were always lorries passing outside their window, and they had only to walk across the car park for meals at the Little Chef. By taking advantage of all the special offers, they had spent an estimated £97,600 on hotel bills over the twenty-two years – the cost of a two-bedroom terrace in the area. 'This is our home,' Mr Davidson said. 'We have everything we need and the staff are like family now – we even get birthday and Christmas cards from them and we often give presents back in exchange.'[57] On their tenth anniversary at the hotel, the Travelodge renamed their room 'The Davidson Suite' and mounted a commemorative plaque in reception.

It was a trunk-road reworking of the much sadder story of Merhan Karimi Nasseri, the Iranian refugee who spent eighteen years at Charles de Gaulle Airport in Paris styling himself Sir Alfred, and who inspired the Tom Hanks character in the film *Terminal*. Perhaps our interest in these stories stems from the fact that they are both slightly absurd and seminally contemporary, speaking to our modern condition of placelessness and exile. Many of us live much of our lives on the motorway; the Davidsons just followed out the logic of our peripatetic existences. But these stories are also oddly consoling. They suggest that non-places are not simply alienating, that their benevolent indifference can be liberating too. It is well-known that homeless people live in airports, wearing Hawaiian shirts and pulling around suitcases on wheels to make it look as though they are about to catch a flight. Service stations are smaller and it's harder to hide, but as long as you can do a passing impression of a motorist, there is no statute of limitations on your stay. You can sit in a service station for hours and, for all the attention you get from the table clearers and floor wipers, you might as well be a ghost. That's why low-level lawlessness has always thrived in the anonymity of the cafés and car parks. Unwanted babies are dumped here, illegal immigrants dropped off, drugs and contraband traded by small-time criminals.

You could probably spend your whole life in a service station, if you had a job you could do remotely with a laptop and a wi-fi connection, and it paid you lots of money. Then you could raid the cashpoints for funds, assuming you were happy for them to charge you for the privilege. You would never starve, although a diet consisting excessively of Ginsters pasties and pick'n'mix would soon begin to pall. Since the sole choice of fruit seems to be slightly mouldy bananas, you might want to avoid scurvy by drinking smoothies. In lieu of a holiday, you could buy a collapsible lounger and some Ambre Solaire from the shop and sunbathe in the car park, passing the time with travel versions of Battleship and Cluedo. If you have forgotten your washbag, a dispenser in the toilets that looks like a gumball machine will sell you a 'chewable toothbrush' for a pound.

Even non-places have their own rhythms and cadences, their own interior lives. Service station workers have long dreaded the phenomenon of 'peaking' – the sudden rush of custom as hundreds of customers arrive at once in coach parties. But there are other times when the service station goes into standby mode: when the lights dim, whole areas are coned off by cleaners, and even the man from the RAC hides his stall in an alcove and goes home. The service station never sleeps, but sometimes its eyelids droop a little. It is then that you see people sitting alone at the tables: lone bikers resting their helmets on tabletops or men in hangdog suits with vacant stares – the sort of sad motorway café people whom the philosopher Alain de Botton has compared to the lone figures in Edward Hopper paintings.[58] These silent, solitary diners encapsulate what has happened to the roadside, and by extension the road itself, over the last few decades. There are no uniformed stewardesses to greet customers, no sightseers on the bridges, no postcards available in the shop, not even anyone to complain to about the food any more. As the roadside stop has come to resemble a small-scale version of Heathrow airport, excited ritual has turned invisibly into banal routine. The act of embracing the new has given way to the melancholy of collective solitude.

6

FAST CARS, SLOW LANES

Slow down, the sea isn't going to evaporate.

Sign on the Autoroute du Soleil between Paris and Marseille

It sounds like an urban myth, but it really happened: the participants simply covered their tyre tracks carefully and have maintained a Mafia-style *omertà* about it ever since. The story begins in October 1986, when Margaret Thatcher opened the final section of London's orbital motorway, just two days after Big Bang, which ended restrictive practices in the City and ushered in a brief, frantic era of take-overs and salary hikes. Some of the high-flying City traders realised that the M25's 117-mile circuit could serve as an illegal racetrack. Boris Johnson sniffed the story out while working as a cub reporter for *The Times*. Cryptic adverts for the 'M25 club' were being placed in the *Enfield Gazette*, and posters appeared all over Essex and Surrey announcing the 'First London Cannonball Run', an imitation of the outlaw coast-to-coast road races held in America in the 1970s as a protest against the new 55 mph speed limit.[1] Drunk on wealth and success, the stockbroking masters of the universe would meet up at South Mimms in the early hours of a weekend morning and race round the orbital in their Porsches and Ferraris, the Dartford Tunnel tollgates serving as an impromptu pitstop. Nothing so vulgar as money changed hands, but the odd jeroboam of champagne went to the winners. The record for completing the circuit was rumoured to be sixty-eight minutes, an average speed of 103 mph. It is not known when the races ended, although the 1987 stock market crash must have put a dampener on the mood of shameless excess and braggadocio that inspired them. But then there was a much darker object on the horizon that would put a stop to these audacious escapades for good.

This device had been invented many years earlier by Maus Gatsonides, a Dutch racing driver who wanted to see how fast he was going round corners, and who used it to help him win the 1953 Monte Carlo rally. The first 'Gatso' camera was installed in October 1992 on the A316 near Twickenham Bridge, where speeding motorists coming off the M3 met a wide, straight dual carriageway suddenly narrowing down to one lane and then turning at a virtual right angle. So many drivers were speeding along this classic blackspot that the camera used up its 200-shot film within half-an-hour. One early offender was caught crossing the bridge at 113 mph and 115 mph within the space of four days. At the insistence of the AA and RAC, police then installed signs warning drivers about the cameras. Within a month, the number of motorists recorded driving above 60 mph in this 40 mph zone fell from nearly 8,000 to just a hundred a week. Meanwhile another twenty of these strange-looking contraptions were installed alongside 50 miles of road in north and west London, and they soon began to inspire a sort of civil-disobedience entrepreneurialism. Start-up firms sold 'flashproof' or foldaway number plates, 'shiny sprays' that promised to make registration numbers illegible in photographs, or maps claiming to pinpoint all the camera locations. The road lined with speed cameras was soon at the front line in the war between the police and that perennially victimised member of the respectable middle classes, the 'otherwise law-abiding' motorist.

The fear and loathing aroused by the Gatsos was probably partly down to their unprepossessing appearance – as ugly grey boxes mounted on thick poles (this was before they were painted canary yellow to give motorists a sporting chance) which seemed to become suddenly and silently ubiquitous, like McDonald's Drive-Thrus. But the main complaint about the speed camera was its mechanical stupidity – its habit of collaring fine, upstanding citizens driving a few miles above the speed limit on deserted roads in the middle of the night. Speeding has always been what lawyers call an 'absolute offence', which means it is no defence to argue that your particular instance of speeding did not harm anyone. But the letter of the law cannot compete with this enduring sense that trivial breaches of limits are victimless crimes. When I started driving in the mid-1990s, I was puzzled by the number of oncoming drivers flashing their lights at me on long, empty stretches of road for no apparent reason. I realised eventually that they were trying to warn me of speed cameras they had just passed. Without being asked if I wanted to join, I had become a member of this half-secret, semi-subversive society of the road.

On the militant wing of this society were the speed camera saboteurs. Its ringleaders were Captain Gatso, the leader of MAD or Motorists Against Detection, who called the cameras 'a cancer spreading across the Western world'; and Angle-Grinder Man, the self-styled 'speed-camera superhero' who named himself after the method by which he decapitated cameras. As well as cutting cameras off their poles, they shot them, blew them up and sprayed them with paint. A popular assassination method, borrowed from a form of summary justice handed out in South African townships, was 'neck-lacing', throwing a tyre soaked with petrol over the camera and setting it alight. The vigilantes celebrated each hit by placing a fuzzy jpeg of the debilitated Gatso on the internet. By 2006 they were destroying half-a-million pounds' worth of cameras a year – an average of more than four a week.[2]

These speed camera renegades often received sympathetic treatment in the media, as modern-day highwaymen carrying the promise of mass wish-fulfilment. In this sense they fitted Eric Hobsbawm's definition of 'social bandits', the near-universal historical phenomenon of 'peasant outlaws whom the lord and state regard as criminals, but who remain within peasant society, and are considered by their people as heroes, as champions, avengers, fighters for justice, perhaps even leaders of liberation'. The broadcaster and journalist Jeremy Clarkson professed sympathy for the saboteurs and claimed that 'speeding is no big deal'.[3] On the hugely popular BBC motoring programme, *Top Gear*, Clarkson and his co-hosts often criticised speed cameras. They rarely filmed on normal roads, preferring to test cars at speed on private tracks, undertake daredevil stunts on deserted beaches, or challenge each other to intercontinental road races, marvelling at the laid-back attitudes of the French police to speeding, or the liberating absence of limits on the autobahns. The programme created a sort of make-believe universe in which the petty restrictions of British roads, with their speed cameras and dawdling caravans, magically melted away.

What is it about speed that makes people so excited and, when denied it, so irritated? The English word 'speed' derives from the old English *spówan*, meaning to succeed or prosper ('God speed the plough'), and speeding has long had associations with wealth, sex and power. But the idea of speed as a natural, instinctual state emerged fairly recently. In the 1840s, risk-averse railway company directors restricted the speed of trains to 30 mph, because medical experts feared that if humans went faster than this, they would suffocate or their skeletons would smash to smithereens. But within a few decades, speeds of 75 mph were the norm and some train passengers, viewing a slowly shifting panorama from the window of a carriage running on level, straight tracks, came to think that speed was rather boring. The train-hating John Ruskin claimed that 'all travelling becomes dull in exact proportion to its rapidity'.[4] Behind the wheel of a car, though, the physical sensation of speed was far more dramatic. Early motorists described the speeds they reached in intensely aesthetic, even mystical terms. As with any drug, the effects of speed wore off with habit, and only bigger hits could achieve the same buzz.

In his 1959 book, *Thrills and Regressions*, the psychoanalyst Michael Balint argued that speed was linked to competitive struggles like wars and races, and was 'symbolically related to erection and potency' – although perhaps one doesn't need to be a psychoanalyst to work that out. But Balint also concluded that besting a slower opponent was only a 'second-order enjoyment'. He identified a condition called 'philobatism' or the enjoyment of thrills, derived from the Greek word acrobat, which literally means 'he who walks on his toes' away from the safe earth. Like all thrills, driving at high speed was a heady mixture of pleasure, fear and hope – the hope that, even in a fearful situation to which you had voluntarily exposed yourself, you could return fairly easily to safety by applying the brakes.[5] So for Balint, speed was both transitive (an affirmation of social power and status) and intransitive (an intensely personal enjoyment).

Perhaps this tension explains why speed exerts such a powerful emotional pull: it is a personal buzz with an inevitably social dimension. Motorists might think that, if they could simply do away with the road and drive alone in the deserted landscapes of motoring programmes, they would experience speed in its purest form. But the reverse is true. It is hard to feel you are driving fast in deserts or prairies, because things always seem far away in a featureless landscape. To really feel speed, you need other things to be slower or stationary. In other words you need a road, with its well-articulated foreground objects like streetlights, telephone poles and other cars. Speed is both a variable and an absolute, something that can be measured by a speedometer but that is always partly a matter of perception, an optical and sensory illusion dependent on your surroundings – so a 30 mph road feels like a slow crawl after a motorway.

But we should know by now that, while we might need roads to feel speed, they offer us less and less opportunity to experience it. The long, open straight where we can floor the accelerator pedal is becoming an exotic rarity. Driving on Britain's roads is mostly about picking your way slowly through the heavy traffic, the hold-ups, the lanes closed after accidents. Somehow the ordinary slowness of the road has come to seem extraordinary, a source of permanent surprise and frustration however often we experience it. Why? According to the French cultural theorist, Paul Virilio, modern society is defined by its ideology of competitive speed, which he names 'dromology', after the Greek word for racing. Industrial progress is 'guaranteed by speeding', he argues, and 'highway casualties are casualties of Progress. Every driver is a "test pilot" for technological expansion.' For Virilio, modernity treats delays and disruptions, like traffic jams and road crashes, as the unacknowledged underside of dromological culture – a perversion or travesty of the culture of speed. Modernity is based on the social denial of human fragility and mortality, on the illusion that we have limitless capacities constrained only by the available technology. So the road crash becomes an obscene interruption into daily life rather than the entirely normal, unsurprising event that it is in a culture ruled by the pursuit of speed. 'To invent the private car is to produce the motorway pile-up,' Virilio writes. 'The multiple security systems with which our vehicles are equipped will do nothing to change this fact: in the course of the twentieth century, accidents became a heavy industry.'[6]

→

The speed camera saboteurs saw themselves as part of a victimised majority of ordinary, decent drivers going about their normal business. In the early years of motoring, though, speeding was more openly acknowledged as an aggressive, competitive act. The German historian Wolfgang Sachs observes that the invention of the car at the end of the nineteenth century coincided with a new idea of competitive speed, with modern timed sports like track and swimming founded on the quantitative measurement of the best performances, calibrated in centimetres or fractions of a second. Participants were not simply competing against each other but against the official 'record' – a word that only appeared in the German (and English) language in the late nineteenth century. The first modern Olympics, 'the world ritual of records', was held in 1896 – the same year that pioneering British motorists held their emancipation run from London to Brighton.[7]

Even the most extreme speed camera opponents acknowledge that the road is not a racetrack, that there are other people who may not want to drive as fast as them. But this was not always the case in the early years of motoring, especially on the continent where motor racing took place on ordinary roads and was a lethally popular spectator sport. This practice reached its inevitably grim conclusion one Sunday in May 1903, when 100,000 people poured out of Paris in the middle of the night to watch the start of the Paris–Madrid car race at Versailles, crowding on to the road itself with their Chinese lanterns for a better view. The first driver to set off, Charles Jarrott, wrote later that 'a wedge-shaped space opened out in the crowd as I approached, and so fine was the calculation made that at times it seemed impossible for the car not to overtake the apex of the human triangle and deal death and destruction'.[8] Many motorists and spectators were killed, their mangled bodies discovered only after the clouds of dust created by the speeding cars had dispersed. The French government stopped the race at Bordeaux, and ordered that the cars be pulled by horses to the railway station and sent back to Paris by train. When news of this 'race to death' reached British newspapers, the public mood turned decisively against speeding. The next month thirty MPs signed a circular condemning the abuse of public roads by unidentifiable drivers travelling at 'furious speeds'. The Motor Car Act of that year, which imposed a blanket speed limit of 20 mph and made car number plates compulsory, reflected this hostility towards so-called 'flying millionaires'.[9]

In Britain, racing on the King's highway, the open road for use by all his majesty's subjects, has always been illegal. In the 1890s, this traditional distrust of speed fell on young men bicycling fast or 'scorching' through towns. As a teenager in 1901, the future land speed record holder Malcolm Campbell was fined thirty shillings for driving a bicycle down Bickley Hill in Kent at the astonishing speed of 27 mph, 'to the confusion and terror of two elderly ladies'. Many horse-loving magistrates were hostile to motorists, and motorists responded by developing their own *esprit de corps*. After being fined £5 by Norfolk magistrates in 1898 for driving a vehicle over 12 mph, Charles Jarrott spearheaded the movement to protect motorists from 'unEnglish' police speed traps. In the early 1900s, Lord Russell tried to persuade the RAC to publish a 'speed trap map', and to encourage its members to throw confetti or red dye on the road, or agree a signal to warn each other of police ambushes.[10] The AA was formed in 1905 with the specific aim of warning members about police speed traps by organising platoons of bicycle patrolmen, whose salute was a way of signalling that the coast was clear. Motorists also countered these restrictions with fantasies of revenge and flight, of defeating the killjoys by escaping the road altogether. In William Randolph Booth's short 1906 film, *The '?' Motorist*, a couple in a car run over a traffic policeman, drive up the front of a building and fly through the air into space, ending up on Saturn, whose gas rings they put to use as a racetrack.

Resentment at speeding motorists mingled with sneaking admiration for their fugitive glamour. Aviation was seen at the time as an offshoot of motoring, a form of 'aerial automobilism', and in the sky there were no speed limits or sluggish pedestrians. Graham Gilmour, a pioneer aviator and motorist, was often in the newspapers for both his airborne stunts and his string of convictions for speeding. Young, pulchritudinous and rich, he was punished only erratically for his crimes. He was once caught speeding on the London–Brighton road while trying to keep up with his fellow aviator Oscar Morison, who was making the first ever cross-country flight. But the chairman of Woking magistrates was so taken with Gilmour that he imposed a nominal fine and invited him home for tea. Even being charged with manslaughter for killing a young boy while speeding did not dent Gilmour's box-office appeal. When word got round of his intention to fly to court, thousands of Salisburians lined the streets as he circled the cathedral spire several times on the way to Wiltshire assizes. He must have charmed the jury as well as the judge this time, for he was again acquitted – and remained a celebrated figure until he was killed in a plane crash in 1912, aged twenty-seven. Speeding above the 20 mph limit soon became quite routine, the pursuit of respectable citizens as well as daring young men in their non-flying machines.

The 1930 Road Traffic Act abolished this limit, on the basis that widely ignored rules brought the law into disrepute and were a short-cut to anarchy. The transport minister, Herbert Morrison, argued that 'the British police have enough common sense not to be too meticulous in enforcing laws which are not in accordance with the general body of public opinion'. But the growing number of deaths on the roads also made speed a contentious issue. Lord Buckmaster attacked motorists who thought they had a monopoly of the road, so that pedestrians 'had to scurry out of their way like black beetles out of a lighted room', and he argued that we were 'offer[ing] up year by year to the Moloch of speed more children than were ever sacrificed to the Moloch of fire in the days of Carthage'. In 1937 a British psychologist warned that 'the desirability of speed, even at the cost of a few thousand lives per annum', had become 'part of our cultural mosaic'. For many young male drivers, 'driving skill and prowess were equated with speed'.[11]

The press excitedly collated new speeding records, and it was not only racing drivers who caught the bug. Caravanners also held speed trials, and 'Mit' Harris, the daredevil editor of *Caravan and Trailer*, founded a Guild of Master Caravanners for those who had attained the awe-inspiring speed of 60 mph, although he may have been the only member. The racing drivers who wrote about cars in the newspapers brought a certain expertise to the emerging consensus that there was no such thing as a single, unsafe speed. In his *Daily Express* column, Lord Cottenham argued that there was nothing dangerous about speed *per se*. 'Speed is like certain forms of poison such as strychnine, arsenic, or alcohol, which may be very good for us in reasonable quantities and given at the right time,' he wrote. 'If, however, wisdom does not prevail, and we are careless with those poisons, it is quite on the cards that we shall not live to realize the full extent of our stupidity.'[12] For Cottenham, speed on the road was a matter for individual judgement, not the letter of the law.

$$\rightarrow$$

After the Second World War, speeding became symbolically entangled with a more general rejection of wartime state controls and a reassertion of individual liberty. On 7 December 1950, police constable Harold Muckle stopped a liberal councillor, Harry Willcock, for speeding on Ballard's Lane in Finchley, and asked to see his identity card. Willcock refused, saying he was a liberal and 'against that sort of thing'. He then managed to turn this incident into a national campaign against the use of identity cards in peacetime, culminating in a mass rally in Hyde Park. Willcock's case went all the way to the appeal court, where the judges upheld his conviction but went on to express their approval at the magistrates' decision to give him an absolute discharge, and criticised those police who demanded identity cards for 'minor' offences. The clear message was that the police should not waste their time on speeding motorists and concentrate on catching 'real' criminals. Similarly, when the police introduced radar speed guns in the late 1950s, the AA complained that they were 'a quite unnecessarily extravagant method of enforcing the law'.[13] This decade was the golden era of British motor racing, when many of the leading drivers were British and the cars they drove were built by ordinary car manufacturers like Aston Martin, Lotus and Jaguar. Speed stood for shaking off the restraints of austerity and embracing a new world of glamour and abundance. The nation's favourite racing driver, Stirling Moss, was fined several times for speeding and other motoring offences and, when he was banned from driving in 1960, almost lost his competition licence.[14]

By now, the foolhardiness of imposing a blanket limit had become received wisdom. A new breed of motoring journalist – the eccentric, buccaneering, probably public-school-educated enthusiast – served as the champion of liberated, post-austerity motoring. Its doyen was the motoring journalist, Leonard (L.J.K.) Setright, an unforgettable character in the flesh and in print. His engineer father had made a modest but significant contribution to the cultural history of the road, by inventing the classic Setright ticket machine used by bus conductors. But his son was no busophile; instead, he became a tireless advocate of the freewheeling motorist. With his long, wispy beard, wide-brimmed hat, cape and black leather gloves, he looked like 'an Old Testament prophet suddenly arriving at a Hell's Angels meeting'.[15] The legendary column he wrote for *Small Car* magazine from 1962 was an exhilarating mix of engineering knowledge and esoteric classical references that made speed-limit advocates seem like soulless pedants.

Setright's unconventional views on road safety boiled down to one basic idea: speed was safe, especially for skilful drivers like himself who had been blessed with exceptional peripheral vision and lightning-quick reflexes. One day in London when the traffic was sparse, he tested out the theory of the racing driver Kenelm Lee Guinness, that the best way to negotiate junctions was simply to drive across them at breakneck speed, since you would then be in the danger zone for the shortest possible time. 'It seemed to work,' he wrote later, 'or maybe I was lucky.' Even his fellow motoring journalists refused to accompany him on his daredevil test drives and, when one of them asked if he had a death wish, he replied that it was his moral duty to test the car within its 'full performance envelope'. He was convinced that, when the national speed limit of 70 mph came in, car manufacturers cynically neglected to test how well their cars performed beyond that limit. The Hillman Avenger, for example, 'became quite unpleasant beyond seventy, although entirely amiable until it reached that speed'.[16]

Setright saw speed limits as a tool of political repression, which helped to 'coerce the populace to remain where they are, instead of roaming around being inquisitive or simply escaping to where the grass appears to grow greener'. He was a libertarian with an indifference to social conventions and a distaste for government busybodies who tried to stifle our natural urges. But these views about speeding tended to cross the political divide. The left-wing media don A.J.P. Taylor so often used his newspaper column to extol the delights of driving at speed that his academic critics dismissed him as 'the motoring correspondent of the *Sunday Express*'. One of his pieces argued that road accidents were caused by motorists driving too slowly. ('What it is,' commented another columnist dryly, 'to have a highly trained mind.'[17]) Motorists of all political colours embraced the Tory anarchism of the road, this right of every freeborn Englishman to drive on the Queen's highway in the manner of his choosing.

→

A common piece of folk mythology about the British road is that speed-limit enforcers are legislative dinosaurs, throwbacks to a time when men walked in front of vehicles with red flags – although, in fact, the Red Flag Act was repealed in 1896, so it barely impinged on the momentum of the internal combustion engine. Another motif recurs in this mythology, of a golden age when Britons briefly and guiltlessly embraced speed: the lost Arcadia of the early motorway era.

The first motorways had no speed limit and, in the first few hours after the M1 opened to traffic, the police's radar checks recorded many speeds over 100 mph. But average speeds soon settled down and after a few days they had fallen to 50 mph. Two weeks later, the *Daily Express*'s motoring correspondent, Basil Cardew, confidently declared: 'For thirteen days I have practically lived on the M1 – day and night. In that time I have kept a log on drivers' behaviour which convinces me that the wise-after-the-event pessimists who are crying for speed limits are shouting through their sunshine roofs.'[18]

In fact, if you somehow drove through a wormhole in the time–space continuum on a slip road and found yourself on one of those early, unrestricted motorways, you would be astonished by the low speeds. On the Preston Bypass, the Lancashire constabulary recorded average speeds of between 35 and 45 mph, with speeds above 70 mph almost unknown. A civil servant concluded: 'I do not think that the average British motorist wants to travel at fast speeds and, certainly, we have heard of a number of people who have said that they would not go on the motorway because they feared the speed of cars over-taking them.' Five years after the M1 opened, the top speed in the left lane was still about 40 mph and 98 per cent of all cars were travelling at or below 70 mph.[19]

But if any of these timorous motorists were bumbling along the M1 at dawn one Sunday in June 1964, they would have seen something terrifying in their rear-view mirror. The racing driver, Jack Sears, using the motorway to test drive his AC Cobra before the 24-hour race at Le Mans, was clocking up speeds of over 180 mph. Sears set off from Toddington services at 4.30am and did four runs up and down the motorway before knocking off at 6.30, when the traffic got busier. His speeds were recorded by a Bedfordshire police patrol who decided to turn a blind eye. News of Sears's drive somehow found its way on to newspaper front pages, one leader thundering that 'the very thought of being passed at 183 mph on the public highway must give the ordinary motorist the willies'.[20] In the ensuing furore, Ernest Marples met the president of the Society of Motor Manufacturers and Traders, who reassured him that it was an isolated incident. In fact, Midlands-based manufacturers like Jaguar and Aston Martin regularly tested their high-performance cars on the nearby M1. The motor industry couldn't see what all the fuss was about; Maserati tested its cars on the autostrade all the time. The managing director of AC cars said it was a pity they had to use the motorway but blamed the poor quality of British racetracks, which could not cope with runs over 160 mph.[21]

The Sears ride has entered folk history as the legendary last hurrah for the high-speed motorway. In a recent BBC documentary, the *Top Gear* presenter James May stood on an M1 overbridge and held up a copy of the *Daily Mirror* front page story about Sears's ride, before repeating the orthodoxy that the motorway in its early days was 'like a drag strip' and that this incident scared the authorities into introducing speed limits. 'What a pillock,' May concluded, presumably blaming Sears for spoiling the fun of unrestricted roads.[22] In fact, speed limits on motorways were mooted even before they opened, and only rejected on the grounds that they were illogical in the absence of a speed limit on other non-urban roads. (At the time there was no speed limit on rural roads and 40 mph limits were only just being introduced on the outskirts of towns.) The Cobra episode was no watershed: the government decided that Sears's behaviour was covered under existing laws on dangerous driving.

Motorway speed limits were part of a general move towards restrictions on all roads, after the Road Research Laboratory suggested they helped reduce accidents. The most compelling evidence came from Germany, where experimental speed limits on certain autobahns in the late 1950s had drastically reduced the accident rate – although this did not sway the speed-loving Germans, for whom the experiment was short-lived. For a long time the government was against a 'global' limit and in favour of speed bands within particular motorway lanes (50, 60, 70) or ad hoc limits for particular bits of road – until they realised the expense and clutter of so many signs. The Ministry of

Transport probably settled on 70 mph because it was the design speed of the motorways – how fast the driver could go, according to the road's alignment, and still be able to stop in an emergency.[23]

Today's motorists often complain that this is an anachronistic limit based on the flat-out speed of a Harry Potter-style Ford Anglia. In a sense they are right: all speed limits are unnatural, a product of historical expediency. A blanket limit is always partly arbitrary, a compromise between the demands of road safety and what is acceptable to most drivers, who will mainly be observing it unwatched. When motorway speed limits were imposed, the same arguments used in the 1930s, about the need for laws to embrace pragmatic reality, re-emerged. Some cabinet members opposed the limits – such as Roy Jenkins, who made the traditional case that laws needed to carry public opinion along with them, and the maverick George Brown, who insisted that driving at 100 mph on the motorway was quite safe.[24]

The transport minister, Tom Fraser, imposed an experimental 70 mph limit on all previously unrestricted roads in December 1965 – although it was his successor, Barbara Castle, who became a media hate figure when she extended the limit indefinitely. (She also received mountains of abusive mail for introducing the breathalyser and making it compulsory for all new cars to have seat belts.) Stirling Moss railed against 'socialist hypocrisy', while an RAC committee member complained that doing 70 mph on the motorway was 'extremely dull in a fast car'.[25] Members of the protest group, Motorists' Action, staged an anti-speed limit rally at Newport Pagnell services. The organisers had predicted that 20,000 outraged motorists would turn up, but only about 800 did. They planned to recreate peak traffic conditions to show the dangers of speed-constrained cars 'bunching' on the motorway. But the experiment failed miserably. The only bunching occurred when about 150 cars left the service area at the same time, and they quickly spread out, not very dangerously.

Britain's car manufacturers also argued that the speed limit would harm the development of its high-performance cars. In fact, L.J.K Setright later attributed the decline of the British motor industry to the introduction of the national speed limit, while the German car industry was able to carry on refining powerful Audis and Mercedes for its unrestricted autobahns[26] – a theory that overlooks the troubled history of British industrial relations and the wretched saga of British Leyland. It is true that the first half-decade of the motorway era did see the launch of some classic British sports cars, such as the E-type Jaguar, the MGB and James Bond's beloved Aston Martin DB5. But it was family runarounds like the Morris Marina, memorably described as 'a skip on wheels', and the Austin Allegro, with a gearbox that felt like 'trying to stir a bag of marbles with a knitting needle', which cemented the British car industry's dire reputation.[27] It has carried on making beautiful sports cars to this day.

Just as the 70 mph speed limit was introduced, motorists on the M1 were taunted by a visible sign of their newly shackled state. British Rail had finally completed the electrification of the west coast mainline and began its InterCity service from London Euston to Manchester and Liverpool. Parts of the line ran directly along the motorway, separated by just a verge and a wooden fence. In 1959, speeding motorists had overhauled the steam trains; now a 100 mph train was overhauling them. It also looked fast, with a smart, blue-grey livery, rake-backed, yellow-panelled power cars at each end (nicknamed 'flying bananas'), and – perhaps the ultimate insult – clean new lettering designed by Kinneir and Calvert, the architects of the motorway signs. There is a story, probably a myth, that the drivers of these locomotive gazelles were instructed to go at full speed whenever they were alongside a motorway. Just two years after the Beeching report had initiated the culling of branch lines, the motorway age seemed to have turned rather improbably into the age of the train.

In some cars, 70 mph may now have seemed quite slow. If you drove fast in an old car, the harsh suspension and overworked engine let you know about it. But the cars produced after the early 1960s gave no such clues. The independent springing adjusted itself to the road surface; the power-assisted steering needed the merest touch to round a corner; and the streamlined bodywork eliminated airflow and engine noise. Enclosed in a well-sprung car on a smooth motorway, your sense of speed was skewed. In the mid-1960s, the Road Research Laboratory noted a trend for average vehicle speeds to rise by about 1 mph per year. By now it was not just sports cars but souped-up saloons like the Ford Cortina Super and the Morris Minor 1000 de Luxe that could reach 80 mph, with a following wind. Motorists had renamed the left, middle and outside lanes of the motorway the 'slow', 'cruising' and 'fast' lanes, a slight semantic shift that redefined the first as a space for stragglers and slowcoaches and the last as a space for the big beasts of the road.

The introduction of the national speed limit did not alter these attitudes dramatically, partly because it was so hard to enforce. Checking speeds on the motorway was a hazardous business. Police could not see vehicle number plates from the tops of bridges, so they assembled their radar equipment on the ground between the bridge stanchions, not to hide behind them but to protect themselves in the event of a crash. The police's radar guns measured up to 80 mph and it was only when the needle ran off the clock that they bothered stopping motorists – a 10 mph leeway known as the 'mercy margin'. And it was impossible to read a registration plate at 80 mph in the dark, so in effect the speed limit was only enforceable in the daytime. After the limit was introduced, police calculated that the number of vehicles travelling above 70 mph on the motorways fell by 19 per cent, and the number travelling above 80 mph fell by 7 per cent. So even speeding motorists were reducing their speed to fit within the semi-official band just above the limit. But the average speed of the family saloon went *up* by about 10 mph. One police officer reasoned that 'the man who drove at sixty now uses his full ration'.[28]

The motorway underlined the fact that speed was a matter of collective psychology and impressionistic judgements. Motorway slip roads soon became the most dangerous roads in the country. Cars would crash at the terminal roundabouts as motorists habituated to the high speeds failed to slow down fast enough. 'Reduce speed now' signs were put up and parallel lines painted on the road, at first evenly spaced and then coming closer together as the roundabout approached, to give drivers a visual cue to brake – an attempt to second-guess the motorway's mischievous habit of playing tricks with the senses. After speed limits were temporarily reduced to 50 mph to save petrol in the desperate fuel shortages at the end of 1973, the Monty Python actor Michael Palin encountered the relativity of speed when he drove from London up the A1 to his in-laws' house in Cambridgeshire. Noting the drivers diligently sticking to the new limits, he thought 'it was rather like being in a slow-motion film'.[29] Fifteen years earlier, these speeds would have seemed thrilling.

$\rightarrow$

But what is slow and what is fast? The view through the windscreen offers no real clues, being an invitation to solipsism and subjectivity. Motorists tend to view speed in terms of their own capacity to accelerate, and blame other motorists for blocking their way or making them slow down. But speed on the road has as much to do with preserving momentum as accelerating. We would get there much quicker if, instead of trying to overtake each other all the time, we could work out some collective choreography that allowed us to maintain a constant speed and never have to touch our brake pedals. Speed was uncontentious in the early motorway age because the new roads were so underused that cars running at different speeds could coexist peacefully. A month after its opening, Lancashire police calculated that 2,300 vehicles were using the Preston Bypass each day, 'well below the capacity of the road and whenever one drives along it one has the feeling that the road is very empty'. The deserted motorways were politically embarrassing, as ministers wanted to show that the country was getting its money's worth out of the new roads. As late as 1963, when Ernest Marples opened another section of the M6, he was talking up the traffic, reassuring the public that motorway usage 'was still rising at an annual rate of about 7 per cent – rather more than the national average on other roads'.[30]

The government's motive for building the motorways was not to increase speed but to reduce delay – an idea with a long history. The sociologist Richard Sennett traces our concern with traffic circulation back to the 1628 publication of William Harvey's *De motu cordis*, with its discoveries about the circulation of the blood through arteries and veins. In the eighteenth century, enlightened planners began to apply this new 'master image of the body' to the city, seeking to make it 'a place in which people would move and breathe freely, a city of flowing arteries and veins through which people streamed like healthy blood corpuscles'. The French engineer, Pierre Patte, first used words like 'arteries' and 'veins' to justify the principle of one-way streets. Planners believed that if movement through the city slowed, then the 'collective body suffers a crisis of circulation like that an individual body suffers during a stroke when an artery becomes blocked'.[31] British planners adopted this way of thinking relatively late. The word 'arterial', used to describe railway lines in the 1860s, was not applied to UK roads until the 1890s. When the car arrived soon after, this medical metaphor expanded to include the idea of the traffic jam as a disease of modern life, a dysfunctional clot in the circulatory system.

This made sense in the early days of motoring, when there were obvious 'bottlenecks', narrow roads that simply needed to be opened out to increase the traffic flow. The original bottleneck was Brentford High Street, the main western route out of London and no more than 15 feet wide. To the anger of pioneering motorists, this motoring equivalent of the Northwest Passage then became further congested by tramrails. The Brentford Bypass finally opened in 1925 under its better known name of the Great West Road, to a swelling of enthusiasm that anticipated the cultural convulsions over the M1. In Patrick Hamilton's 1932 novel *The Siege of Pleasure*, a female character being driven along it swoons over 'the wide, smooth, deserted spaces of the Great West Road ... Gee! – it was like a racing track – no wonder he put on speed. It was like being in an aeroplane!' But soon these arterials became clogged as well and the experts called for more medical intervention. In 1939 the Royal Institute of British Architects argued that 'we must analyse anew the map of Britain, for if the blood is not to run sluggishly in the veins, and if the arteries are not to harden, then the *roads must change*'. Another author compared a great nation's road system with that of a honed athlete who 'has need of a better circulation than the sedentary worker'.[32]

The first really epic traffic jams came with the end of petrol rationing on 26 May 1950, an event that happily (or, as it turned out, unhappily) coincided with the Whitsun weekend. Motorists symbolically tore up their fuel coupons in cathartic rituals held at petrol pumps, and ancient cars undriven since the 1930s were taken out for a spin. There were colossal queues on main roads out of London, including a two-and-a-half mile snarl-up on the A24 to Worthing and, in the evening, there was a jam virtually all the way from Weston-super-Mare to Bristol. Soon there were multi-mile long jams at weekends coming back from the seaside resorts and the national parks, which the AA called 'Sunday spectaculars'. In 1958, Birmingham's surveyor, Herbert Manzoni, suggested that congestion 'probably started in the organs of this country, which are the urban areas and, like cancer, it has spread ... if we do nothing for a few years, traffic congestion will strangle Great Britain. Fortunately, unlike cancer, it is curable.'[33]

There is no doubt that 1950s traffic jams were bad – and no wonder. When the M1 opened, there were 16,769 more miles of road than there had been in 1911 – an increase of only 9.5 per cent when the number of vehicles had risen by 3,400 per cent. But what tips a jam over from being merely tedious to intolerable? Being stuck in traffic is frustratingly real; but it is also a state of mind that can alter according to your expectations about how quickly you should be going. Sometime in the mid-1950s, as advocates of roadbuilding began to portray the jams as uniquely insufferable, the undrivability of Britain's roads became a potent political metaphor. The Roads Campaign Council handed out leaflets to motorists stuck in Whitsun traffic: 'Get yourself out of this jam – Press your MP for better roads.' It was widely believed that the relief of just a few trunk roads would cure this 'traffic thrombosis' and 'arterial sclerosis', because 1 per cent of the roads was carrying 25 per cent of the traffic.[34] The prescription was a brand new motorway system, a sort of emergency heart bypass on Britain's clogged arterial roads.

Many experts thought that congestion was curable, and that motorists could beat the jams by using the motorways and paying attention to the new BBC radio traffic bulletins. In the 1960s some of the worst jams happened in the gaps between motorways, like the bit on the A5 that funnelled all the motorway traffic from the M1 to the M6, and when the motorways finally linked up in free-flowing intersections, these bottleneck jams were supposed simply to melt away. But the chronic motorway jams that arrived in the 1970s put paid to this Whiggish narrative of historical progress. Things only got worse in the next decade, when the earliest motorways came to the end of their projected life and had to be dug up and coned off into contraflows. No more open-heart surgery; all that could be offered now was palliative care. The worst thing about these sorts of jams was their banality, their ability to bring everything to a standstill as a matter of routine, to create turmoil out of one of the most mundane irritations of daily life, heavy traffic. The longest ever traffic jam to occur in Britain was a 32-mile tailback between Milton Keynes and Rugby on the M1 on the afternoon of 5 April 1985. The cause was not a concertina pile-up or a Biblical-scale exodus from Milton Keynes, but roadworks.

Any traffic cop will tell you that a jam is not always the result of a major problem like a crash or a contraflow; it can build up gradually, gaining momentum as small events accumulate to create momentous consequences. Highways Agency workers like to say that a road is 'q' instead of 'quiet' because keeping traffic moving is a delicate game of controlled chaos and they are superstitious that the mere act of saying 'it's quiet today' will be punished for its complacency by instant gridlock. A jam can be caused by the simple matter of a driver changing lanes, a vehicle parked on the hard shoulder or a worker mowing the grass verge, each of them slowing cars very slightly and creating a chain reaction that stops traffic several miles back. In traffic engineering argot, these jams are caused not by accidents but by 'incidents'. The novelist Will Self once described the anticlimactic experience of reaching the end of a jam on the M25. 'You're expecting some Godard-style smash with heads bleeding and tears and body parts lying everywhere,' he said, 'and when you eventually get there, it's nothing, nothing. The traffic starts to move again.'[35] He's right: reaching the end of these phantom jams and not finding anything to explain and justify your delay is strangely unnerving. It's like coming to the end of a boring whodunit and not even having the satisfaction of finding out the name of the villain because the last page is missing.

→

The first person to study the unpredictable nature of traffic jams was James Lighthill, one of the great applied mathematicians of the last century. Lighthill, who preceded Stephen Hawking as Lucasian Professor of Mathematics at Cambridge, was a pioneer of fluid dynamics, the study of how liquids and gases behave in motion. In 1955 he and his research student, G.B. Whitham, theorised that the course of traffic, just like the flow of a river, could be affected by the most trivial incidents. Even a very slight halt in the traffic created a cascade effect because vehicles passing through a jam would have to stop suddenly on entering it, but could only increase speed gradually as they left it. As a keen amateur swimmer, Lighthill put the principles of fluid dynamics to good use in his long distance swims around islands all over the world, planning them by studying the tides and currents and perfecting an unusual swimming method he called the old English backstroke. In 1973 Lighthill became the first person to swim around the island of Sark, and he repeated the feat several times before dying of a heart attack in his last attempt, in 1998, aged 74. It is not known whether Lighthill also practised the principles of fluid dynamics when he was stuck in traffic jams, which would have meant driving at a constant speed to encourage the other cars to break out of their stop/go cycle, even if it meant a gap opening up before him and a queue of irate drivers behind.

Traffic jam theory had gone into abeyance since the 1960s but soon after Lighthill's death it enjoyed a renaissance. Modern traffic jam studies extended his work with the aid of supercomputers and a newish area of theoretical physics, chaos theory. It suggested that modern traffic jams could be caused by the random slowing down and speeding up of cars, similar to the unruly behaviour of fluids or gases. This was a more radical version of Lighthill's thesis, arguing that simple over-accelerating and over-braking, and not just traffic coming to a halt, could cause a jam. If someone comes up too fast behind the car in front, and has to brake for just a second, the driver behind them will see the brake lights and brake too, only a little harder, so there is a kind of autosuggestive, red-light domino effect all the way down the motorway, as quietly contagious as yawning. If you look at slow traffic from the air, you will see strange patterns emerging, waves of congestion passing through the line of cars like ripples on water. As with the classic example in chaos theory of the butterfly flapping its wings that causes a tornado on the other side of the world, traffic jams are extraordinarily sensitive to initial conditions. Any slight change (or 'butterfly effect') on busy stretches of road can cause a shock wave going back for miles, trapping drivers into crawling platoons as the jam moves 'upstream' against the traffic flow.

The chaos theory of traffic is prone to attractively off-the-wall explanations. The regular jams that used to occur between junctions 11 and 12 of the M25, for instance, were blamed on drivers slowing down to look at the giant mushrooms that used to grow there on the central reservation. But the real point is that traffic jams are often simply 'emergent phenomena' – that is, they are not really 'caused' by anything in particular but are just the outcome of countless individual interactions in a system too complex to compute. They are like sand ripples or the billows on a flag, the product of insubstantial perturbations of the breeze that build up for no obvious reason, or a million different ones.

There is one clear lesson to be learnt from traffic jam theory, however. Driving uncompetitively is a good thing – not just good for the soul, but good for getting there quicker. Like the law of karma, every action forms part of a wider cycle of cause and effect. We reap what we sow. A slower, steady speed is better than the quick-slow rhythms of most motorway driving. Modern traffic control systems like MIDAS (Motorway Incident Detection and Automatic Signalling) work on this principle: they have sensors in the road surface that detect where traffic is building up, feed the information to computers which work out automatically what temporary speed limit to impose, and then send warning messages to the gantry signs to slow the traffic down gradually. The notorious 50 mph limits on the M25 are trying to kill the energy of pressure pulses, straightening the sine curves and filtering traffic into the gaps between the waves. Motorists hate these signs because they are counter-intuitive – they are slowing you down to speed you up – and they conjure up the unappealing sci-fi vision of automated cars driving along freeways in tight convoys, perfectly spaced apart. They do themselves no favours by using the words 'Queue Ahead', a disingenuous phrase that suggests a line of stationary traffic when in fact the traffic has simply risen above a certain threshold. The point of the signs is to prevent queues rather than warn you of them. Yet many motorists think they have been tricked into slowing down for a jam that does not exist, and that the government is deliberately trying to delay their journeys. Instead of these mother hennish signs, perhaps what we need is a platoon of four or five cars to drive round and round the M25 at 50 miles per hour, occupying all the lanes, like the safety car they use at grand prix races after a downpour – forcing everyone into a constant speed and gobbling up the nasty traffic waves.

On roads, we have no vivid collective imagination, no easy way of thinking beyond our own experience other than our view of the back-end of the car in front. The nearest thing we have to sociology is the drivetime radio traffic bulletin, that litany of low-intensity aggro with stock expressions as familiar as the weather forecast. On the radio, jams tend to be blamed on chronic conditions like 'sheer weight of traffic', a catch-all term that traffic reporters use when they cannot find a single explanation. At other times they talk as if the road itself, rather than the cars, is responsible for the jams: *The M8 is very heavy eastbound … the M4 is queuing from 24 to 31 … The M6 northbound is still really slow*. Many traffic reporters now have hotlines which motorists, often giving themselves CB radio handles like Diesel Dog or Slow Joe, can ring to report jams they are stuck in – ostensibly so that other listeners can avoid them, but perhaps also so that they can have their own misery witnessed and mentioned. The traffic bulletins are really about collective solace, an invitation to fatalism and even masochism – for the jams, like the poor, will always be with us.

→

What narratives of ended or ruined lives lie behind those pat phrases about a road being shut or a lane closed 'following an incident, earlier'? Whenever the traffic reporters offer an explanation it always seems to be something fairly harmless, like a fuel spillage or a lorry shedding its load. But many of the closures must be down to pile-ups, some of them fatal. Road deaths vanish into the everyday because they happen in ones and twos, not the critical masses of plane or train crashes. On traffic bulletins, the only thing we know about an accident is that it causes a jam – that is, until the reporter announces matter-of-factly that it has been 'cleared' or 'shifted' or, still more blithely, 'the accident's gone'. On average, an accident remains on the asphalt for less than an hour before rapid response teams of paramedics whoosh away the victims, the recovery vehicles spirit the wreck away and the traffic starts moving again. You need to be a careful reader of the road indeed to spot the minuscule evidence that remains – the skidmarks heading for the verge or central reservation, the tiny black fragments of tyre on the asphalt, the slight kinks in the crash barriers.

Death on the roads was not always so invisible. At different times in motoring history, road crashes have bubbled up from the collective unconscious like the return of the repressed. In 1934 the number of deaths on the road peaked at 7,343 – a figure not exceeded for another thirty years. Using a common analogy, the *Daily Telegraph* wrote that 'a year on the roads is more murderous than the three years of the South African War'. In his intriguingly titled memoir, *Something in Linoleum*, the broadcaster Paul Vaughan gives a grim account of growing up in the 1930s in a house overlooking the Kingston Bypass, where from the lounge window he could see the South Lane Junction where the worst accidents happened, and hear 'the screaming of brakes, a sharp bang, a reverberating skitter of metal fragments, followed by even more sinister noises: the moans of the victims, the screams of women bystanders'. In the days before proper research into skid resistance and tyre grip, accidents generated rumour and counter-rumour about their causes. Roads in the south-west, with a surface dressing of Bridport pebbles and coal tar, had a lethal reputation. Crashes on the A1 and A4 were blamed on their bitumen-rich toppings which, when combined with spilt oil, horse droppings and rain, produced a fatal polish. These new roads, complained one motorist, had 'a surface that in its highest and glassiest state of perfection recalls the fearful delights of a Cresta run'.[36]

The road crash was such an emotive topic that many people mined it for political capital. The RAC and AA's response to accidents was invariably to call for more roads, which helpfully deflected the blame from incompetent motorists. 'Five bees in a bottle bump oftener than three,' declared Mervyn O'Gorman of the RAC. 'Give the bees a bigger bottle!' Concrete manufacturers, in their propaganda war against their fierce rival, hot-rolled asphalt, used the slogans 'skidding ends where concrete begins' and 'let concrete save our children's lives'. In 1947 the High Tory novelist Angela Thirkell used road crashes to attack socialist rationing and the welfare state, blaming the deaths on wartime fatigue 'accentuated since the outbreak of peace by deliberate under-nourishment of the people of England to make them too listless to resist petty tyranny'. Many used road accidents to call for motorways to be built. In 1955 *Picture Post* ran a piece by Trevor Philpott about the A5, then the busiest trade route in Europe and just 16 feet wide at its narrowest point. Like many other trunk roads, parts of the A5 had three lanes and no central reservation – the middle lane, used for cars overtaking from either direction, being nicknamed the 'suicide lane' (left side, right side, suicide). 'Every mile has its tragedies,' wrote Philpott, '– of men dead by burning, dead by suffocation, dead by bleeding, dead by pulverisation.' He had himself witnessed the body of a twenty-year-old man being recovered from a lorry at Towcester. The headline read: 'The motorway we MUST build.'[37]

But the building of the motorways only exacerbated people's fears about crashes. Newspapers and magazines stoked popular anxieties with headlines like 'Motorways will be Murderways' and 'M1 for Murder'.[38] Of course, a well-watched road will forever remind you of its dangers and, when the motorways opened, the police and motoring organisations were all surveying them closely. Inevitably, the most notable events they had to report were crashes. The first ever motorway crash happened at Bamber Bridge at 11.15pm on 7 December

1958, two days into the life of the Preston Bypass. A twenty-two-year-old man drove a stolen Ford Zephyr at speed off the road and over a seven-foot ridge, overturning in the field below. Two days later a fourteen-year-old boy borrowed his father's Vauxhall Velox without asking, and span it off the motorway into a field at 70 mph. Both cars were write-offs but their drivers sustained only minor bruising.[39] Most of the early accidents were minor ones like this, the general emptiness of the road preventing serious collisions.

Motorways were the safest roads in Britain statistically, but drivers had difficulty squaring this reality with their own anxieties. Human fears respond to images, not numbers. Six months after the M1 opened, a rumour circulated that 'phantoms' were appearing on it at night, shadows under bridges that looked like parked cars. They had already caused one fatal accident, when (according to her widower) a woman driver swerved to avoid what looked like a furniture lorry parked with no lights on. Newspapers printed photographs of dark shapes under motorway bridges with captions like 'Is this the phantom van on the M1?' (As usual when newspaper headlines resort to asking questions, the answer was 'no'.) The Road Research Laboratory even published a report, 'Phantoms on the M1 motorway', which found no evidence of ghostly apparitions and blamed the fatal accident on the headlights of the family's car not being full-on.[40] At the speeds reached on motorways, the risks seemed greater than normal and crashes tended to be spectacular ones involving tyre blowouts, multiple pile-ups and crossover collisions. Articulated lorry crashes looked horrific, the whole vehicle folding like a jackknife around its axis. 1960s caravans were so flimsy that in a crash they just disintegrated, flew apart at the seams to leave their domestic interiors eerily exposed. It took years for caravan-towing drivers to shake off an undeserved reputation for recklessness.

The biggest fears of all were generated by motorway fog – and in this case the fears were justified. Even after the 1956 Clean Air Act, which created smokeless zones in cities, smoke from factories and coal fires would merge with low mists to create miasmic pea-soupers. Not since Victorian London had fog carried such a threat of confusion and chaos. Flat stretches of motorway like the southern end of the M1 and the M6 near Stafford created notorious fog belts, and British Rail laid on 'fog specials' to lure commuters from their cars. On the first motorways, drivers had no collective signal to slow down in fog and, worried about fast cars hitting them from behind, they ploughed on into the white-out and caused horrific pile-ups. Then, in 1964, the police began installing roadside fog warning lamps – vertical pairs of alternately flashing amber lights. When fog descended the police would drive along the motorway activating the lights with radar guns; they staged competitions with each other to see who was the best shot. But even after these lights were installed – and many of them were stolen or sabotaged by vandals – the suicidal behaviour of motorists did not noticeably improve. One chief inspector complained that 'a large percentage of motorists are just damned fools … They get the idea in their noddles that there will never be anything they can hit.' The Ministry of Transport attacked these 'lunatic drivers' and one Tory MP, Dudley Smith, condemned 'the lemmings of the internal combustion age' who drove fast through thick fog as if they had a death wish. Or as the Jak cartoon in the *Evening Standard* put it: 'Put your foot down, Sid, I can't see a thing!'[41]

→

For J.G. Ballard, the laureate of the Westway, the road crash embodied the 'lurid mythologies' and 'special logic' of the 1960s. In 1969 he curated an exhibition of crashed cars at the Camden Arts Laboratory, made up of the mangled remains of road accidents, salvaged from north London breakers' yards. The opening night descended into confusion, as guests poured wine over the cars and smashed the windows, a topless model hired for the evening claimed to have been sexually assaulted in the back of a Pontiac, and a *New Society* journalist interviewing Ballard became 'so overwrought with indignation … that she had to be restrained from attacking me'. Convinced he had uncovered some dark underbelly of the collective psyche, Ballard began to investigate the car crash in his fiction. He believed that, far from being senseless calamities, crashes happened with our unconscious collusion, a sort of shared Thanatos or death wish – since 'the rough equivalent of speeding on unchecked tyres along a fast dual carriageway at the end of a tiring day at the office is lying in a hot bath with a blazing three-bar electric fire balanced on the edge below a half-open window rattling in a rising gale.'[42]

The crashes in Ballard's fictions typically happen on west London's elevated roads, the striking new landscape created as the motorways lined up with the old arterials. The semi autobiographical narrator of his 1991 novel, *The Kindness of Women*, is driving along the Hammersmith Flyover sometime in the late 1960s and crashes into a car which turns out to be driven by one of his amphetamine-addicted acquaintances. Another of his more toxic friends drives 'in a deliberately careless way, as if trying to express a casual nothingness', and kills several people while driving the wrong way along the same flyover, his headlamps flashing as he forces the approaching cars against the safety barrier. Soon after this incident, the narrator arrives at a crash on Chertsey Bridge in Surrey, involving two of his friends. He is 'struck by their self-conscious pose, like dancers arrested in an audience-catching flourish at the end of their performance', and by the onlookers who gather round the car, inspecting it 'with the practised eyes of enthusiasts judging a display of aerobatics'. After no one makes an effort to help the victims and one man protests when the paramedics arrive and block his camera shot, the narrator concludes that 'a new street theatre had been born'.[43]

In Ballard's novel, *Crash*, voyeurism and the death wish come together explosively on west London's fast roads. Its anti-hero, 'hoodlum scientist' Dr Robert Vaughan, obsesses over the deaths of film stars like James Dean and Jayne Mansfield in car accidents, and leads a small cadre of fetishists who, tuning in to police radios, descend on car crashes and experiment erotically with and among the victims' bodies. Finally Vaughan kills himself on Heathrow's perimeter roads, seeking a kamikaze erotic communion with Elizabeth Taylor as she drives to the airport from the Shepperton Film Studios. Vaughan races towards Taylor's limousine but instead crashes through the flyover railings and plunges through the roof of a bus filled with

airline passengers. The publisher's reader who first saw the manuscript wrote, 'The author of this book is beyond psychiatric help.'[44]

Ballard's vision was certainly avant-garde but he was tapping into
widely held anxieties of the time. When elevated roads first arrived
in west London, residents feared that lorries would crash through the
barriers and drop on them; one parish priest worried that his church
tower could be knocked down in an accident. Ballard's theories about
the voyeuristic appeal of road crashes were also being voiced by others.
The term 'rubbernecking', first used to describe the steady motion of
sightseers looking down at their guidebooks and then up towards a
tourist attraction, was now beginning to be applied to onlookers at
road accidents. In 1972 an AA official identified an 'alarming new
trend' of motorist 'ghouls' stopping on the hard shoulder, central reservation and even the motorway itself to watch rescue operations and
take photographs of crashes.[45] Recovery teams began sending vehicles
to both carriageways in anticipation of shunts on the opposite side of
an accident, as motorists slowed down to take a look.

Ballard's experiences in an internment camp in China during
the war had left him with a heightened awareness of the violence in
human nature, and he saw the car crash as one of the few places in
western society where the reality of death broke through the cara-
pace of shiny consumerism. He treated the crash as a seminal event,
a connecting rod for all sorts of contemporary cultural obsessions
about sex, sadism and celebrity. But we now know that Ballard began
writing about crashes just as public fears about them were beginning
to recede. 1966 was the worst year for road deaths in Britain before
or since, with almost 8,000 dead.[46] Most of these deaths were not
on motorway flyovers but on crowded urban roads and unrestricted
rural lanes, just before the arrival of compulsory seat belts, breatha-
lysers and speed limits. Thanks to the radial-ply tyre revolution led
by Michelin and Pirelli, the growing use of crash-test dummies to
simulate collisions and the Road Research Laboratory's work on skid-
proof surfaces, hard science was now helping to prevent accidents.
Roads were designed to be 'forgiving' – that is, to be able to absorb
driver error. Crash barriers, rather than bouncing the car back on to

the road, would trap it in their grooves and bring it to a juddering halt; lamp-posts would absorb energy and crumple acquiescently on impact; rumble strips were laid by the roadside to wake up drivers who fell asleep and veered off the road.

That the roads now had a duty to 'forgive' our mistakes was a peculiar take on what Ruskin called the pathetic fallacy, the attribution of human qualities to inanimate objects. A similar sort of personification occurs in Ballard's fictions, in which the flyovers take on a strange, sinister life of their own, almost as though they are willing accidents to happen. Novelists, like psychoanalysts, tend to search for the design and order of narrative in the seeming arbitrariness of life, imagining 'accidents' to be the result of unconscious desires or hidden obsessions. But surely the scariest and most disturbing thing about road crashes is not their fatal glamour but their crushing ordinariness, their statistical regularity. If crashes were solely the fault of sex-crazed psychopaths stalking celebrities on motorway flyovers, there would fortunately be few of them.

→

One of the most common causes of road crashes is a naturally occurring phenomenon: falling asleep. Until at least the end of the Second World War, drivers who fell asleep were not blamed for causing accidents. Solicitors generally argued in court that, since their clients were asleep at the wheel, they could not be said to be driving and were therefore not responsible for their actions. The government only began to take the problem seriously when the motorways arrived, and safety experts worried about monotonous stretches of road inducing 'driver-hypnosis'. But even in the early 1960s, Ernest Marples was urging motorists to drive through the night to avoid holiday jams. 'I am sure that the isolated lack of one night's sleep hurts no one,' agreed the *Birmingham Mail*'s motoring correspondent. 'You get tired, it is true. Then the sensible thing to do is to drop your speed … while you do feel a bit tired in the early hours of the morning (especially if your passengers are sleeping), I find this passes off and I usually arrive in good order.'[47] The most common all-night journey was down to the West Country during the holiday season. It was only in the summer of 1972, at the Somerset-Devon border, that police erected the first 'Tiredness Kills' signs at lay-bys, offering exhausted drivers light refreshments and mild admonishments.

Even now, when governments castigate tiredness as a deadly sin of the road, nodding off at the wheel is still seen as blackly comic – as in the old Bob Monkhouse joke, 'I want to die like my dad, peacefully in my sleep, not screaming like his passengers' – and the phenomenon is surrounded by myth and misunderstanding. If you fall asleep for more than a few seconds on the road you will probably crash, but to know you have been asleep it must last for a minute or two – so drivers can nod off, cause an accident and then sincerely protest their innocence. Unlike drink or drugs, sleep leaves no trace in the blood for the autopsy. The giveaway is the absence of skidmarks and the timing of many of these crashes – between noon and 4pm, or 2am and 6am, when our circadian rhythms are at their lowest ebb. Breakfast show traffic reporters will often mention that a road has been blocked by a lorry turning over at around 6am, perhaps driven by a trucker who set off early to avoid the morning rush while his body clock had other ideas.

Falling asleep raises the discomfiting question of how much control we actually have over our behaviour on the roads. Do we drive on the road or does the road drive us? Car crashes tend to be confusingly multi-causal: they are amalgams of individual error (clumsiness, speeding), unconscious handicaps (sleepiness, inattention) and things outside the driver's control (road layout, bad weather). The road claims its victims in predictable regressions to the mean, not spectacular smashes on motorway off-ramps. The most dangerous roads are the older, rural ones with the unforgiving designs. Northern roads are more lethal than southern ones because their twisting, hilly routes and lighter traffic make it easier to drive fast and overtake. The most treacherous road in the country statistically is the A682, which winds picturesquely from the M65 in Lancashire to Long Preston in the Yorkshire Dales.

Road accident statistics have always rendered death unreal.

Cost-benefit analyses reduce it to a simple calculus of profit and deficit. Even before the M1 was built, the Road Research Laboratory calculated that it would prevent 520 casualties, including twenty deaths, each year – and, since fatal casualties cost the country £2,500 per 'unit' (that is, per person), serious casualties £650 and slight casualties a very reasonable £50, this represented a saving of £215,000.[48] Statistics are serenely indifferent to the fate of individual lives, allowing them to blur into impersonal graphs and euphemistic acronyms like RTCs (road traffic collisions) and KSIs (killed and seriously injured). Just occasionally, though, the statistics can reveal disturbing random patterns. When the M25 opened, there were more accidents clockwise than anticlockwise. Some thought that this was because motorists driving in a clockwise direction were more likely to have the sun shining in their eyes. Others laid the blame on Guildford, which generates a large tribe of commuters driving clockwise in the early morning.

The unsettling thing about these statistics is not that they are unexplainable – odd clusters like this can occur through pure chance and are quite normal – but that they seem to have broken their unspoken contract with us. They don't do what accident statistics are supposed to do, which is to actuarialise the road crash, finesse it into columns of figures that make it seem like a rare but predictable event, part of the normal run of things instead of unknowable fate. Perhaps this also explains why some motorists get upset and even angry at those impromptu roadside shrines to crash victims, usually consisting of rotting flowers wrapped in cellophane and fluffy toys tied to railings, that have fairly recently arrived in this country from the Catholic Mediterranean. Like those seemingly surreal M25 accident statistics, these shrines serve as memento mori, reminders of a ubiquitous but increasingly hidden event on our roads.

Eventually it will happen. You will see the aftermath of a road crash, on a well-lit, well-laid out junction that you drive through every day. As the cars pass slowly in single file you have time to register the blur of crumpled metal, flashing lights and yellow jackets. Suddenly, the everyday stops being invisible and the road is no longer about the

endless movement of traffic. For a brief moment, the smooth continuum of daily life, the illusion that it has no past or future, has been
broken like a spell – just like in Philip Larkin's poem, 'Ambulances',
when the fleeting interruption of a siren dissolves 'the unique random
blend of families and fashions' into a 'solving emptiness'.[49] But as you
pass the same spot the next day you will find that everything has been
brushed over, cleaned-up, disappeared. The road has shrugged off the
accident like a 24-hour headcold and is acting as if nothing had happened. The price we pay for fast roads is their resilience in the face
of death, their ignorance of the finite trajectory of individual lives.
People may be fragile and ephemeral, but the road goes on.

7

YOU CAN STUFF YOUR MOTORWAY

*Why is the motorway culture drearier in Europe than any-
where in America? Perhaps because it is so imitative and
looks hackneyed and unstylish and ill-fitting, the way no
European looks quite right in a baseball cap.*

Paul Theroux[1]

When I first got a car, I was frightened of roads, especially motorways. I was living in Brighton then and, determined to conquer my
phobia, I used to make dawn raids on the sparse motorway system of
the southern counties, when the traffic was light. This is how I came
to be driving through junctions 10 and 11 of the M3 not long after
sunrise one Sunday in the spring of 1995, less than a year after this
section of road opened. I had already seen the cutting in photographs,
but it still left me unprepared for how huge and unrepentant it seemed
in the flesh. From the south you approach it from an angle, on a sharp
incline, and at first the gap in the Downs seemed too narrow to pass.
It reminded me of that scene in *Jason and the Argonauts* when the
ship's crew have to row mightily through the Symplegades, the rocks
at the mouth of the Bosphorus that clash together, crushing boats to
smithereens. Once I was inside it was like driving through a dry ocean
bed. The sides of the cutting had been left as bare chalk and, although

the first vegetation and petrol fumes had already dulled it a little, the dirty white still looked stark against the gunmetal grey asphalt. Probably because I first saw it through eerie, early morning vapours on a deserted road, the image has remained with me of a scar, a gaping wound in the earth. It does not surprise me that road protest veterans still make sure they never have to drive through here, or even avoid the whole of the M3 on principle. This place is called Twyford Down.

This mere 400 yards of motorway should really be marked on OS maps with crossed swords – for it was here, in 1992, that Britain erupted into a civil war that was to last for the next five years. In fact, there *is* an impromptu war memorial, but it's on the edge of the downland above the cutting so you can't see it from the motorway. This menhir-shaped stone was part of the spoil from the blasting through the cutting, and it still bears the deep grooves left by the holes drilled to insert the TNT. A stonecutter has inscribed it with the legend, 'This land was ravaged by', followed by various names, some of which – R. Key, J. MacGregor, M. Thatcher, J. Major – seem vaguely familiar.

As civil wars tend to do, this one forged unlikely alliances between aristocrats and outcasts, brought together people of all ages and backgrounds, employed its folk heroes and folk devils on both sides. Like all wars, it had a tipping point and a much deeper set of causes. The anti-road campaigns of the 1990s were sometimes linked to the rise of 'single-issue politics' – but there was nothing singular about them. They drew on a rich body of ideas about democracy, land ownership and the countryside dating back to the English Civil War. And the battles were not just about particular stretches of tarmac but about how roads are thought about and felt, how they feed into our collective desires and fears.

→

Of course there never was a golden age of asphalt, when everyone excitedly welcomed new roads. If roads are palimpsests, then so are the anti-road crusades that form around them, picking up the narrative threads of much earlier campaigns like an organic folk tradition.

It takes about a dozen years to build a road, from the first dotted lines on a ministry map to the ribbon-cutting opening. The longest time is spent agreeing the preferred route, which can take about a decade, compared to which the actual ground-clearing and building are fairly quick. So if you really want to stop a road, you have to start early, preferably before it gets included in the National Roads Programme and certainly before the public inquiry – assuming you know about it before then, which is unlikely. Plans for new roads can disappear but then come back, sometimes many years later under new guises and disguises. It is almost as though the protagonists are actors in endless variations on the same play, performing a series of stock roles from rough-hewn outlaws to Whitehall villains. And the play almost always has the same ending: the road gets built.

In a sense, the road protests slotted into a ready-made narrative; in the immediate postwar years, they were prefigured, and perhaps even found some of their inspiration, in works of fiction. In the late 1940s and early 1950s there was a series of films which drew on British traditions of localism and scepticism towards state power, refuelled by widespread resentments about the survival of wartime red tape, rationing and top-down planning. These films celebrate the cussed-ness of little people in the face of authority, a well-mannered flirtation with anarchism underpinned by an entrenched conservatism. In Muriel Box's 1952 film, *The Happy Family*, the Lord family endure a Whitehall siege after refusing to let their home and shop be bulldozed to make way for a road to the Festival of Britain site on London's South Bank. After a week behind the barricades living without light and water, the Lords win and the government agrees to bend the road around either side of their home. Pa Lord (Stanley Holloway) raises his glass to toast 'living quietly and being left alone and not being led about like sheep, to our Englishman's castle and to all the millions of little castles belonging to little people all over the country'. In the 1953 Ealing comedy, *The Titfield Thunderbolt*, an alliance of the local squire, the vicar and the town clerk keeps an ancient steam train running by getting the better of a nouveau riche bus company and the faceless bureaucrats of British Railways. The squire (John Gregson) succeeds in rallying a local crowd to the cause by imagining a grim future in which 'our lanes will be concrete roads, our houses will have numbers instead of names'.

Real protests against the building of motorways began before the first one was even finished. In 1958, when it emerged that the second section of the M1 planned to cut through Charnwood Forest near Leicester, 32,000 people signed a petition against the destruction of the city's green lung. The London–Yorkshire Motorway was swiftly renamed the London–Birmingham Motorway because its route through Leicestershire was so contentious that it was clearly not going to reach Yorkshire for several years. In the early 1960s, farmers and racehorse trainers protested even more fiercely about the route of the M4 through the Berkshire Downs – which partly explains why this stretch of motorway is so dull, the road hidden forever in a bush-strewn ditch.

Public feeling about roads really shifted when the motorways edged their way into London, and people began to protest about roads them-selves rather than specific routes. When the Chiswick–Langley section of the M4 opened in March 1965, the newspapers picked up on the pioneering anti-road group, the Chiswick Motorway Liaison Com-mittee, and the growing reaction against 'the monster roads nosing into Britain's cities'. Reporters found residents of nearby houses who complained that the sodium lamps gave them headaches, vibrations shook their houses, loose chippings pinged off their windows and exhaust fumes dirtied their washing. A familiar newspaper photo-graph of the time showed bewildered council tenants standing in their back gardens with the stub of an uncompleted slip road rearing above them. But at first the proponents of efficient traffic circulation airily dismissed the objectors. 'Even if a fleet of bulldozers was turned loose in London and all the drivers were blindfolded,' said the West Riding county surveyor and motorway advocate, Stuart Maynard Lovell, 'they could not do much unnecessary work because of the immensity of the problem.' The old-school RAC chairman, Wilfrid Andrews, described London as an 'orphan city' whose growth was being stifled because its roads stopped at the city walls. 'I am staggered,' he said, 'by the colossal impertinence of those who complain of the aesthetic atrocities of urban motorways.'[2]

The first large-scale protest against an urban motorway was the campaign against London's Western Avenue Extension, a two-and-a-half mile flyover planned to run between White City and Paddington Basin, making it the longest elevated road in Europe. The protest movement emerged out of the community workshops in north Kensington, set up by middle-class radicals who had settled there. One of them, an ex-Aldermaston marcher called George Clark, saw the area as a testing ground for the ideas of the French new left, which were partly a response to France's own experiments with transport planning. During the 1950s and 1960s, Paris's working-class residents had been dispersed to the suburbs, forced out by compulsory purchase and rent increases. Streets were widened, the one-way system was made the most extensive in Europe and an expressway on the right bank of the Seine was built. French radicals thought that this new urban landscape had created a unique kind of human alienation. The Situationist International, a revolutionary Parisian movement, protested that commuting was nothing more than unpaid labour and that traffic circulation was 'the organization of individual isolation'.[3]

But in north Kensington Clark saw an opportunity. He thought the building of the Western Avenue Extension might be a chance to reclaim public space, particularly for children, in the traffic-clogged streets nearby. In May 1968, while students from the Sorbonne barricaded the Latin Quarter with iron railings and paving stones, the North Kensington Play Space Group successfully campaigned for an adventure playground underneath the motorway. Laing, the contractors, generously agreed to pay for it. Then came a much bigger victory. The Play Space Group discovered that the council had not granted itself planning permission for the massive, walled-off car park it planned to create under the motorway – and the group managed to reclaim the whole space for use by locals.

When the road, rebranded 'Westway', was officially opened in July 1970, protesters drove up an unopened off-ramp, dodged a police block and advanced the wrong way down the motorway towards the official motorcade. A junior minister, Michael Heseltine, conducting the opening ceremony, was met by protesters armed with placards. *Ramps rape residents' repose. You can't fly over human lives. Help: our street is being killed. Rich fly over the poor. Get us out of this hell.* Some shook their fists at Heseltine but others were more deferential, crying out, 'It's a lovely road but we're living in misery, sir.' Many seemed remarkably stoical about the distress the road had inflicted on them. 'What I really like is talking to friends out of my window,' said one elderly woman resident of Acklam Road, which was only twenty yards from the carriageway. 'Some of the passing motorists are very friendly and wave at me, but it isn't the same thing.'[4]

→

The Westway was just one of the radial arms of an ambitious scheme of four concentric 'ringways' circling the capital, the building of which was meant to take up the rest of the century. The aim was to transform London's road pattern from the spokes of a wheel to a spider's web, with traffic not bound for the centre diverting round the ringways. Ringway 1 was the notorious 'motorway box', shaped less like a ring than a wobbly rectangle, with corners at Willesden, Hackney, Blackheath and Clapham Junction – about as close to the heart of London as a motorway could get. The number of homes it would destroy was fiercely disputed, estimates ranging between 15,000 and 80,000.

Roadbuilders are pragmatists: they go where they think there will be least topographical and popular resistance. So it is no surprise that the only bits of the ringway to be built were in poor areas, like north Kensington and Hackney's Victoria Park, amid the new concrete deserts of tower blocks and subways. But the ringway planners reckoned without the phenomenon of gentrification, which brought middle-class bolshiness and articulacy to the protests. The motorway box aimed to cut a swathe through new property hotspots like Notting Hill, Islington, Greenwich and Battersea. The route plan of Ringway 1 was almost a 'gazetteer of gentrification', as one historian puts it, because it cut through the Victorian urban rim where middle-class colonists were drawn to the period houses.[5] 'Ringway bashing' by motorway action groups soon became a popular metropolitan pastime.

The ringway saga was C.P. Snow's 'two cultures' argument in action. Snow had argued in 1959 that British culture was split between scientists and 'literary intellectuals' with a reflex antipathy towards one another. Even before he joined the Ministry of Technology in the new Labour Government of 1964, it was clear where Snow's sympathies lay. 'If the scientists have the future in their bones,' he wrote, 'then the traditional culture responds by wishing the future did not exist.' The Cambridge literary critic F.R. Leavis attacked Snow as the embodiment of 'technologico-Benthamite' civilisation.[6] The arguments over urban roads replayed this enduringly British clash of cultures. The engineers and designers responsible for the early motorways, like James Drake, Owen Williams and Jock Kinneir, were Snow's 'new men', the arch-meritocrats who had high status in the years of postwar reconstruction. Now the literary intellectuals were fighting back, marshalling the forces of history and culture against the future-oriented technocrats.

The first signs of a fightback had been seen in the protests against a planned inner ring road across Christ Church Meadow in Oxford in the mid-1950s. The proposed road came so close to the college walls that it seemed like the barbarians were at the gate. One Oxford don wrote that it was 'a pity that Ruskin is not alive to castigate such barbarism as it deserves!' (What Ruskin would have thought is not perhaps so straightforward. In 1874 he led his students, including a young Oscar Wilde, to dig a road at Hinksey Ferry near Oxford to learn about the dignity of manual labour, which he thought 'as much an art as the mere muscular act of rowing'.[7]) A decade after the Oxford ring-road debate, the anti-ringway movement was headed by the largely Oxbridge-educated members of the cultural professions who had moved into up-and-coming areas of north London – artists, writers, journalists, academics, architects. They formed the pressure group, Homes Before Roads, which in the 1970 London local elections won 100,000 votes, but no seats.

In these campaigns against urban freeways, which soon spread beyond London, the new radicalism of the young – born in the protest movements and alternative subcultures of the late 1960s – united with a deeper vein of elegiac conservatism. The most high-profile anti-ringway advocate was John Betjeman, who railed against 'plansters' and called the motorway box a 'line of death' around inner London. Defender of the Euston Arch and St Pancras Station and celebrant of branch-line suburbia, Betjeman worried that England was becoming 'a few acres of preserved countryside between concrete flyovers, spanned by cafeterias thrumming with canned music and reeking of grease'. The anti-roads movement brought together this strand of preservationism with a left–liberal disdain for the takeover of cities by cabals of political and business interests. The Bristol University English lecturer, Fred Inglis, dispensed with scholarly detachment to attack the 'blitzed and poisoned landscape' created by a new flyover cutting through his city. Inglis added a political edge to Leavisite humanism, arguing that the road planners' 'flow-chart efficiencies' were 'a brutal and irrational effort to solve a trivial difficulty by destroying everything in the way'. The urban motorway was a symbol of 'intellectual tunnel vision … It is as if, like American policy in Vietnam, you annihilate all natural and human life in an area, strip the trees and drive out the homesteaders in order to call the country pacified.'[8]

In 1972 the Department of the Environment acknowledged the public disquiet and conceded that 'the day of the supremacy of the motor car and the road-builder has come to an end'. The urban motorway programme ground slowly to a halt. Leeds managed to complete its inner ring road, but in an ill-advised PR campaign, it persuaded the Post Office to frank mail from the city with the proud slogan, 'Motorway City of the Seventies'. The Guardian journalist and native of Leeds, David McKie, thought the phrase had a 'chilling ring';[9] by the 1980s, when it was still being used on postmarks, it had become a source of humour and derision. Liverpool had planned a non-stop fast road from the M53 Wirral motorway, through the new Mersey Tunnel, on to an eight-lane inner ring road sweeping through the city on its way to the M62. The plans were scuppered by fierce local opposition and spending cuts – so the M62 begins illogically at junction 4, a few miles from the centre of Liverpool. For similar reasons, the other end of the M62 stops 16 miles from Hull near North Cave, merging diffidently with the A63. The change of political mood was starting to reverberate on the roads themselves, turning the motorway system into an unfinished narrative.

→

The sweetest moment for the growing anti-roads movement came in April 1973, when the now Labour-controlled Greater London Council scrapped the motorway box. Even without the protests, it would probably have been scuppered by rising land costs from the early 1970s property boom. The government redirected funds towards Ringway 3, an outer road that lay outside the GLC's jurisdiction. But if they thought this would give them an easier ride, they reckoned without the Upshire Preservation Society, founded by a redoubtable local magistrate called Joyce Woods. Upshire was a pretty village in the middle of Epping Forest, right in the projected path of the northern section of Ringway 3, then called the M16. At the lunchtime traffic peak one day in February 1973, Upshire residents assembled their combine harvesters, tractors and horseboxes in London's Parliament Square. Then, led by Vanessa the goat, they marched in a slow-moving line down Whitehall carrying banners with the legend, 'Not Epping likely'. Civil servants began privately to describe the M16 as 'the Epping nuisance'.

But when Labour returned to power in 1974, it proved to be as keen on this outer ring road as the Tories. The environment secretary, Anthony Crosland, believed that roads were a force for social mobility and the middle classes should not 'pull up the ladder' of car ownership behind them. In his classic 1956 book, *The Future of Socialism*, Crosland had called for the left to ditch its Fabian-style Puritanism, arguing that Britain should be 'a more colourful and civilised country to live in' and that there was more to life than 'total abstinence and a good filing system'.[10] In the 1970s, while environmental campaigners were beginning to point to the folly of pursuing unlimited growth, Crosland remained committed to greater prosperity for all. Sadly, his faith in the politics of pleasure bequeathed the nation the most unpleasurable road in Britain. In November 1975, he was instrumental in the decision to end the ringway saga by deciding on a single orbital route around London. This route would ratchet together different halves of two planned ring roads – the northern section of Ringway 3, the M16, and the southern section of Ringway 4. Running between 13 and 22 miles from Charing Cross, it was now to be known by a single number: M25.

The sparsely attended public inquiry into the route of the M16, held at the downbeat Epping Forest Motel, had been repeatedly abandoned because of one noisy protester. John Tyme, a Sheffield Polytechnic lecturer and leading light in the Conservation Society, pronounced motorways 'a consummate evil' and 'the greatest threat to the interests of this nation in all its history'. A keen amateur historian, he believed the parliamentary system, conceived to fight Stuart absolutism, needed to evolve to fight a new tyranny, the 'Divine Right of the Technological Imperative'.[11] At the time, the remit of public inquiries into roads was limited; objectors could not argue that the road should not be built, only that it should go through someone else's front room instead of their own. Tyme believed that, since the government both set up the inquiry and adjudicated on its findings, the whole thing was a sham. His aim was to disrupt the inquiry so much that it would have to be abandoned and the road could not be built. He became an itinerant protester, hired by local campaigners for the same nominal fee of 50p. One newspaper profile described him as 'the self-appointed Don Quixote of the motorways' with 'the righteous glow of an Old Testament prophet – a twentieth-century Moses leading his people out of bondage'. 'I have a formula,' Tyme told this reporter. '$T + C + N = I$, truth, plus courage, plus numbers equals invincibility. I supply the truth. The people themselves must supply the rest. In the end we cannot lose.'[12]

When the anti-road protests reached England's historic capital of Winchester, Tyme was to play a key role. The completion of the M3 to the north and south of Winchester had left a twelve-and-a-half mile gap in the motorway around the town. Traffic had to pour on to the congested A33, one of the oldest dual carriageways in the country. So the Ministry of Transport planned to drive the M3 through the Itchen Valley water meadows, where Keats had written his 'Ode to Autumn' and declared the air around St Catherine's Hill 'worth sixpence a pint'. A petition against the motorway had been signed by more than half the adult population of Winchester, handed to the Lord Mayor in April 1973, and quietly buried in a filing cabinet. Winchestrians were virtually united in wanting to protect their ancient city from more roads. One resident noted wryly that after a packed protest rally, in which opposition to the motorway was unanimous, 'the meeting broke up to a tumultuous applause and a sustained banging of car doors and revving of car engines'.[13]

In the stifling heat of the drought summer of 1976, several hundred protesters massed at the public inquiry. Among them was John Thorn, the liberal-minded headmaster of Winchester College, who called the road 'a monstrous piece of desecration' and accused the council of selling 'the heritage of a thousand years'. Thorn received several letters from outraged old Wykehamists because he permitted senior boys to attend the inquiry and appear on television dressed in casual clothes. He later admitted to being rather intimidated by Tyme, who throughout the inquiry kept doing the same drawing on a pad – 'a pair of huge car headlights like the eyes of a devil'.[14] Tyme and Thorn disrupted the inquiry with shouts from the floor and were ejected along with several others, including a man dressed as King Alfred who had arrived on a horse. The remaining protesters shouted 'Sieg Heil' and 'fascist' at the inquiry inspector, Major-General Raymond Edge, before drowning him out with a rousing chorus of 'Rule Britannia'.

Tyme reappeared a few months later at the ill-tempered campaign to stop the widening of Archway Road in north London, when Hugh Rossi, the local Conservative MP, accused the middle-class anti-road demonstrators of 'fascist tactics' of intimidation and bullying.[15] This inquiry had to be adjourned on several occasions, most dramatically when police were called in to disperse demonstrators who were hammering on the door of a room in which the inquiry inspector and his team had locked themselves and then retreated to the fire escape.

This was not a good time to be a roadbuilder. One civil servant later recalled that up until about 1972, ministers were desperate to appear at inaugural ceremonies for roads, but by 1976, he couldn't find anyone to open the York Bypass or the last section of the M62. Apart from these protests against roads, the spending cuts and price hikes for oil-based asphalt made governments less keen to build them. In the mid-1970s, petrol prices rose so steeply that many now felt there would not be enough cars to fill any new roads – a judgement endorsed by the Leitch committee on trunk roads in 1978, which argued that governments should properly compare road schemes with alternatives like railways and that roads should be gradually improved rather than built all at once without regard to local conditions. In the same year, the BBC filmed a one-off drama by Alan Bleasdale, *The Black Stuff*, about a gang of Liverpudlian tarmac layers who lose their jobs after a moonlighting job in Middlesbrough. The drama was not shown until 1980 and the 1982 series it spawned, *The Boys from the Black Stuff*, came to be seen as a bleak commentary on Thatcherism's abandonment of the north – but it had its roots in the retrenchment of the Callaghan years, a bad time for the black stuff. At a 1980 conference commemorating twenty years of British motorways, the mood was sombre. One RAC representative lamented the 'unreasonable opposition from the "buttercups and daisy brigade".'[16]

→

One motorway carried on being built, futureproofed against the growing road-weariness. While the ringway had been horribly public, the M25 was built almost in secret, progressing by the 'salami tactic' of splitting the public consultation up into lots of local inquiries, thirty-nine in all. None of these inquiries stopped a single stretch of tarmac being laid, but they did change the way it was built – a foreshadowing of how all roads would be built in a more disbelieving age. Noise-reducing earth mounds, false cuttings, 'sound-baffle' fences and a cosmetic screen of two million trees and shrubs hid the motorway from the world. High cut-off lanterns reduced light spillage, and some bits of the road were unlit. But while the motorway was built furtively, the property market knew what was going on. A surge in house prices in neighbouring towns, all the way round the perimeter, accompanied its completion in 1986, even though it was only the northern section that was new. House prices in west Kent, in towns like Sidcup and Sevenoaks, rose by a quarter that year, exceptional even for the south-east equity bonanza of the Thatcher years. Estate agents put it down to the M25 effect, the property-boom version of a Mexican wave.

Even as the political temperature changed, one politician was still happy to attend road openings. She had, after all, been born above a Grantham grocer's shop fronting the Great North Road and, according to the first line of her memoirs, her 'first distinct memory [was] of traffic'.[17] On 29 October 1986, Margaret Thatcher cut the ribbon across an eight-mile section of the M25 near Watford, the final and crucial bit that closed the circle and linked it up with the M1 and A1. For fear of disruption by protesters, the ceremony was held a quarter-of-a-mile from the nearest bridge, with 550 specially bussed-in guests assembled on the carriageway. In her speech, Thatcher celebrated the M25 as 'a showpiece of British engineering skills, planning, design and construction', reminding her audience that 98 of its 117 miles had been built since she took office. She then tackled the nay-sayers head-on: 'I can't stand those who carp and criticize when they ought to be congratulating Britain on a magnificent achievement and beating the drum for Britain all over the world.' That so many motorists were already using the motorway was a mark of its success, she argued; those who complained about the congestion reminded her of an old saying that 'nobody shops at Sainsbury's because of the queues'. Interviewed by journalists after the ribbon cutting, she berated them: 'Now have you got the message? It's a great engineering achievement … Fly the flag for Britain.' An insufficiently enthusiastic television reporter got a flea in his ear: 'Do you think you can really accentuate the positive? Go on, accentuate the positive. Can you bring yourself to say "it is a splendid achievement for Britain"?' 'It *is* a splendid day for Britain,' he replied sheepishly.[18] Harold Macmillan never had to be so strident on the Preston Bypass.

Whoever wrote the glossy brochure produced to celebrate the motorway's completion also seemed a bit prickly. 'The M25 is, of course, not perfect,' it conceded. 'But – for all the carping at occasional congestion or teething troubles – it IS a tremendous achievement. The Victorians would have blown many trumpets; our generation uses the road, and, if forced to slow down temporarily to 50 mph, grumbles.'[19] In fact, the inauguration of the M25 was probably the last major road opening to generate real public excitement. The queues at both ends of the final section were much longer than usual because drivers were itching to be the first to complete an orbit. When the *Guardian* journalist, Terry Coleman, drove along this section shortly after the cones had been removed, he saw crowds waving from the bridges just as they had done on the Preston Bypass. Coleman's only complaint was that, at just three lanes, the M25 was not big or bold enough. It was 'absurdly too far out from the centre, which must be obvious even to those bicycling protectors of disused allotments and the like who ensured by their protests that it should not be closer in'. The M25, he argued, summed up 'the mangy poverty of our present expectations'.[20]

The birth of the M25 was still less protracted than the building of the last big stretch of motorway to be completed in Britain: the M40 extension from Oxford to Birmingham. The protests against it became more intense the nearer it got to the road-hating university town at its southern end. In the early 1970s it had emerged that the proposed route of the M40 ran across Otmoor, a wild area of fenland just a few miles north-east of Oxford. This was where, in protests against enclosure between 1813 and 1833, villagers cut the dykes, tore down fences and reclaimed the area as common land, crying 'Otmoor for ever!' When the landscape was finally squared off with hawthorn hedges and ditches, an Oxford don called Charles Lutwidge Dodgson looked down at Otmoor from Noke Hill and was inspired to recreate it as the chessboard world, the 'most curious country' of *Alice Through the Looking Glass*. Apart from an old Roman road and some green lanes, Otmoor remained a roadless wilderness. The architectural historian James Lees-Milne called it 'an oasis of medieval England', and declared that if it was lost to the developers 'the conservationists may as well pack up, abandon England to the philistines and emigrate'.[21]

The Otmoor saga rumbled on until the early 1980s, when Joe Weston, a local coordinator for Friends of the Earth, hit on a canny way of mobilising support. He bought 2.3 acres of land off a fellow Friends of the Earth member, Terence Holloway, whose farm the proposed M40 route bisected, for £5,000. Weston named the land Alice's Meadow, and sold 3,100 tiny plots to people from all over the world for £2 each. These buyers in turn divided and sold their plots to create 100,000 landowners. Since the government had to take all reasonable steps to find every owner before making compulsory purchase orders, this obviously complicated things. In November 1985, the government finally gave up and picked a new route, diverting around Otmoor in a long, un-motorway like loop. Otmoor remained so anti-road that in 1998, local campaigners managed to stop the national cycleway running through it because it would have meant tarmacking one of the bridleways.

→

After the M40 saga the government might reasonably have concluded that building motorways was more trouble than it was worth. Instead, in May 1989, it published a short but incendiary white paper called *Roads for Prosperity*. This proposed 2,700 miles of new and widened roads at a cost of £6 billion, more than doubling the roads budget; for just as the Macmillan government had seen the motorways as a symbol of the affluent society, Thatcherism viewed these new roads as the dynamo of an enterprise economy. In March 1990 the prime minister quoted Rudyard Kipling's poem 'The Glory of the Garden' in a speech to the Royal Society: 'Our England is a garden, and such gardens are not made, / By singing: "Oh, how beautiful!" and sitting in the shade.' This, she said, was a warning to think realistically and not 'in an airy-fairy way' about the environment. She concluded that, although we might need to find more economical ways of using petrol, 'we are not going to do without a great car economy'. 'What vision!' wrote Richard Mabey in his journal. 'Britain as a nation of garage-keepers, the Venice of the trunk roads.'[22]

A single line from *Roads for Prosperity*, promising 'the biggest road-building programme since the Romans', proved to be a PR disaster. Repeated *ad infinitum* in anti-roads literature, it allowed the protesters to portray themselves as indigenous Englanders against an invading militia. One anti-roads group produced a comic book called *Asterix and the Road Builders* which reworked the cartoon series about a Gaulish village fighting against the Romans as a struggle between plucky road protesters and the 'yellow army' of roadbuilders. The only flaw in this narrative of imperialist hubris brought down by native resistance is that the notorious line did not actually appear in the white paper, or anywhere else – although the transport minister, Paul Channon, did describe himself, with atypical overstatement, as 'the biggest road and bridge builder since Julius Caesar'.[23]

In fact, this roadbuilding programme began to be scaled down almost immediately in the face of budget cuts and protests from established environmental groups like Friends of the Earth. The most important battle of the civil war erupted on long-disputed territory, the site of a route planned years before *Roads for Prosperity*. After the Winchester protesters of the 1970s had pushed the M3 extension away from the water meadows, the planners went back to the drawing board and found a new route. This ran mainly through undisputed arable land, apart from a small area of chalk grassland about three miles south of Winchester. Winchester College had sold the land to the Ministry of Transport and, since it was some distance from the school, was happy for them to build a motorway on it. The roadbuilders would need to make a large cutting, about 400 feet wide, through this designated Area of Outstanding Natural Beauty: Twyford Down.

In March 1985, two local councillors, Barbara Bryant and David Croker, founded the Twyford Down Association to oppose the road. They had a smart eye for the visual statement, like marking the sides of the planned cutting with six-feet-wide lines of black polythene sheeting, to show everyone the huge hole it would make in the hill;

holding candlelit dinners in evening dress on the site; and, during the 1992 general election, marshalling hundreds of people into lines on the Down to make a giant 'X'. After the pro-road Tories won the election, though, Bryant and Croker believed they had exhausted all the formal sources of appeal and prepared to concede defeat.

Just as this polite protest was winding down, young people from outside the area – a disparate group of gap-year students, recent graduates and new-age travellers – began arriving on the Down. Their aim was to set up camp and continue the fight. They were the late twentieth-century equivalents of what the historian Christopher Hill called the 'masterless men' of the English Civil War era – the beggars, squatters and pedlars who, as nobody's servants, were ripe for conversion by radical religious and political sects.[24] They had imbibed the spirit of the back-to-the-land movement that flourished in the free festivals and Albion Fairs of the 1970s, with its nomadic lifestyles based on the summer solstice and other pagan rituals. They named themselves the Donga tribe, after the ancient tracks that crossed Twyford Down. These masterless men and women directed their energies against the new enemy of the motorway.

In the Thatcher years, when new-age travellers were involved in a series of skirmishes with the police near Stonehenge, the right-wing tabloid press demonised them as yobs and dole scroungers. With their dreadlocks and noserings, the Dongas looked the part, but they shrewdly struck up an alliance with the middle-class Winchester residents who opposed the road. The Bishop of Winchester, whose predecessor had led a successful campaign in 1935 to stop the original Winchester Bypass cutting into St Catherine's Hill, even held a service at the Donga camp in which the tribe sang 'Jerusalem' with locals, from pensioners in waxy anoraks to young mothers with baby buggies. The Dongas garnered still more public sympathy after the infamous events of 9 December 1992. Just before dawn, about eighty security guards employed by the roadbuilders descended on their camp, destroying their possessions and throwing them off the hill. The conservationist David Bellamy, who witnessed the battle, compared it to the Somme. Thirty-two guards, shocked by their colleagues' behaviour, handed in their notice immediately. Police reinforcements arrived for the second day of battle and, because the security guards wore high-visibility tabards and the police wore uniforms, the events went down in Donga mythology as 'Yellow Wednesday' and 'Black Thursday'. By the end of the two days, the camp had been cleared.

The battle may have been over but the war continued. In August 1993, at the end of a dinner at London's Park Lane Hotel, the junior transport minister Robert Key rose to speak. Key announced that he had a confession to make. 'I love cars,' he said. 'I loved my father's cars and my mother's cars, especially when she lent them to me. I loved my first car, a wonderful Sunbeam Rapier convertible of 1958 vintage. I adored and worshipped my MGB. I even polished the copper pipes on the engine. I love cars of all shapes and sizes. Cars are a good thing.' This encomium was well-aimed at his audience of about 200 car makers and motoring aficionados, at an awards ceremony sponsored by *Auto Express* magazine. 'I also love roads,' he went on. 'Looking back on my childhood … I remember my father doing a diversion to Lincolnshire because he had heard there was some dual carriageway there. And of course we saw the first motorways. The car is going to be with us for a very long time. We must start thinking in terms that will allow it to flourish.' He ended his speech with a dig at the railways, arguing that they 'carved up the countryside' and 'spewed out polluting gases'.[25] After this rousing speech, Key earned a nickname from the road protesters: the 'Mr Toad of the motorways'.

$$\rightarrow$$

The Donga tribe eventually dispersed and many of its members moved on to other protests, financed by compensation for wrongful arrests at Twyford Down. Quite a few fetched up in east London at the 'No M11 Link' campaign. The M11 Link was to be a three-and-a-half mile fast road to the London–Cambridge Motorway, smashing through the Victorian terraces between Hackney Marshes and Wanstead's Redbridge Roundabout. Since 1976, action groups had opposed it through conventional petitions and demos. Then the Department of Transport made a mistake. After compulsorily purchasing houses in the way of the road, it did not flatten them but loaned them to ACME, a London charity founded in the early 1970s to find affordable studio space for artists by offering cheap lets on rundown council houses. By the 1980s, they were home to mass squats of artists and other bohemians ready to be radicalised by the campaign against the road.

There were no water meadows here. People's homes were at stake and the protest would be politically spikier – but it began, in traditional eco-mode, over a 250-year-old sweet chestnut tree. In November 1993, contractors built an eight-foot fence around a small area of George Green, Wanstead, which locals had been promised would survive intact as the road tunnelled underneath it. A few days later, a crowd pushed down the fence and occupied the land, at the centre of which was the tree. The protesters started living in the tree, gave it a letter box, declared squatters' rights, and managed to turn it into the first treehouse to receive recognition from the courts. Its residents had to be served with an eviction order and were not removed until December. The campaign moved to some large Edwardian houses on the nearby Cambridge Park Road, which on 9 January 1994 declared itself the Independent Free Area of Wanstonia.

Wanstonia's inspiration was another real-life Ruritania, born in the no man's lands underneath the urban motorways on the other side of London. In November 1977 the residents of Freston Road, a squatted street in the shadow of the Westway, were threatened with eviction to make way for an industrial estate. The location was significant because, in the seven years since this flyover had opened, it had become a symbol of youthful alienation and inner-city grunge. The Clash's lead singer, Joe Strummer, had dubbed their guttural, aggressive music 'the sound of the Westway' and celebrated the road in the song 'London's Burning'. On the cover of their 1977 debut album, the Jam lean moodily against the Westway's stanchions.

Freston Road's residents held a plebiscite and unilaterally declared independence from Britain as the Free Republic of Frestonia. They sent telegrams to the EEC and the UN asking for membership, adding that they might require a peacekeeping force should the GLC decide to invade. Frestonia printed its own coat of arms, passports and stamps, clearly owing more to the Marx Brothers' Freedonia than Marx, more to *Passport to Pimlico* than Proudhon. The future Tory minister, Geoffrey Howe, wrote supportively: 'As one who had a childhood enthusiasm for G.K. Chesterton's *Napoleon of Notting Hill*, I can hardly fail to be moved by your aspirations.'[26] One of Frestonia's leading citizens, and its ambassador to Britain, was a 1960s radical, Heathcote Williams, who was inspired by the revolutionary ferment of the English Civil War, when groups like the Diggers and the Levellers created utopian communities in protest against the appropriation of common land. In 1974 Williams had set up the Ruff Tuff Creem Puff Estate Agency, a squatters' self-help bulletin listing empty properties. Ruff Tuff filled up nearly the whole of Freston Road with squatters and it became a commune, with all the garden walls removed and the party walls of the houses knocked through to create a vast shared dwelling. Williams later published the epic anti-car poem 'Autogeddon', which described streets as 'open sewers of the car cult' and 'alfresco gas-chambers'. When word reached him of Cambridge Park Road he declared, 'Long may Wanstonia reign and may it bring England back to civilisation!'[27]

Like its west London prototype, Wanstonia asked the UN for recognition, produced its own passports, had its own flag (an inverted Union Jack called the Union Jill) and a Declaration of Independence which upheld the rights of trees and banned all cars and roads. Its national anthem, 'Free Wanstonia', ended with the rousing lines: 'I believe what the hedgehogs say / You can stuff your motorway.' Wanstonia finally fell on 16 February 1994 – Ash Wednesday, renamed Bash Wednesday by manhandled evictees. Hundreds of protesters had barricaded themselves into just five houses. They dug a huge trench, removed all the staircases and chained themselves to washing machines filled with cement. It took 800 police, security guards and bailiffs the whole day to evict them.

The campaign moved west to Claremont Road, a cul-de-sac backing on to the railway line, mostly emptied by link-road blight. One of the few remaining residents was a 92-year-old woman, Dolly Watson, who had lived at Number 32 all her life. While Dolly and eight other tenants remained in their homes, the other houses began to be occupied by road-protesting squatters, and residents and new-comers united against the road. By now, the protesters probably realised the M11 Link would be built anyway, and they transformed their campaign from a protest against a specific road to one of sym-bolic resistance against road culture in general. The street became an artwork, the road and pavement turned into a living space with armchairs, sofas and carpets. The protesters painted a chessboard on the tarmac, using hubcaps and traffic cones as pieces, and cut a car in half, the two halves being placed at each end of a home-made zebra crossing. The pièce de resistance was a 100-foot scaffolding tower, painted pink and christened Dolly, poking through a hole in the roof of one of the houses. On another roof, a protest veteran known only as Mick built a fully working gallows. It was meant to symbolise the death of the road, but many of the bailiffs believed that Mick was preparing to hang himself if they tried to evict him – a rumour that Mick understandably did nothing to discourage.[28]

In April 1994, eight Claremont Road activists carried off the most audacious stunt of all when, in the dead of night, they climbed on to the roof of the transport secretary John MacGregor's house in Muswell Hill Road. Unveiling a huge banner with a six-lane motor-way painted on it – to symbolically drive a road through his home – they remained there for five hours while a small group of supporters on the ground echoed earlier battles by shouting 'Homes not roads!'

Short-lived mini-republics were soon springing up all the way along the link road's route. There was Greenmania, a verdant land near the inaptly named Green Man Roundabout (there were no pagan fertility deities in this barren ring of concrete); Munstonia, a creepy-looking house like the one in *The Munsters*; and the State of Euphoria in Leytonstone's Fillebrook Road, whose citizens touchingly wrote to the prime minister saying they would still like the Queen to be their head of state. All these principalities had their proud symbols of nationhood – flags, anthems, constitutions – albeit with the minor complication that many of their people continued to depend on the mother country for dole cheques.

But Claremont Road was the campaign's Alamo. On 28 November 1994 several hundred police and bailiffs entered the road to encounter a deafening soundtrack of music by the Prodigy and three protesters lying casually on mattresses. When the police tried to lift them, they found their arms were buried in the mattresses; when they tore through the mattresses they realised their arms were also buried in the asphalt. Others were locked on to chimney pots, hanging in nets suspended across the road or ensconced at the top of Dolly the Tower. It took four days for them all to be evicted, while a crowd of demonstrators in an adjoining street chanted 'Power to the tower!' The last man to be caught was dragged from a treetop screaming repeatedly, 'You're killing the earth!'

→

Successful revolutions need to reach beyond a committed vanguard of activists and win over the normally well-behaved and apolitical. While Twyford and Leytonstone erupted into protest, the mood was changing more subtly in the shires, at letter-writing stalls in markets and at meetings in draughty church halls. John Major's tiny majority after 1992 meant that he was vulnerable to local constituency campaigns and backbench revolts against roads, particularly in southern England. It was this respectable groundswell that really turned the tide against roads – probably because, however theatrical dreadlocked protesters buried in asphalt might be, what really interests the mainstream media is a slightly distorted mirror of itself: the misbehaving middle class.

Even before the Battle of Twyford Down began, the prosperous residents of Surrey were crowding into school halls to protest against a scheme to widen the M25 to fourteen lanes, a Los Angeles-style freeway threatening to descend on the home counties. Distinguished Oxonians, led by the historian Alan Bullock and the former ambassador to Moscow, Sir William Hayter, were planning to lie down in front of the JCBs to protest against the building of two bypasses around their university town. And in Essex, Ingrid Channon was fighting against a new motorway running from the M25 to Chelmsford by holding a fundraising garden party and wearing a T-shirt with the legend, 'Stop the M12!' Her husband was Paul Channon – the minister of transport at the time of *Roads for Prosperity*.

But the middle-class protest that generated most media interest was the campaign against the Batheaston–Swainswick Bypass near Bath. This planned to cut into Little Solsbury Hill, a local beauty spot celebrated in a Peter Gabriel song about a spiritual experience he had after leaving Genesis. The SOS (Save Our Solsbury) campaign became a cause célèbre through the involvement of Batheaston resident Bel Mooney, the author and then wife of the broadcaster Jonathan Dimbleby. Mooney had a crusading zeal that put other prominent anti-road activists in the shade. On 13 May 1994, she entered a Mongolian yurt, equipped with kilims and a tape recorder on which to play Gregorian chant, to begin what she described as 'a solemn fast – to symbolise my despair at the starvation of spirit which allows this mania for roadbuilding to destroy the country of which I am so proud'. Mooney survived for eight days on vegetable and fruit juice and the occasional 'finger of red wine'. 'I will starve myself, so help me God, until the land is at least granted a short reprieve,' she wrote in a vigil diary for a newspaper. 'As I get angrier and angrier about the bypass, I feel a fire starting to burn in my stomach. There's no room for food there.'[29]

The media interest in Mooney was not simply down to her hunger strike, which lasted just over a week and cost her a stone in weight. Protesting middle-class women have long been the subject of satire, from the Edwardian 'suffragettes' (a derogatory term coined by the *Daily Mail*) to the eccentric, breast-baring anti-motorway protester Lady Maud Lynchwood in Tom Sharpe's 1975 novel, *Blott on the Landscape* (played with gusto by Geraldine James in a 1985 TV adaptation). Mooney received similar treatment from unsympathetic journalists, one *Mail on Sunday* columnist accusing her of showing 'hypocrisy ... as tacky as the wax on a new Barbour jacket'.[30] In particular her Mongolian yurt came to be seen as the height of luxurious radical chic – unfairly, because it was intended as a PR centre for the whole camp and did not belong to her.

Robert Key dismissed the Batheaston protesters as 'rentamob', a small clique of nimbies and nomadic rebels who were out of step with the road-supporting locals. Behind the insult was a by now familiar argument: the protesters were a vocal and articulate minority who could skilfully segue vested interests into moral principles, while those who would benefit from new roads formed a quieter majority. The SOS campaign meanwhile claimed that the so-called 'bypass' was an attempt to dupe locals into thinking that the ministry had only their traffic jams at heart, when the road was actually going to be part of a dual-carriageway trunk route running from Southampton to the M4. The government's refusal to acknowledge that the bypass was part of this wider scheme was, said Mooney, 'like saying that the middle of the sausage bears no relationship to its ends'.[31]

In late 1994 Mooney's cause received a boost from an unlikely source: a government advisory committee published a report conceding that new roads generate their own traffic. This phenomenon of 'induced traffic' is not, of course, a recent discovery. In the late 1960s, Michael Thomson of the London School of Economics questioned the idea of predict-and-provide planning by arguing that the ringways would increase traffic on other roads, not ease it. In the 1970s, transport specialists talked glumly about the 'Braess paradox', a counter-intuitive theory by a German mathematician which held that building extra roads increased journey times. And even before the M25 opened, another LSE academic, Martin Mogridge, was making grave (and accurate) predictions that it would worsen London's congestion problems.[32]

So why was the government now acknowledging something that had been obvious to many people for years? The Department for Transport is unusual in spending much of its money on capital projects – so while it is hard to cut health or education budgets, which mostly cover running costs, new roads can always be shelved on the principle that no one grieves over what doesn't yet exist. The surge of anti-roads sentiment meant that the Treasury, in the middle of a recession, could identify roads as a soft target for savings and sell this as a growing concern for green issues. Road schemes – the M12, the

Oxford bypasses, the 14-lane M25 – gradually bit the dust. By the time Sir George Young became transport secretary in July 1995, the government seemed to be in full retreat. This 'bicycling baronet' was reputedly a member of Ealing Friends of the Earth and was definitely chairman of the House of Commons Cycling Club. Young slashed the roads budget by another third. Out of the 80 road schemes cancelled, 60 were in the south of England, where the middle-class militia was strongest.

By now, though, the road protests had developed a momentum that would not be halted by road cancellations. The revolution had become a wider one, moving on to roads that already existed. Within three months of the fall of Claremont Road, some of its veterans joined up with their northern cousins, graduates of the M65 protest near Blackburn, to form 'Reclaim the Streets'. They aimed to claw back the road as common land, used by all the people and not just motorists. Their tactics echoed the seventeenth-century 'Skimmingtons', riotous protests against enclosure accompanied by music, foolery and the removal of fences. In order to show that the triumph of tarmac was not inevitable, they would turn the everyday world upside down. For a short time, the traffic would stop and people would be made aware of a possible world without that bullying road hog, the car.

The first Reclaim the Streets party took place on a Saturday afternoon in May 1995 on Camden High Street. Around 1pm, two cars crashed headlong into each other and blocked the road. The drivers started arguing and one of them smashed the other's windscreen. This wasn't road rage; it was street theatre, the cue for 500 people to surge out of the pavement crowd and unfurl a banner: 'Reclaim the Streets – Free the City – Kill the Car.' They carpeted a 200-yard stretch of road and spread a rainbow zebra crossing across it, then poured sand on to another stretch of tarmac and lounged about in deckchairs, in a literal but upside-down reworking of the old 1968 slogan, 'Beneath the paving stones, the beach.' For the next few hours, people danced to music blaring out from a stereo run on eco-friendly cycle-pedal power while they gleefully dismembered the two crashed cars, a crumbling Citroën and Talbot Samba. Drivers caught in the jam were offered tea and cakes.

The most daring street reclaiming of all took place around Saturday lunchtime on 13 July 1996, when thousands of people poured out of Shepherd's Bush Tube station and congregated on the nearby green. Fearing a lightning raid on the Holland Park Roundabout, the police sealed it off. Instead the protesters diverted down a backstreet and, just after two o'clock, ran unopposed on to the M41 motorway. The former West Cross Route of the defunct ringway scheme, this was a half-mile stub leading from the Westway which dumped all its traffic on to the already congested roads of Shepherd's Bush. As a symbol of the futility of roadbuilding, it was well chosen.

Two lorries pulled on to the hard shoulder and the partygoers unloaded huge sound systems, scaffolding and mock road signs saying 'Fuck The Car' and 'Cars Come Too Fast'. Until early the next morning, about 7,000 people danced, drank and threw frisbees on the carriageway. The central reservation became a stage for firebreathers, stiltwalkers and a bewigged barrister cross-examining a car in a mock trial. Two carnival figures, 30 feet high with 10-foot-wide skirts, were wheeled up and down the motorway as bagpipe players in Restoration wigs sat on top of them. Hidden inside, and drowned out by the sound of techno, were people drilling into the tarmac with Kanga hammers, and planting saplings rescued from the path of the M11 Link. After the protesters had dispersed, the Highways Agency had to close the motorway for several days for resurfacing.

→

Even as the roadbuilders seemed to be on the run, the road protests grew more rancorous. Half an hour before leaving office as transport minister in 1995, Brian Mawhinney had bequeathed his successor a headache by approving the building of a road a few miles north of Twyford Down. A bypass for the Berkshire town of Newbury had been mooted since before the war, and as long ago as 1963, Colin Buchanan's report, *Traffic in Towns*, had used it as the model of a small town with chronic congestion. The main cause of the jams was the A34, a major route between the south coast ports and the Midlands where Ian Nairn had discovered subtopia in the 1950s. The bypass would sweep the lorries west of the town through 120 acres of woodland. Most Newbury residents supported the road, but the town was also steeped in the history of radical and environmental protest: Greenham Common, Aldermaston and Watership Down, the inspiration for Richard Adams's 1972 novel about a community of rabbits whose warren is destroyed by builders, are all nearby.

The protesters who began arriving on site in late 1995 were old lags – a mobile university of agit-professionals ready to share their awkward-squad expertise with newcomers. For months they built compost toilets and food dumps, appointing quartermasters and quartermistresses to stock up at cash'n'carries. They scrounged polypropylene rope, climbing equipment and motorcycle D-locks, needed to chain themselves to diggers. They drew 'phone trees', flow charts where each person called would have to ring several other numbers, so that people could be assembled quickly during evictions. Thirty-one separate camps were set up and each built a postbox near a road and sent themselves a letter to let the Post Office know they were there so that they could receive mail.

By now the protesters had developed an entire belief system, an eco-paganism with ideas drawn from Wicca, Druidry and anarchism, which framed the protests as a fairy-tale struggle between untainted nature and tyrannical humanity. They used chants and charms to invoke protective rings of magic around protest camps, and held full moon rituals and energy-raising sessions. Some of the protesters, perhaps under the influence of entheogenic mushrooms, claimed to have had encounters with King Arthur's knights and 'fairy dudes', who offered them pointers about the anti-roads struggle. Protesters used the term 'pixieing' for any act of cheeky defiance, such as stealing a roadbuilder's hard hat or filling JCB petrol tanks with sugar. When accused of criminal damage, the protesters blamed it on the pixies.

This anti-roads mysticism centred on trees, because tree-clearing was often the first stage of roadbuilding. The first treehouses of the road wars had been built in July 1993, at Jesmond Dene near

Newcastle, to try and prevent the Cradlewell Bypass cutting through a public park. A group of protesters called the Flowerpot tribe gathered in the woodland and, to evade the builders, climbed up the trees, remaining there all summer. Their treehouses were hastily improvised and pretty basic, mostly hammocks with sheeting slung over them. By Newbury, though, the treehouses were more varied. Some were just 'twigloos' – tiny redoubts with coppiced hazel whips bent over and tied together, covered in tarpaulin, sleeping two at a squeeze. Others were like small houses, built of old pallets and doors, with glass windows, chimneys, carpets and wood-burning stoves – everything except the kitchen sink. The 'Mothership' treehouse by the river Kennet, at the halfway point on the Newbury Bypass route, stretched across nine or ten trees, with its own kitchen and plenty of space for a dozen people. An intricate network of overhead ropes and cargo nets enabled protesters to skip from tree to tree – a virtual village in the sky. In tribute to the Newbury protesters, nightclubbers began wearing climbing harnesses as fashion items. The tree-dwelling denizens of the anti-road protests were often compared to the women of the Chipko movement in the Himalayas, who hugged trees to prevent the industrial logging of their ancestral forests. (The word Chipko means 'hug', which may be the derivation of the disparaging term 'tree-hugger'.)

Trees were not just a good way of evading roadbuilders. Ancient woodlands of beech and oak appealed to the English imagination in the same way as water meadows and downland. Ironically, much of this dates back to the birth of scientific forestry in the late seventeenth century. In *Sylva: A Discourse of Forest Trees*, published in 1664 to encourage tree-planting to provide timber for the navy's warships, John Evelyn was probably the first to use the phrase 'hearts of oak', which David Garrick later reworked for his 1759 sea shanty, now the Royal Navy's official marching tune: 'Hearts of oak are our ships / Hearts of oak are our men.'[33] For the Newbury tree-dwellers, the older and sturdier the tree the better. Some of the trees along the bypass route, it was mooted optimistically, had been around since the English Civil War, when the first two battles of Newbury took place.

Trees were ancient, organic, alive – the antithesis of modern, grey, dead tarmac.

Some protesters refused even to violate the trees by banging nails into them while building their treehouses. Others felt that trees should never be felled because the earth was a living being and this would be like cutting her hair (although what was so wrong about this was a bit unclear). Wrapped up in all this was the folklore of the free greenwood, an evocation of the English idyll since Saxon times, when William the Conqueror's son Rufus razed entire villages to turn the New Forest into a private hunting ground. In the greenwood, lord and subject happily co-existed in the absence of political intermediaries – notably in the Robin Hood myth where it is the Sheriff of Nottingham, not the king, who is Robin's enemy. The Newbury protesters liked to think they were on the side of the ancient oaks, the common people and the abiding spirit of Albion against the upstart politicians. Union Jacks were raised in many treehouses – a significant moment in the reclaiming of this flag from the right-wing nationalism of the National Front, mirrored in mainstream culture by Noel Gallagher's Union Jack guitar and other patriotic paraphernalia of Britpop.

In fact, music was one of the main purveyors of Newbury mythology – but Gallagher, with his rock-star Rolls Royce, would probably have been unwelcome at the camps. The protesters' tastes ran more to anti-road folk music groups like the Space Goats and Tragic Roundabout. The Mothership treehouse was named after a song by the ex-Teardrop Explodes singer Julian Cope, who supported the protesters by playing a benefit gig, Kar-Ma-Geddon, in Portsmouth, and spending time at the camps 'weirding out the security guards'. Cope later wrote an eccentric but scholarly survey of Britain's ancient megaliths which railed against linear roads and linear thinking, arguing that 'before the Romans foisted their straight lines upon us, these isles undulated with all that was the wonder of our Mother Earth ... the death of meaninglessness will only truly be born when we free ourselves from the choking stranglehold that 2,000 years of patriarchal Mr Stork rules have brought us to.'[34] In the Newbury greenwood, a new generation of troubadours sat around campfires telling stories and composing ballads about those modern-day Romans, the roadbuilders.

The Newbury treehouses also carried potent cultural associations, from the Swiss Family Robinson to Winnie the Pooh. They reminded many of Lothlórien in *The Lord of the Rings*, the magical woodland where the Hobbits occupy underground burrows and their allies, the Elves, live in giant Mallorn trees. Given the ages of most of the protesters, they were probably also inspired by the Ewoks, the bear-like characters in *Return of the Jedi* who live in villages built high among the trees in their planet Endor's forests, and who help Luke Skywalker and the Rebel Alliance destroy the energy shield around the Death Star. Like the Tolkienesque imagery of Lothlórien light struggling against the darkness of Mordor, the story of the Rebel Alliance's battle against the Empire suited the protesters' tendency to view the world in Manichean terms, to see themselves as underdogs fighting huge, hostile forces. They were the mischievous pixies against the spoilsport humans, the natives against the invading Romans, the custodians of nature against a brutalising technocracy.

On 9 January 1996, the Third Battle of Newbury, the biggest anti-road confrontation in history, began. Four hundred security guards arrived from London and began making arrests under the 'aggravated trespass' provisions of the new Criminal Justice Act. The arrests went on for the next two months while the protesters did everything they could to delay the groundclearing. They managed to halt construction for several weeks while the fate of a rare snail – the Desmoulin's Whorl, about as big as a grain of rice – was discussed in the high court, and its habitat of sedges and reeds was painstakingly relocated. Their aim was to delay the builders until the songbird nesting season in late spring, when, according to EU law, no one was allowed to fell trees.

But they ran out of time. The separate camps were evicted in turn, each eviction following a familiar pattern. Security guards and police surrounded the camp at daybreak, and the lookout woke the protesters with a siren and the warning cry 'arrooga arrooga!' The tree-dwellers threw pink paint, mushroom soup and, occasionally, excrement and urine bombs ('bailiff-decorating') on to the contractors. Eventually professional climbers employed by the bailiffs shinned up the trees to make arrests. Diehards occupied the rope walkways to stop them being cut, the braver ones lying face down on top of the rope, then unclipping their harnesses and putting their hands behind their backs, so that the slightest move by the climbers would send them plummeting to their deaths. The last of the settlements, Tot Hill and Castle Camp, was cleared on 2 April when a lone protester, dressed in a pantomime cow costume, left the last of the treehouses and the tree was felled. A single oak was spared a meeting with the chainsaw. It ended up in the middle of a roundabout.

→

This felt like the end of the war, but there was a coda. It occurred along a 13-mile dual carriageway scheme on the A30 in Devon between Exeter and Honiton. The main protest camp, at Fairmile, was built around an oak-tree copse, and residents named themselves, after the Latin for oak, the Quercus tribe. The camp had the usual quota of treehouses, included a rowing boat tied on to some branches and covered in sheeting. Beneath the trees, however, the protesters perfected a technique pioneered at Claremont Road: a network of Vietcong-style tunnels inhabited by 'tunnel rats'. Digging out a 40-inch section and shoring it with timber struts took about a week, with two diggers and two bucketeers working solidly with broken-handled axes and shovels and, for tight corners, a child's bucket and spade. They built them as narrow as possible, on the probably sound principle that bailiffs would be fatter than tunnel rats. By the time they dug in for Christmas 1996, the Fairmile catacombers had created a complex tunnel system, dropping between 14 and 40 feet below ground, with lots of changes of direction to foil the evictors. The tunnels led to living chambers which were quite cosy, with posters on the walls, white fairy lights and dashboard lamps powered by car batteries. The tunnel rats used intercom to converse with Pixie Pete, who relayed them news from above ground and played them music to alleviate the boredom. They sustained themselves with their 'eviction stash' of food: cornflakes, biscuits and fruit kept in rat-proof boxes.

The evictions came at the end of January 1997, masterminded by the Undersheriff of Devon, a title that hinted at a sworn enemy of the greenwood (although his name, Trevor Coleman, was less evocative). The Undersheriff's 'molehunters', many of them potholers from the Peak District, used air compressors and ground radar to locate the tunnels, sometimes falling back on the low-tech method of listening for coughing. Meanwhile about two dozen protesters above ground made their job more difficult by sustaining a constant cacophony with mandolins, penny whistles, drums and didgeridoos.

The molehunters took days to reach the tunnel rats, digging each hole wider and strengthening the shoring as they went. The last man out was evicted from the Big Momma tunnel after seven consecutive days underground. If they had emerged last, fame might have befallen one of the other members of the Fairmile Five: Ian, Animal, Welsh John or Muppet Dave. Instead the bright TV lights awaited a twenty-three-year-old with a very muddy face who had first become a protester at Newbury, his hometown. He had achieved local notoriety as 'Newbury's Most Arrested Man', but was largely unknown to national media. He came out of the tunnel blinking rapidly, smiling beatifically and coughing prodigiously, an effect of Drum tobacco as much as tunnel-living. He revealed that he had passed the time on his own reading Douglas Adams's *Hitchhiker* series – which, it will be recalled, begins with Arthur Dent's house being demolished to make way for an intergalactic highway – and, also appropriately, *The Secret Diary of Adrian Mole*. When the bailiffs reached him he was 'lying down reading my book, eating some bourbon biscuits'.[35] The media identified him as Daniel Hooper, whom fellow protesters had nicknamed – because he was always the muddiest – 'Swampy'.

Overnight, Swampy became the poster boy of the anti-roads movement. The 'brave burrower' had a ghostwritten column in the *Sunday Mirror*, *Just Seventeen* christened him 'alternative totty', he appeared on the BBC's *Have I Got News For You* and under the headline 'Look what emerged from the swamp', a *Daily Express* photoshoot dressed him in an Armani suit. Not everyone in the road-protesting fraternity was impressed. There had long been arguments between the 'fluffies' and the 'spikies' – those who called for non-violence in all circumstances, and those who thought that violence was sometimes necessary to defend one's ground. Before any potentially violent encounter with the roadbuilders, someone would cry, 'keep it fluffy' – and, almost always, people would. But the spiky anti-roads collective, Aufbehen, saw fluffiness as pandering to wussy middle-class liberalism. It despaired of the semi-mystical school of road protesting that reached its zenith along the Newbury Bypass and A30. The fluffy, it complained, 'is the Situationist's nightmare come true, the rarefied thought of the postmodernist personified – virtual politics'.[36] Soft-spoken Swampy was fluffiness made flesh, and his embrace by the tabloids symbolised both that the road protests had gone mainstream, and that its wider political aims had been blunted. But then the protests had always been a loose alliance of anarchists and conservatives, radical greens and shire Tories – which was why they had made such an impact.

After this, the protests fizzled out quickly. In March 1997 a PO Box in Newbury published *Road Raging: Top Tips for Wrecking Road-building*, a vade mecum for road protesters with tips and wrinkles about everything from building treehouses to locking-on to JCBs. It was meant to be widely circulated, the copyright page declaring that 'any part of this publication may be freely reproduced, circulated, transmitted in any form, or quoted out of context in hostile newspapers, with no prior permission required whatsoever'.[37] But by then it was more of a historical curio than a practical manual. Fairmile was the last major anti-road camp. Swampy was next heard of occupying the route of the second runway at Manchester Airport, before disappearing from public view as quickly as he had entered it.

'We cannot go on simply pandering to the motor car': not Swampy's words, but those of the former transport minister Steven Norris, interviewed a few months after Fairmile on the BBC's *Panorama*. It was the same Steven Norris who had argued only two years earlier that the car was better than public transport because 'you don't have to put up with the dreadful human beings sitting alongside you'; and who had written in his 1996 autobiography, 'I doubt there are many more effective recruiting sergeants for the Conservative Party than the great unwashed appearing on television, clambering over the tops of cherry pickers, screaming abuse at policemen.' Norris was a more thoughtful politician than his petrolhead caricature suggested, but his *Panorama* comments were seen as a sign that the most improbable people were coming on message. John Watts, his successor as transport minister in the dying days of the Tory government, just sounded tired and exasperated. 'I couldn't care less what Swampy says,' he declared. 'I would happily bury him in concrete.'[38]

→

The civil war was over. Given the proximity of deadly machinery, the precarious heights reached by the tree-climbers and the risk of tunnel cave-ins, it was fortunate that no one had died in battle. But after Twyford Down, although the protesters had achieved some isolated victories, no road scheme had been halted after the roadbuilders had arrived. All the protesters usually did was add a few weeks or months to the land clearance, but this was such a small part of the project that the time lost could be retrieved during the building of the road. Road protests could simply be built into work schedules. The disruption they caused ran into millions of pounds, and was meant to dissuade governments from approving similar roads in future. But what was probably more significant was the change in public mood that occurred gradually and almost imperceptibly during the road protests – the growing sense that the protesters had right on their side.

Most of us don't calmly weigh up the pros and cons of road schemes, don't conduct our own private road inquiry in our heads before coming to a rational, objective decision about it. Political arguments feed into our mental habits and gut reactions; we respond to poetic turns of phrase, arresting images, powerful rhetoric. In this sense the protesters' most powerful weapon was that they managed to create enchanting forms of street theatre that were more like performance art than a political campaign. If the Vietnam war was lost in American living rooms, then the roadbuilders probably lost the tarmac wars in those unforgettable images of protest sites on the evening news, with treehouses glowing like fairy lights and lone protesters balanced precariously on branches, their outlines sharp against the setting sun.

A useful gauge of the shifting mood was that throughout the 1990s, road openings became an increasingly secretive affair. Contractors often kept the opening date secret so that protesters wouldn't be able to organise demonstrations. A few activists might get word of the opening and hold a symbolic vigil, outnumbered by security guards, as happened when the M3 through Twyford Down opened in the quiet of the summer holidays in 1994. But after the high drama of the tree clearings and the JCB lock-ons, it was all a bit of an anticlimax. There was, however, one memorable ceremony. In November 1998, a former Bonham's art dealer and performance artist called Rodolph de Salis, who had also been one of Newbury's more blue-blooded tree-dwellers, unofficially opened the Newbury Bypass. In front of a small crowd made up mostly of bemused police, de Salis stood on a pedestrian bridge over the bypass at Skinners Green and claimed the road as his own, before kindly bequeathing it to the nation as 'Britain's longest drive-through sculpture, a £15 million per minute, £12 million per mile theme-drive allowing access to previously undiscovered southern British images'. With a nod to Anthony Gormley's iron sculpture erected the previous year near the A1, he called the road 'Angel of the South: Porous Asphalt on Earth'. De Salis noted in passing that the word 'asphalt' comes from the Greek *asphalton*, meaning 'of foreign origin', and he likened the shape of the road to an Islamic crescent with Chieveley services, at the M4 junction, its accompanying star.[39]

The bypass's official opening, held the following Tuesday, was less momentous. Swampy had just become a father and received a friendly visit from the police the night before, just to check he was on road-protesting paternity leave. The contractors bussed in coachloads of security guards but only seven protesters turned up. In thick fog, the head of the Highways Agency cut the tape in front of a few local VIPs. Police removed the cones and sign covers before waving on the traffic, which consisted of a lone woman driver in a Volkswagen. It was 1.25am.

Ten months later, on 1 September 1999, the bypass had to be closed for repairs. Loose pebbles and holes had appeared on the road, and traffic was once again diverted through Newbury so residents were reminded of what the traffic was like before the bypass arrived (terrible). As de Salis correctly noted, the bypass had been made of 'porous asphalt', a more expensive variety which, like its sister material, 'whisper concrete', was increasingly employed on unpopular new roads for its noise-reducing qualities. But porous asphalt is a fickle surface. If it is not laid at the right temperature the chippings can pull away from the rest of the blacktop. As the road was still under its one-year guarantee, the contractors had to come and redo it at a cost of £2.2m. No one was quite sure what had gone wrong – and the phlegmatic Highways Agency spokesman summed up the low status of roads at the end of the millennium, the draining of all romance from the business of laying them. 'Building roads,' he said, 'is like baking a cake. Sometimes you just get one where a bad egg makes it flop.'[40]

8

THE END OF THE ROAD

And the wind shall say: 'Here were decent godless people:
Their only monument the asphalt road
And a thousand lost golf balls.'

T.S. Eliot[1]

The protest roads of the 1990s soon retreated into routine, betraying nothing about their painful births. The Batheaston Bypass protesters argued all along (and rightly) that it was intended to be part of a much longer trunk route across the south-west, but these plans were abandoned in the anti-roads momentum of the mid-1990s. Now, as you drive north along the bypass, the white arrows guide you left as it changes back into the old, bendy single carriageway. The Newbury Bypass merges quietly into the old A34, the only sign of the join being where the road starts to arc round the town in a long Cupid's bow. Swampy's Honiton–Exeter road is today just an unassuming section of the A30. A narrow, deserted road that looks like the old A30 runs right along it for some of its length, returning villages like Fairmile, once in the middle of a busy trunk route, to sylvan quietude.

We think of roads as living in a historical vacuum, a perpetual present of roadworks, jams and dot-matrix signs warning us about spray or strong winds. Roads are continually looking ahead, their traffic always moving forward, albeit often quite slowly. But then you come across these time-warped roads, outdoor museums that look much like they must have done years ago, and you realise that the history of the road is uneven: it goes backwards as well as forwards. The quiet lane that used to be the A30 now looks very much like its interwar incarnation, when it was immortalised by Daphne du Maurier as the clear, straight, white road along which Maxim de Winter drives the nameless heroine of *Rebecca* as they make their way from London to the rhododendron-backed driveway of Manderley.

The other great protest site, the M11 Link, isn't called that any more; it's just part of the A12, hidden in a deep cutting behind a yellow brick wall, clearly meant to blend in with the stock bricks of the surrounding terrace houses. It's hard to imagine that it was once a dense network of Victorian streets, home to the walled city of Wanstonia. There is one way of re-imagining its former life, however. All you need to do is pick up an electronic headset and a map, in return for a deposit of £5, from one of the public libraries that dot along the route. Then you are ready to walk the line of an invisible artwork called *Linked*, by Graeme Miller.

Miller moved to the artists' haven of Leytonstone's Grove Green Road in 1984 and stayed there for ten years, witnessing the growing movement against the new road. Returning home periodically from Salisbury where he was working on another project, he would notice that whole streets of houses had vanished. Soon he was evicted by police in riot gear who, wrongly believing him to be one of the protest ringleaders, smashed his door down early one morning and ransacked his house. Miller's act of revenge was to make a piece of living art, to reclaim the deep ecology that the link road had destroyed by 'sending out seed crop'.[2] He hired a team of five researchers to talk to local residents and road protesters, and ended up with hundreds of hours of recorded interviews.

The artwork runs over three miles, following roads next to the link road and crossing bridges over it. Your headset is tuned to one wavelength and there are twenty transmitters fixed to lamp-posts, continually broadcasting on the same frequency. As you approach each lamp-post, the receiver registers the signal – you first hear gentle murmurings, then whole sentences – and then shuts down as you walk away from it. These speech fragments are set to phrases of music like a violin playing just two notes, or sound effects like the clinking of bottles and the low hum of a long-gone milk float.

You can hear unnamed Leytonstonians remembering the area in the 1940s – before the M11, never mind its link road, was even a twinkle in a road planner's eye. Then different, younger voices start to talk about the link road evictions of the 1990s, about standing in rubble where their houses used to be. There are little gaps in the road's yellow brick wall every few hundred yards, with padlocked gates and stepladders leading down to the road, presumably for maintenance workers. You can look through one of these gaps at the whooshing traffic and hear someone say through your headphones: 'I know that if my house was still there, it would be hanging in space above the inside northbound lane. I can still feel myself in that place, that bit of air, the place where I lay down to go to bed.' The transmitters have stable computer chips and no moving parts to wear out, and are under guarantee for a hundred years. As long as they have a supply of electricity, they might last even longer than that, perhaps outlive the road itself. The history of the M11 Link may remain hidden, but the curious will be able to recreate it in sound.

The fate of these famous protest roads of the 1990s – the bitter battles of the recent past visible only in fragments, or audible only in invisible artworks – is a neat summation of what has happened to roads in the intervening years. For while the politics of roadbuilding should have become ever more urgent, as congestion worsens and the environmental impact of roads is more keenly felt, the battle lines seem less clearly drawn than in the age of Swampy. Perhaps we need to think carefully about what we can learn from the history of roads since the beginning of the motorway era – and what this suggests about how (or whether) roads will be built, imagined and remembered in the future.

→

Miller's archaeology of the forgotten lives buried under tarmac is a useful corrective to the way that roadbuilding has been rationalised in these years – by insisting that progress is inexorable, that we are help-less in the face of change, that we must pay blind obeisance to traffic predictions and growth projections. New roads continue to be justi-fied according to narrow calculations about the time and money they save; but time is for living in, not for chopping up into fiscal units. The people who protested against the link road and other motor-ways in the 1990s turn out to have been farsighted in their critique of the pursuit of infinite growth in a world of finite resources. The problem with roads, almost everyone now agrees, is that they kill the earth twice – eating up vast amounts of energy to produce and lay the asphalt, and then choking the atmosphere with the carbon from car exhausts.

And yet in castigating roads as the universal enemy, the anti-roads movement also drowned out some important historical nuances. The movement became a sort of religion that brooked no argument, right down to the curse its members visited on the roadbuilders for 'killing the earth'. But no motorway cut up virgin land; it simply found another use for land that had already been worked and reworked. And although a road mutilates the land in obvious, abrupt ways, it is not the worst thing that can happen to it. The anti-road campaigns often railed against the destruction of irreplaceable landscapes like water meadows and wildwoods. But the slow loss of the commonplace can be as catastrophic as the rapid loss of the conspicuously beautiful. The featureless boredom of a countryside taken over by agro-industry may not be as stark as a line of grey asphalt, and not so easy to raise an army against – but the monocultures created by intensive farming have done far more harm to biodiversity than rural motorways.

As for urban motorways, when they arrived in the 1960s people laughed hollowly at the planners who claimed that flyovers would make less noise than normal roads, because fast-moving cars would not be making grinding gear changes. Whisper it under the Westway, but the planners had a point. Being underneath a flyover seems no noisier to me than being next to a busy surface road. I have walked the length of the dead zone under the elevated A40, along the cobbled paths of Paddington Basin and into a netherworld of football pitches, studio spaces, roller-skating parks and horse-riding stables that would not exist without the road above them. I have smelt cut grass and heard birdsong under the Mancunian Way. I have navigated the footballers' wives housing estates and golf driving ranges next to the Worsley Braided Interchange and the joggers and dogwalkers all behaved as though the road, mostly hidden behind earth banks, did not exist. I have walked down Gravelly Hill to Spaghetti Junction, through a quiet suburb with Tudorbethan semis, gravel drives and faded Neighbourhood Watch signs – and it is surprising how near you get before the sweeping parabolic curve of the Aston Express-way dominates the landscape. I have hiked just a few hundred yards inland from Newport Pagnell services, and the sound of M1 traffic was already a distant murmur, a babbling brook. Around the M11 Link road, people and cars have brokered an uneasy but durable truce. Leytonstone lives. Roads can be ruinous, but they are not a concrete napalm that renders all human life around them unbearable.

A rallying cry of the fin-de-siècle road protesters was that, once a precious bit of countryside is taken away to build a road, it disappears forever. When she lost the fight to save Twyford Down, the indomi-table councillor, Barbara Bryant, suggested that a permanent fund should be started to pay for the restoration of the Down by filling the chasm with chalk again and landscaping it, when the motorway became obsolete in two or three centuries' time.[3] But the earth is more resilient than this narrative of loss suggests. The reclaiming of the road by nature began almost immediately as part of the environmen-talist bargains struck to build these roads. During the road protests, trees had been the conscience of the landscape, the reverse image of the road. But trees did well out of new roads, being replenished by roadside planting or 'translocated' to nearby fields as complete woods.

After the M3's Twyford Down section opened, the 1930s Winches-ter Bypass was closed. The road was recontoured with chalk from the Down and covered with turf, thus rejoining St Catherine's Hill with the Itchen Valley water meadows and creating an area of grassland nearly three times larger than that lost at the motorway cutting. The only clue about where the road used to be is at the railway bridge near Compton, which once stood 20 feet above it but is now surrounded by grass. The dual carriageway that carried millions of motorists each year has simply vanished as though it never existed.

→

The civil war over roadbuilding, from *Roads for Prosperity* to Swampy's last stand, began at the end of the Thatcher years and ended in the final days of the Major era. The doomed roads programme came to seem like the symptom of a tired, dying government that had been in power for too long. A few months after Fairmile, the Tories lost the election and Tony Blair swept to power on a Labour landslide. Blair's government had developed its transport policy in opposition, while the protests were at their height, and was determined not to make the same mistakes. The new deputy prime minister, John Prescott, declared: 'I will have failed if in five years time there are not many more people using public transport and far fewer journeys by car. It's a tall order, but I urge you to hold me to it.'[4] The 1998 white paper, *A New Deal for Transport*, cancelled many road schemes and declared that new roads would be built only as a last resort. The trunk roadbuilding programme begun in the late 1950s, which had created over 2,000 miles of motorway, seemed to be over. The year 2000 was the first since 1956 that Britain wasn't building any motorways.

Gradually, though, this agenda changed, with extra bits of money here and there for road schemes. Perhaps worried about losing the support of Mondeo man – that semi-mythical, aspirational but insecure resident of middle England defined by his ownership of a mid-range saloon car – the government stepped back from what the *Daily Mail* liked to call its 'war on the motorist'. When Alistair Darling became transport secretary in 2002, he volunteered a rare snippet of family memoir: his father, Sandy, had been an engineer on the Chiswick–Langley section of the M4 and he kept a photograph of the road taken when it opened in 1965, showing 'maybe fifty cars'.[5] But Darling did not make the mistake of Tory pantomime villains like Robert Key or Steven Norris, by professing his love of roads or badmouthing the people who used public transport. His road openings, while no longer conducted with armies of security guards under cover of darkness, were cannily low-key. When, just before Christmas 2005, Darling unveiled a plaque to commemorate the completion of the widening of the M25 near Heathrow, Britain's first proper twelve-lane motorway, he did not try to mimic the oratorical flourishes of an Ernest Marples or a Margaret Thatcher. The project, he explained flatly in his gentle Edinburgh solicitor's tones, was 'part of our commitment to improving the road network'.[6] This softly-softly approach concealed a subtle shift in policy. By 2008 Labour had quietly approved massive widening programmes for the M25, M1 and M6 along with many local roads and bypasses – a roadbuilding programme more than double the size of the Tory one that had sparked the protests of the 1990s.

Most of these new schemes inspired local protest campaigns, but they failed to coalesce into a wider movement. There were no treetop communities or tunnel occupations. A new generation of green activists had grown up inspired by the road protesters of the 1990s, but they were more interested in a different sort of tarmac. When environmental campaigners were planning direct action against the proposed expansion of Heathrow, one of the organisers predicted that it would be 'the mother of all battles … the Newbury Bypass of the skies'.[7] But why were there no neo-Swampys, ready to dig tunnels and climb up trees to stop new roads? The answer was that in our increasingly outsourced and contracted-out public sphere, no one who wanted to protest against a road could be sure who or what to protest against. *Roads for Prosperity* had listed and costed all road schemes under a single budget, but now the roadbuilding programme had fragmented into tiny pieces. In order to feed the post-Thatcherite shibboleth that private companies were shining beacons of competence and efficiency, many new roads were built and paid for by private finance in design-and-build 'procurement solutions', with the government gradually refunding the money in a complicated form of hire purchase. Paying for roads on the never-never conveniently erased the investment from the Treasury's books, but in the long run it was more expensive than paying for them through public borrowing. A concession company would finance the road and operate it for forty years, with the government repaying this company over time through shadow tolls, based on the number of vehicles using the road. More traffic meant more profits: so much for fewer car journeys.

Meanwhile 'roadbuilding' had become a dirty word, the government preferring to talk about 'widenings', 'improvements' and 'extensions'. A new language of rationing and austerity suggested that traffic problems could be solved by 'tweaking' the road system, focusing on 'choke points' and 'better use' options. If you had to build something as distasteful as a road, the trick was to present it as part of an inexorably unfolding narrative with an obvious endpoint – by arguing, for instance, that it would widen the last bit of single carriageway on a long stretch of dual carriageway. The trouble with roadbuilding is that its narrative structure is inevitably linear. A new, wide road joining up with an old, narrow one automatically creates pressure for 'upgrading'. The idea that this narrative has a natural endstop is a roadbuilding version of the gambler's fallacy, the belief that one last throw of the dice will solve all our problems – rather than simply generating more demand in a process of eternal regress.

At the heart of this new philosophy were the New Approach to Appraisal (NATA) rules introduced by Labour in 1998, which assessed all new transport schemes, including roads, against set criteria. This practice dates back to a computer programme called COBA, invented in the early 1970s to work out the cost-benefit calculations of road schemes. With COBA you could simply factor in building costs, journey times and other things that were easily calculated, and the computer would work out losses and gains automatically. In response to the growing anti-roads sentiment, the 1978 Leitch Committee recommended that the government factor in environmental issues, without actually proposing that they should be costed. But NATA now gave everything, including environmental aspects like biodiversity and quality of landscape, a costing, collating all the information on a standard AST or 'Appraisal Summary Table'. The entire case for and against building a road, from 'reduced traveller stress' to 'estimated increase in people annoyed', could now be summarised on a single side of A4.

Some of NATA's costings were rather telling. Every minute a new road saved a car driver was worth 44p – and all those 44ps added together over the road's projected sixty-year lifespan could be offset against the cost of building it. But a minute saved for a bus user was only worth 33p, and for a cyclist 28p. Each life saved by building a new road could be given a figure: the Highways Agency predicted that one of the M1 widening schemes would prevent 2,081 accidents over sixty years, including four deaths, adding £105m to the project's 'value'. They even factored in the millions of pounds in tax revenue that all the extra petrol sold would generate. Environmental damage could also be costed – £1m per kilometre of new motorway lane, say, or £70 per tonne of carbon produced. But these sums were tiny when weighed against a road's economic 'benefits'.[8] Everything could be given a price, corralled into this self-contained, ledger-book world of profit and loss, debit and credit, receipt and expenditure. But the bookkeeping seemed to have been done by a very creative accountant.

$$\rightarrow$$

In the future this triumph of political arithmetic will have one certain consequence: charging people for using roads. Rod Eddington, the author of a major government report on transport in 2006, used his native Australianese to describe road pricing as an 'economic no-brainer' – necessary both to ration an increasingly scarce commodity, road space, and to make the cost of using it reflect the environmental damage it caused.[9] In fact, charging for the use of a road has long antecedents – notably the turnpike trusts, which in their final days were loathed for levying extortionate tolls. Things came to a head in the south-west Wales village of Efailwen in the summer of 1839, when about 400 local men, mostly farmers, wearing women's clothes, wigs and horsehair beards, demolished the turnpike with sledgehammers, set the tollhouse on fire and chased the collector or 'pikeman' off into the night. They called themselves the Daughters of Rebecca, after the ringleader's nickname. The Rebecca Riots spread throughout south Wales, lasting five years and prompting the setting up of a Royal Commission which recommended removing the turnpikes, just as the railways were beginning to make them unprofitable anyway.

In the 1960s, when economists revived the idea of road pricing as a way of controlling congestion, they found that Rebeccaism had left a residue of resentment against road charging. Road pricing is a classically free-market principle – you pay for what you use – but it was first mooted by a Labour transport minister, Barbara Castle, in the late 1960s, and rejected twenty years later by Margaret Thatcher, who feared it would prove as unpopular as the poll tax. It took an old Labour rebel, London mayor Ken Livingstone, to introduce the capital's congestion charge, in 2004. Meanwhile, the government followed the American example of allowing private companies to build and operate toll roads, where drivers prepared to pay a surcharge could escape the congestion on the public roads. The first was the M6 toll, promoted on illuminated advertising panels at service stations with a picture of two indigestion pills and a tumbler of water above the words: 'Eases congestion: fast, effective relief from the M6.'

It is one thing to invite motorists to relieve the dyspepsia of commuting by escaping into the private sphere; it is quite another to expect them to pay for using roads as a matter of course. Once they have coughed up for their tax disc and their heavy-duty petrol, motorists feel they have rendered unto Caesar and earned the right to consume as much road as they like – in a road-hogging Hummer if they so wish. So it's not surprising that the most popular petition on Downing Street's e-petitions site was created by Peter Roberts, who described himself as an 'ordinary motorist and account manager from Telford' – although it transpired he was also a member of the Association of British Drivers, which campaigned against speed cameras and believed global warming to be 'the biggest con trick ever perpetrated on the human race'.[10] Roberts's petition invited people to agree that road pricing was an 'unfair tax' and that 'the idea of tracking every vehicle at all times is sinister and wrong'. More than 1.7 million people signed up, and Tony Blair sent a conciliatory email to them all, reassuring them that no decision had yet been made.

New Labour had put its faith in a kind of post-political politics that cast aside petty conflicts of interest. According to the Blairite mantra, what mattered was what worked: policies should be servants of the people rather than outdated dogma. And the people could be treated as a single constituency, because all ordinary, decent people agreed about what was fair and right. So NATA-speak fell back on banal, uncommitted language about 'route management strategies', 'multimodal studies' and 'mode-neutral perspectives' – poker-faced phrases that brushed off the arguments and ill-feeling that new road schemes inevitably generate. Wading through all these acronyms and euphemisms, even on a single side of paper, was like trying to swim in viscous asphalt. All the words and parts of speech were in the right order to make sentences, but they seemed drained of meaning and sense. Roads were no longer part of history, politics and culture: they had been wrenched from their local contexts and soaked in the deathly phrasing of the policy wonk.

→

Just as everyone's daily life is part of a shared history, you can travel on any road and see the postwar story of roads in miniature. Whenever I drive home to the Peak District, the route delivers me a pointed reminder that its history does not begin and end tidily like a NATA spreadsheet: it is full of loose ends and detours, unfinished stories and stalled narratives. As you turn off the M60 for Glossop at the Denton Roundabout, you drive along one of the shortest motorways in the country: the five-mile M67. It was built in the mid-1970s as two separate roads, the Denton Relief Road and Hyde Bypass, which just so happened to be joined together to make a single motorway. It is often said that a British motorway is the shortest route between two bottlenecks, and in the M67's case it is literally true. It starts from a congested dual carriageway coming east out of Manchester and then disgorges all its traffic on to another roundabout at Mottram, the last eastern outpost of the city before it thins out into the Derbyshire hills. Whichever way you approach it from, all the motorway does is nudge a traffic jam a few miles further up the road. When it was opened the local journalist Simon Bain described this three-lane carriageway, built to relieve two small, depressed Mancunian suburbs at a cost of £6 million a mile, as 'the whitest of all elephants'.[11]

As you may already have guessed, the M67 was not built to relieve the teeming metropolises of Denton and Hyde. This midget motorway was meant to be just the first section of the 'Manchester to Sheffield All-Weather Route', first mooted in the late 1960s. If you want proof, you can find it at the Denton Roundabout, where there is another of those concrete-and-steel follies – a bit of elevated motorway pointing towards the city centre and leading into thin air. Known to natives as the Ski Jump, it was supposed to form part of the motorway and lead all the way into Manchester. The unbuilt M67 would have left the city at the Mancunian Way, joining the current M67 before running all the way over the Pennines to meet up with the M1.

As the first planned motorway to cut straight through a national park, the Manchester–Sheffield route crashed against the first wave of road protests in the mid-1970s. In 1974 the Labour transport minister Fred Mulley made the familiar complaint that 'the people who will be making most objections will be from London and Scotland and the south-west, who have never been within fifty miles of Manchester or Sheffield'. 'Longdendale,' he added gratuitously, 'is not exactly the most marvellous scenery in the world.'[12] The motorway was meant to be part of the brave new post-Beeching world in which roads would supplant railways. When the Woodhead Tunnel was sealed up in 1981 and Glossop lost its rail link to Sheffield, there were dark rumours that it had been deliberately run down because it was in the motorway's path. Unlike most conspiracy theories, this one turned out to be true. The new Woodhead Tunnel had opened in 1954 as a state-of-the-art, electrified tunnel – the pride of British Railways. But in the late 1960s the government hatched a secret plan to convert the rail bed and tunnel into a motorway. After the tunnel was closed, they discovered it was too small for a dual carriageway, and even a one-way road would have had to ban lorries and impose a 40 mph limit.

By the mid-1980s, the Manchester–Sheffield Motorway had died a quiet death. So as you reach the Mottram Roundabout at the eastern end of the M67, it feels like the modern road system has come to a sudden halt. On the roundabout you can see the blue signs for the motorway, a McDonald's Drive Thru, a Premier Inn and the clean sweep of the M67 arcing back towards Manchester. But looking east there is just the narrow single carriageway of the A57 disappearing over the top of Mottram Moor.

The dotted line of the Manchester–Sheffield Motorway, however, lives on. Just past the roundabout on the A57 is a sign saying 'Stand and deliver the bypass now', sponsored by 'the Longdendale Siege Committee'. They mean the Longdendale Bypass, a three-and-a-half mile road planned to skirt round the congested villages of Mottram, Hollingworth and Tintwhistle. The route would follow that of the unbuilt motorway, heading north-east from the roundabout, before curving south to end on the Woodhead Pass. You can walk the projected line of the bypass by finding a single-track road just above it, which leads into a dirt track and then out into open moorland where swallows dart about at head height and the sheep, happily ignorant of the planning process, timidly make way for strangers. The route ends near Swallows Wood, a sixty-acre nature reserve of bluebell meadows and copses at the centre of the campaign against the bypass. In the wood there are stiles with painted white lettering spelling out 'No Bypass Boneheads'.

The bypass route loops around Hadfield, which doubled as the town of Royston Vasey in the BBC comedy series, *The League of Gentlemen*. Presciently, the first series revolved around the increasingly Gothic efforts of Edward, who runs the local shop with his wife, Tubbs, to stop the building of a new road through the town. 'I wish for an end to the plague of strangers, for our futures to remain local, and for new road to be totally destroyed,' he declares. The only resident in favour of the road is the vicar, who fulminates from the pulpit that 'if God had meant us to walk everywhere, he wouldn't have given us Little Chefs'. It is easy to see why the series creators chose this small town overshadowed by moorland for their satire on Anglo-Saxon attitudes, in which a new road represents the unwelcome invasion of modernity into an insular community of sadists and secret cannibals. 'We had to have the hills,' said one of the writer-performers, Steve

Pemberton, 'because then it looks as though you can't get out of the place.'[13]

I doubt *The League of Gentlemen* had the Longdendale Bypass in mind, but it's another reminder that roads are insistently intertextual, that they can't easily be disentangled from their cultural associations. Roads are both real and imagined – a tension that is sharpest when the road is being planned and it becomes a compelling story with interested parties all arguing about the ending: what will happen when the road arrives. The long-running saga of the Longdendale Bypass hasn't quite been *Blott on the Landscape* crossed with *The Wicker Man*, but it has excited similarly strong feelings. Locals have been campaigning for this bypass for nearly thirty years and its on-off progress mirrors the more general history of roads in recent times.

Plans for the bypass appeared in the notorious 1989 white paper *Roads for Prosperity*, but in 1994, at the height of the anti-roads movement, the road was cancelled. In 1998 New Labour's New Deal reinstated it, but as some time had passed since its cancellation the planning process had to start all over again. A Public Participation exercise, including a very New Labour 'stakeholder seminar', found that 90 per cent of local people favoured the bypass and 70 per cent agreed with the preferred route. The Longdendale Siege Committee travelled to London to deliver a 9,000-strong petition to Downing Street in favour of the road. But a group of local activists were also now campaigning against the road, arguing that it was another step by stealth to a motorway across the Peak District. The anti-bypass movement even had its own unlikely celebrity supporter: the fashion designer Vivienne Westwood. Just after the war, long before she invented the punk look from her shop in Chelsea's King's Road, she had been brought up in Tintwhistle, and played in woodland in the bypass's path.

In another sign of the post-Thatcherite times, the public inquiry into the bypass was outsourced to a private company called Persona Associates and in June 2007 it opened at Stalybridge Civic Hall. But the Inspector had to stop the inquiry three months later when the Highways Agency owned up to getting its figures wrong and went away to recalculate its traffic forecasts. As I write, the inquiry has yet to be restarted and it is beginning to resemble the interminable case of Jarndyce *v* Jarndyce in *Bleak House*.

The Longdendale Bypass may be an extreme case, but these seemingly endless planning sagas are scattered all around the country and the arguments tend to seem similarly intractable. You can see why locals want this bypass to be built: there is a near-permanent queue of traffic on the existing road and it only takes one broken-down lorry to wreak havoc. The millstone terrace houses next to the road are blackened by years of petrol fumes and have the occasional chunk taken out of them by wayward juggernauts. But you can also see why others oppose the road so ardently: it would cut through a landscape that most people, with the possible exception of Fred Mulley and the League of Gentlemen, think is surpassingly beautiful, and the history of roadbuilding over the last half century suggests that it would defer rather than solve the problem, inducing traffic rather than quelling it. Whether this road should be built is a question I still don't know the answer to. All I know is that we might make better decisions about roads if we acknowledged that our feelings about them are entrenched in a rich and complex cultural history – a history that can't just be abridged on a side of A4, brushed over by computer-generated images of new roads or buried under a pile of abstract nouns.

→

Roads carry on being built, but they no longer form such a vivid part of our cultural imaginations. Who, like le Corbusier and others once did, now imagines the future as a road? A few years ago the architect Will Alsop unveiled his visionary plans for a SuperCity, 'Coast to Coast', sited on a 15-mile-wide strip along the length of the M62. Alsop dreamed of a 'beautiful urban sprawl' where people would live in Hull, shop in Manchester and work in Liverpool. He cruised along the road in his 4x4 vehicle for a Channel 4 series, visions of the future appearing magically in his side window. Fifteen-storey villages called Stacks, piled high in asymmetrical shapes like chaotic games of Jenga, would 'litter the landscape as objects of curiosity and wonder, in the manner of the castles of the Welsh marches', he suggested.[14] But Alsop's motorway city was a car-free zone, reserved for Japanese-style bullet trains.

Roads may look resilient but their lives are finite and, in the great scheme of things, short. What would happen to roads if humans disappeared from the earth – the kind of chastening thought experiment that Alan Weisman conducts in his book *The World Without Us*? Our buildings will last long after we are gone; the oldest have already survived for over 6,000 years. But roads, being closer to the earth, will fare less well. Civil engineers often say that a road is unique because it only leaves the ground on a bridge and only escapes the rain in a tunnel, so it is fighting constantly against the soil and the elements. If the traffic were eternally diverted, the first problems would occur in early spring, when the constant freezing and thawing of the ground would break up the asphalt. Water would fill the cracks and, when it froze, widen them. Weeds would make their way into the cracks, which would widen a bit more. After a decade the road would be overgrown with vegetation; a decade later, it would be impassable except in the sturdiest off-roader. After half-a-century, a small wood would have grown through the blacktop and, since thorn bushes gravitate towards abandoned roads, it would probably be even more impassable for having been a road.[15] A deserted road will eventually surrender to the wild, just as Rudyard Kipling imagines it in his poem, 'The Way Through the Woods', about a disused highway now hidden under coppice and heath. The only evidence that it ever existed arrives late on summer evenings, when you hear 'the beat of a horse's feet, / And the swish of a skirt in the dew, / Steadily cantering through / The misty solitudes'.

It is worth remembering that even modern roads age with use, that they too will acquire a history. Interviewed about *Linked*, Graeme Miller nicely summarised a common idea about roads: 'Motorways sterilize the land: they kill the ecology of narrative. You can't make up a story about a motorway. When you break down on the side of a motorway, there's this incredible lack of meaning. Time stops.' Miller's comments connect with a recurring argument in modern environmental writing – that our lives gain purpose and meaning from the concrete particulars, the texture and detail of individual existences knotted together in unique localities over many years. In this argument, the problem with roads is not just that they destroy the planet but that their levelling sameness undermines this parochial quest for meaning. They make the whole world reachable and despoilable, cutting through common ground on the way to some elusive elsewhere. Roads add to our growing sense of what Robert Macfarlane calls the 'retreat from the real … a prising away of life from place, an abstraction of experience into different kinds of touchlessness'.[16]

It's a powerful idea – slow, vernacular traditions give us a sense of belonging and identity, and characterless, mobile modernity destroys it – but it's not, in fact, a modern one. We do feel a pull to the local and familiar, but our sense of what this is changes over time. In the nineteenth century, railways were hated destroyers of natural landscapes, and the crooked cabals that brought them into being make today's road lobbyists seem like benevolent amateurs. But we can become accustomed to the most brutal interventions into the landscape. In 1955 W.G. Hoskins believed the arterial roads of the inter-war period were the epitome of modern hideousness, but he thought the Victorian railways, which made even straighter, harsher lines on the landscape, gave us 'new vistas' to enjoy.[17]

Railways today wear both a pleasing patina of age and a virtuous air of environmental friendliness. In his recent history of postwar Britain, A.N. Wilson accuses Dr Beeching of being in cahoots with the motorway lobby and waxes lyrical over vanished branch lines that were 'heavy, in summer, with cow parsley and rose-bay willow herb, or swathed in autumn by cow-breathed fogs and river mist'. Now there are few parts of England, he writes, 'where the noise of birdsong and insects chirruping is not drowned by the destructive hum of the distant *Autobahn*'. Note the hard Germanic word, in italics, to underline the alien intrusiveness of the motorway. At the new St Pancras Station there is a lovely statue of John Betjeman by Martin Jennings, with the poet holding his hat as he gazes up in wonder at the huge span of William Barlow's train shed, which he helped to save from demolition. Standing by this statue for an affectionate BBC documentary about railways, the writer-presenter Andrew Martin invited his viewers to 'imagine a poet battling to save a motorway'.[18] From the tone of his voice, he clearly thought it unimaginable.

But I am not so sure. Roads have always defied any attempt to render them meaningless. The engineers who built them wanted to create pristine asphalt ribbons with no potential for human anxiety or doubt. So they boxed them off with science and statistics, made them a matter of soil mechanics, bearing ratios, strain distribution and computer-calculated alignments. But roads refused to be just taciturn pieces of engineering. They took on new meanings, and their history became the history of much else besides: our desire for community and our fears about its fragility; our natural instinct to expand the possibilities of life set against our premonitions of death, destruction and loss; and our fierce arguments about what is valuable and beautiful about the world. Nothing more eloquently demonstrates the human craving for meaning-making than our talent for weaving myth and narrative out of these narrow strips of bitumen decorated with little more than sheets of coloured metal and streaks of paint.

Will Self offers some speculations on the future meaning of motorways in his short story, 'Scale', in which the unnamed narrator has a borderline pathology – an unhealthy obsession with the M40. He is writing an impenetrable doctoral thesis on the hermeneutics of motorway signs and composes verse based on the rhythmic incantation of place names on the signs, which *The Times Literary Supplement* calls 'affected as well as asinine'. But in an epilogue set many years into the future, this Casaubon of the trunk road system has achieved an unlikely eminence after publishing his magnum opus, *A History of the English Motorway Service Centre*. Only electric cars with a maximum speed of 15 mph are allowed on the motorways, and the now elderly narrator sometimes drives his golf buggy out to the M40's Stokenchurch Gap, where the National Trust has granted him permission to build his mausoleum. He wonders if archaeologists of the distant future will note the 'similarities in construction between my tomb and the great chamber tombs of Ireland and the

Orkneys' and 'posit a continuous motorway culture, lasting some 7,000 years'.[19]

This link between the road system and our prehistoric earthworks and stone monuments is not as far-fetched as it sounds. In her study of Stonehenge, Rosemary Hill argues for a direct lineage between this ancient edifice and a very British example of traffic engineering. In the mid-eighteenth century the architect John Wood modelled the Grand Circus in Bath on the beautiful proportions and sacred geometry of Stonehenge, about which he wrote a classic architectural account. The Grand Circus inspired other traffic circuses in London and elsewhere, eventually devolving 'into that favourite piece of traffic planning, the roundabout'.[20] Amateur historians like leyline hunters often have a compressed idea of the prehistoric era, seeing all its megaliths and mounds as similarly 'ancient', when in fact they may have been built as much as three millennia apart. So it is possible that some amateur archaeologist three millennia from now will conflate our own era with the prehistoric and assume that the Colonais standing stones and the elevated roundabout at the Lofthouse Interchange were once offered up to the same angry god.

Nostalgia is such a powerful and omnivorous human urge, a weed that flourishes in the most unlikely places, that it is not too big a leap to imagine that our motorways might one day be cherished as examples of human ingenuity and communality, just like leylines or donga tracks today. Perhaps the motorway heritage society of the next century will campaign to save the precious Jock Kinneir signs, our country's brief flirtation with modernist design, or compare the regimented, white-line landscape of the road with the classical regularity of Georgian terraces. Industrial archaeologists will purr over the motorway main-tenance depots and the rock salt barns used for gritting. Some A-road Pevsner will call for the Little Chefs, with their uncommon fusion of neo-vernacular folksiness and American diner flashiness, to be listed. If the roads are unused and overgrown, then maybe we will simply experience what Rose Macaulay calls that 'morbid pleasure in decay' that the Romantic poets and painters felt among the ruins of Gothic abbeys and Greek temples.[21] But surely small groups of enthusiasts will keep tiny bits of the system open – the unspoilt, eight-mile M45 springs to mind – like the steam-railway buffs who run narrow-gauge lines today. They will polish the road signs, retouch the chevrons and allow motorway tourists to drive on them in their vintage Ford Focuses and Vauxhall Astras. And then today's motorway enthusiasts will no longer be dismissed as ironists and kitschophiles but celebrated as John the Baptists crying in the asphalt wilderness, keepers of the flame at a time when roads were most unloved.

Perhaps it is already happening. As I was finishing this book I heard that the School of Life – a new cultural enterprise based in Bloomsbury offering 'ideas to live by' – was organising a weekend break on the M1, a package tour to 'unearth the story of the motorway's construction, reveal the poetry of its monumental architecture, dine in its historic service stations and recover the utopian thrill of its early days'.[22] The tour would start in central London, stop at the famous Ace Café on the North Circular and pitch camp at the Donington Park Travelodge. I was tempted to sign up. But I had already spent a whole day driving several times up and down the first section of the M1, and a whole weekend at the Welcome Lodge at Newport Pagnell. I decided that joining a coach party on the M1 would have felt too much like a busman's holiday – and then regretted my decision, whiling the weekend away wishing I was there with them, talking to the lorry drivers who rode the motorway in its early years and one of the original serving staff at Leicester Forest East.

→

What goes around comes around, and that goes for roads. If the motorway is ready to be celebrated, albeit as a minority sport, then it is only a return to its original utopian associations. A few days after the M1 opened in 1959, the BBC broadcast a radio programme called *Song of a Road* – one of the classic radio ballads assembled by the folk singer Ewan MacColl, his partner Peggy Seeger and the producer Charles Parker. For almost two months, they travelled the length of the M1 building site in a battered Morris Minor, talking to the road workers and composing folk songs about them. They wanted to celebrate the 'two-legged machines', the pick-and-shovel men who did all the hard work, while the state-of-the-art diggers were getting all the credit.

The workers interviewed talked lyrically about 'the old muck-shifting', describing the soil as their 'harvest' – a sort of quasi-pagan attachment to the earth which curiously anticipated the attitudes of the road protesters a generation later. I'm not sure what today's hi-vi army of road maintenance workers, who are regularly pelted with coins, nuts and bolts by motorists for undertaking one of the most dangerous jobs in Britain, would make of this evocation of the motor-way navvy as folk hero. But then they could hardly envy the lives of the *Song of a Road* workers, who told heartbreaking stories about drifting in and out of work, near-vagrancy and loneliness. MacColl and Parker spent one night in a hostel with two or three hundred workmen – an unspeakably squalid ex-army camp on the site of the future town of Milton Keynes, where they found homesick workers from Kilkeel in County Down sobbing on beds or staring blankly into space. They were both deeply affected by the young man who started crying when describing his ten-hour shifts breaking up con-crete – 'such a naked expression of human agony,' wrote Parker later, 'that I switched the tape recorder off in embarrassment'.[23]

It's sad that these workers' stories are now lost underneath an immovable pile of scepticism and resentment about roads. But at least the M1 workers have a ballad to remember them by, which is more than can be said for the navvies who built the seven-mile section of the M62 that climbs over the Pennines to 1,422 feet, the highest stretch of motorway in England. They took seven years to complete it – blasting their way through the gritstone moorland, shifting 700 million tonnes of peat, battling against the drifting snow, driving rain and fierce crosswinds that put icicles on their beards. For seven years, as the chief engineer Geoffrey Hunter later recalled, they 'ate mud, walked in mud, sat in mud and were aware of mud. And there was mud in the sandwiches.' Now you can drive over it, only slightly above the speed limit, in seven minutes.[24]

In the early motorway era, they laid plaques at the opening cer-emonies naming all the road's midwives, from the architects to the consulting engineers. Today a road is laid without any expectation of thanks or applause, which is just as well since it never receives any. While star-name architects invest their energies in urban flag-ship projects like millennium bridges and giant gherkins, roads are designed and built by unknown, unsung subcontractors. When the new Bingley Bypass in Yorkshire won the prime minister's 'Better Public Building' award, there was much amusement in the newspa-pers – as if it was inherently absurd to acknowledge that roads do not magically appear out of the ground but have to be designed and made. (Admittedly, the honour was slightly tainted when they had to close the bypass down soon after to fix the drainage system.)

Roadbuilding now reflects these shifting cultural attitudes. No longer seen as an obvious social good, roads are cobbled together from society's leftovers. Road aggregate is made of everything from pulver-ised car tyres to recycled china clay waste. The Newbury Bypass reused the concrete runway from Greenham Common Airbase, despite fears that it might be radioactive after a fire in the 1950s. Newspaper gossip columnists gleefully reported that a million unsold copies of Robbie Williams's 2006 CD, *Rudebox*, had been ground up to make roads in China – the ignominy of low sales being somehow compounded by being remixed as hardcore. Perhaps the most intriguing example of recycled material is unwanted words. Every year, more than 120,000 new books are published in Britain, creating millions of volumes that will never be opened, let alone read. Many of these unread books are shredded into tiny fibre pellets called bitumen modifier, which can be used to make roads, holding the blacktop in place and doubling up as a sound absorber. A mile of motorway consumes about 50,000 books. The M6 Toll Road used up two-and-a-half million old Mills and Boon novels, romantic dreams crushed daily by juggernauts. So thank you, reader, for saving this book from being buried under one of the new lanes on the M1. Mind you, if I had to be pulped I can think of worse fates. Having your unread books vanish into the authorless anonym-ity of a road feels pleasingly melancholic, like having your ashes scat-tered in a vast ocean.

The motorways I have come to know best are the M60 and M62, the main route from the Peak District back to my current home in Liverpool. As I'm looping round the south Manchester suburbs on the M60, I wonder how many of my fellow motorists – hardened orbital veterans casually cutting me up with their perilous lane-changes – are aware that they are driving over a piece of history. Although the complete orbital did not open until 2000, it roughly follows the line of the outer ring road mentioned in the 1945 City of Manchester Plan, and includes the first piece of motorway building. In early 1956, even before work began on the Preston Bypass, a Trafford steelworks was trying to get rid of 400,000 tons of slag. Lancashire county council took it off their hands to build up the embankments for the new Barton High Level Bridge over the Manchester Ship Canal, which would form part of the Stretford–Eccles motorway. The only snag was that the minister of transport had not actually given the go-ahead for the motorway yet, but the council took a chance that he would and, fortune favouring the brave, it got the first bit of motorway for free.

The building of the bridge was marred by strikes, go-slows and the deaths of six workmen when scaffolding collapsed. This meant that the Stretford–Eccles Motorway came in a year behind schedule. On 16 October 1960, twelve days before traffic was allowed on it, the bridge was opened to pedestrians, 50,000 people taking the opportunity to walk along a motorway for the first and last time in their lives. But the opening ceremony was not held until the following March and the county council, bucking the contemporary trend, announced that this would not be an extravagant affair but 'a cup of tea and a bun to speed the traffic on its way'.[25] Every time I drive over the eighteen spans of the Barton High Level Bridge, I can't quite believe that they celebrated the hard-won completion of this beautiful piece of engineering with the sort of low-key get-together more suited to a village fête.

But then, at the Liverpool end of the M62, there is at least an inkling of how roads may one day be remembered and re-enchanted. As the red lights bring you to a halt at the Rocket Junction, you can see the 1,030-foot viaduct of the Queens Drive Flyover carrying the

Liverpool ring road over the end of the motorway. The flyover has recently been sandblasted, fitted with LED lighting strips and turned into a piece of highway art. It's the sort of makeover they normally give to historic urban buildings, cleaning them up and bathing them in floodlights. The road's stanchions have been encased in steel and at night a projector shines the words 'Welcome to Liverpool' on to the underside of the concrete deck, visible to drivers coming off the motorway. The road has scrubbed up well, looking sleek and elegant as it curves round, like a white scimitar laid on its side – much like it must have looked as it was hoisted into place in the drought summer of 1976, when they struggled to fit the prefab sections together because the joints kept expanding in the beating heat. Road protesters were disrupting inquiries from Winchester to north London that summer, and the roads themselves seemed to take it personally, as waves of caloric heat rose up from them and their asphalt melted. When the Rocket Junction opened that November, it marked the completion of the final section of the M62, the last great cross-country motorway. But no national newspaper covered the opening. The early excitement about motorways had already subsided into bitterness and boredom.

Psychologists call it cognitive dissonance: that feeling of stress and discomfort we get from holding two ideas that oppose or undermine each other, so that we unconsciously discard one of the ideas or shape it into a new, less painful form. Perhaps this explains why we can't for the moment hold these two seemingly antithetical impulses in our heads simultaneously – to acknowledge the environmental destruction and human alienation wrought by roads but also the physical achievement of all those smooth lines of asphalt carved out of unforgiving earth. At least the Rocket Junction is getting its moment of glory at last – maybe it, and the mini-break on the M1, are a sign of things to come.

For now, though, the public image of roads is so poor that you wonder why anyone would want to enter this hellish land of jams, pile-ups, shed loads, road rage and contraflows. So, for the benefit of any future obituarists of the British trunk road system reading this book in, say, the twenty-second century, I would like to add this demurral: not everyone hated the roads. In fact, whenever I talked to the people who used them, even those with daily commutes like Homeric odysseys, they seemed quite fond of them. Although we knew it was as guilty a pleasure as smoking, we were still drawn to that dead time alone on the motorway, that brief hiatus where we could count off the junction numbers and take stock of our lives while the road rumbled beneath us. One of my students told me that on Second Life, that virtual world online, no one bothers to use the roads. Nothing comes between the cyber-citizens and their real estate; everyone simply teleports to their destinations. And part of me thought: what sort of life is that?

Apart from those infantilising dot-matrix motorway signs ('have you got enough fuel?'), the road does one thing right: it treats us like real, grown-up people. There is something rather touching about traffic weaving in and out on a motorway, like the end-of-over field changes in a cricket match or a dance on a crowded ballroom where the couples never bump into each other – a human community silently, endlessly and (most of the time, anyway) peacefully recreating itself. Roads can be places of alienated solitariness, cocooning us in wordless tin boxes with only our stereos and the wish-wash of the windscreen wipers for company. But they are also about the inextinguishable desire for connecting with other human beings and sharing our experiences of the world. Black Box Recorder, in a song that I find every bit as haunting as Kraftwerk's more famous 'Autobahn', once declared that 'the English motorway system is beautiful and strange'. It's true that the beauty is an acquired taste, and the strangeness has had its edges taken off it by the universal narcotic of habit. (And, needless to say, I rather disagree with the next line of the song: 'It's been there for ever, it's never going to change.') But for good or ill, we spend our lives travelling in this semi-strange, almost beautiful land. Maybe we will learn to love it, before we run out of road.

NOTES

1. In road country

1. Andrew Cross, *An English Journey* (London: Film and Video Umbrella, 2004), frontispiece.

2. Roland Nicholas, *City of Manchester Plan: Prepared for the City Council* (Norwich: Jarrold and Sons, 1945), pp. 205, 43.

3. John Baxter, 'Eye-pleasing highways', *The Times*, 9 June 1970.

4. Matthew Hyde, Peter Porter and Aidan O'Rourke, *Around the M60: Manchester's Orbital Motorway* (Altrincham: AMCD Publishers, 2004), p. 142.

5. Bob Roberts, 'Banish yob families to steel container homes', *Daily Mirror*, 21 June 2005.

6. Department for Transport, *Transport Statistics Great Britain 2008* (London: The Stationery Office, 2008), p. 125.

7. Marc Augé, *Non-Places: Introduction to an Anthropology of Supermodernity*, trans. John Howe (London: Verso, 1995), p. 7.

8. Daniel Defoe, *A Tour Through the Whole Island of Great Britain* (London: Dent, [1724–27] 1963), p. 130; Gibbon quoted in C.W. Scott-Giles, *The Road Goes On: A Literary and Historical Account of the Highways, Byways, and Bridges of Great Britain* (London: Epworth Press, 1946), p. 126.

9. Kenneth Grahame, *The Wind in the Willows* (London: Methuen, [1908] 1962), pp. 38–39.

10. W.G. Howell, 'Motorways and the landscape', *Guardian*, 15 November 1963.

11. *The Secret Life of the Motorway*, Episode 2, 'The honeymoon period', BBC4, 22 August 2007; 'Compulsive listening at the wheel', *The Times*, 20 May 1972.

12. Duncan Campbell, *War Plan UK: The Secret Truth about Britain*'s *'Civil Defence'* (London: Paladin, 1983), pp. 149, xvii.

13. Thomas Hardy, *The Woodlanders* (London: Penguin, [1887] 1998), p. 5.

14. Iain Sinclair, *London Orbital* (London: Granta, 2002), p. 3.

15. Department for Transport, *Traffic Signs Manual* Chapter 8: Traffic Safety Measures and Signs for Road Works and Temporary Situations, Part 2: *Operations* (London: HMSO, 2006), p. 54.

16. Ronald N.F. Blake, 'Geoenvironmental factors in the regeneration of military airfields in Great Britain', in Judy Ehlen and Russell S. Harmon (eds), *The Environmental Legacy of Military Operations* (Boulder, CO: Geological Society of America, 2001), p. 204.

17. *The Secret Life of the Motorway*, Episode 3, 'The end of the affair', BBC4, 23 August 2007; see also Peter Hall, *London 2000* (London: Faber, 1963), pp. 207–8.

18. Martin Parr, *Boring Postcards* (London: Phaidon, 1999).

19. Pierre Nora, 'General introduction: between memory and history', in Pierre Nora (ed.), *Realms of Memory: Rethinking the French Past*, Volume One: *Conflicts and Divisions*, trans. Arthur Goldhammer (New York: Columbia University Press, 1996), p. 3.

20. Sigmund Freud, 'A note upon the mystic writing-pad', in *On Metapsychology: The Theory of Psychoanalysis*, trans. James Strachey (Harmondsworth: Penguin, 1984), p. 433.

21. Edward Thomas, 'Roads', in *Edward Thomas: The Annotated Collected Poems*, ed. Edna Longley (Tarset: Bloodaxe, 2008), p. 106.

2. The motoring we used to dream about

1. A.A. Gill, 'Last exit to Whipsnade: The M1, February 2001', in *A.A. Gill is Away* (London: Cassell, 2002), p. 241.

2. T.P. Hughes, 'Roads policy at national, regional and local levels and the role of motorways', in *Twenty Years of British Motorways: Proceedings of the Conference Held in London 27–28 February 1980* (London: Institution of Civil Engineers, 1980), p. 8; 'Prime Minister breaks rules', *The Times*, 6 December 1958; Sefryn Penrose, *Images of Change: An Archaeology of England's Contemporary Landscape* (Swindon: English Heritage, 2007), p. 25; 'Draft press notice – 5 December 1958: Prime Minister opens first motorway', National Archives, MT 121/22.

3. Hansard, HC Deb, 17 March 1959, vol. 602, col. 218.

4. Ian Breach, 'Design on the motorway', *Design*, 288 (December 1972), p. 42; Trevor Rowley, *The English Landscape in the Twentieth Century* (London: Hambledon Continuum, 2006), p. 31; 'Silvertown way', *The Times*, 14 September 1934.

5. Matthew Hyde, Peter Porter and Aidan O'Rourke, *Around the M60: Manchester's Orbital Motorway* (Altrincham: AMCD Publishers, 2004), p. 142; Peter Merriman, *Driving Spaces: A Cultural-Historical Geography of England's M1 Motorway* (Oxford: Blackwell, 2007), p. 40.

6. Mick Hamer, *Wheels Within Wheels: A Study of the Road Lobby* (London: Routledge and Kegan Paul, 1987), p. 44.

7. Harold Watkinson, *Turning Points: A Record of Our Times* (Salisbury: Michael Russell, 1986), p. 69; Jeremy Richardson and Geoffrey Dudley, *Why Does Policy Change?: Lessons from British Transport Policy, 1945–99* (London: Routledge, 2000), p. 70.

8. 'The new motorway between London and Birmingham: The job and how it will be done', National Archives, MT 96/84; see also Ministry of Transport and Civil Aviation, 'London–Birmingham motorway: Spectacular start to £20 million road project', 24 March 1958, National Archives, MT 96/84.

9. Merriman, *Driving Spaces*, p. 109.

10. Ultan Cowley, *The Men Who Built Britain: A History of the Irish Navvy* (Dublin: Wolfhound Press, 2004), p. 177; L.T.C. Rolt, *The London–Birmingham Motorway* (London: Laing, 1959), p. 36.

11. L.T.C. Rolt, *Landscape with Figures: The Final Part of his Autobiography* (Stroud: Sutton, 1994), p. 181.

12. Dominic Sandbrook, *Never Had it So Good: A History of Britain from Suez to the Beatles* (London: Little, Brown, 2005), p. 92; 'Conservative Manifesto 1959', in F.W.S. Craig, *British General Election Manifestos 1900–1974* (London: Macmillan,1975), p. 217; Breach, 'Design on the motorway', p. 47.

13. 'Ernest Marples', *Observer*, 3 January 1960.

14. Watkinson, *Turning Points*, p. 90.

15. Mark Arnold-Foster, 'Going slow on M1 is so soothing', *Observer*, 1 November 1959; Patrick Mennem, 'I drive on Britain's space-age highway', *Daily Mirror*, 30 October 1959; Pathe News, 'Motorway progress', 8 September 1958, film no. 1551.11; Pathe News, 'Motorway at last', 29 October 1959, film no. 1599.04; Watkinson, *Turning Points*, p. 90.

16. 'Students in the way', *Guardian*, 2 November 1959.

17. John Cox, road engineer for Tarmac plc, interviewed in *The Secret life of the Motorway*, Episode 1, 'Falling in love', BBC4, 21 August 2007; 'Speech of the Right Hon. Ernest Marples, Minister of Transport at the opening of the London–Birmingham motorway on Monday, November 2nd at 9.30am', National Archives, MT 121/23.

18. '5,000 cars an hour on motorway', *The Times*, 9 November 1959.

19. 'The Queen on M1', *Guardian*, 21 November 1959; 'The Duke drives Queen on M1', *Daily Mirror*, 21 November 1959.

20. Raymond Spurrier, 'Better bypasses', *Architectural Review*, 130 (October 1961), p. 234; Reyner Banham, 'New way north', *New Society*, 4 May 1972, p. 242.

21. Roger Deakin, *Waterlog: A Swimmer's Journey* (London: Vintage, 1999), p. 255.

22. Edward Thomas, *The Icknield Way* (London: Constable, [1913] 1929), pp. 4–5; Edward Thomas, *The South Country* (London: Dent, [1909] 1984), pp. 153, 224.

23. G.K. Chesterton, 'Heretics', in *Collected Works*, Volume 1, ed. David Dooley (San Francisco: Ignatius Press, 1986), p. 62.

24. 'Old roads and new', *The Times*, 5 March 1927; W.C. Sellar and R.J. Yeatman, *1066 and All That* (London: Methuen, 1930), pp. 3–4.

25. Quoted in C.W. Scott-Giles, *The Road Goes On: A Literary and Historical Account of the Highways, Byways and Bridges of Great Britain* (London: Epworth Press, 1946), p. 202; J.B. Priestley, *English Journey* (Harmondsworth: Penguin, [1934] 1977), p. 237.

26. W.G. Hoskins, *The Making of the English Landscape* (Harmondsworth: Penguin, [1955] 1985), pp. 247, 299; W.G. Hoskins, *English Landscapes* (London: BBC, 1973), p. 95.

27. Alan Hamilton, 'It was free and it was fast, but it was soon falling apart', *The Times*, 20 July 1998; Arnold-Foster, 'Going slow on M1 is so soothing.'

28. Rowley, *English Landscape in the Twentieth Century*, p. 51.

29. Merriman, *Driving Spaces*, p. 120; '11½ miles of motorway', *Guardian*, 20 December 1962.

30. Christopher Booker, *The Neophiliacs: A Study of the Revolution in English Life in the Fifties and Sixties* (London: Collins, 1969), pp. 63–64, 59–60, 12.

31. '3-mile viaduct over railway', *The Times*, 15 October 1958; 'Spaghetti Junction – the gateway to London', *The Times*, 25 May 1972.

32. Le Corbusier, *Precisions on the Present State of Architecture and City Planning*, trans. Edith Schreiber Aujame (Cambridge, MA: MIT Press, [1930] 1991), pp. 154, 143.

33. Lord Montagu of Beaulieu, 'London traffic', *The Times*, 21 August 1924; 'London on stilts', *The Times*, 21 August 1924; 'Building on stilts', *Guardian*, 27 February 1928.

34. Geoffrey Jellicoe, *Motopia: A Study in the Evolution of Urban Landscape* (London: Studio, 1961), p. 12.

35. 'Flyover man accuses: "Twice as much, twice as long"', *Evening Standard*, 29 September 1959; 'The gang had a crazy day, but …', *Daily Mirror*, 3 October 1959.

36. 'Road to disillusion for touring MPs', *Guardian*, 18 July 1961; 'New flyover points way to aesthetics in design', *The Times*, 12 December 1961.

37. Hansard, HC Deb, 12 April 1961, vol. 638, col. 220. For the Mrs Marples rumour see, for example, Hamer, *Wheels Within Wheels*, p. 50 and Andrew Marr, *A History of Modern Britain* (London: Macmillan, 2007), p. 174. The rumour seems to have emerged in a joke made by a Labour MP in the House of Commons. See Hansard, HC Deb, 29 April 1963, vol. 676, col. 835.

38. Quoted in *Ian Hislop Goes Off the Rails*, BBC4, 2 October 2008.

39. Bridget Cherry and Nikolaus Pevsner, *London 3: North West* (New Haven, CT: Yale University Press, 2002), p. 214; 'Flying down to Slough', *Observer*, 21 March 1965.

40. James Campbell, 'J.G. Ballard: Interview', *Guardian*, 14 June 2008; Martin Amis, 'J.G. Ballard', in *Visiting Mrs Nabokov and Other Excursions* (London: Penguin, 1994), p. 79.

41. J.G. Ballard, 'Shepperton past and present', in *A User's Guide to the Millennium: Essays and Reviews* (London: HarperCollins, 1996), p. 183; Tim Adams (ed.), *City Secrets: London* (New York: The Little Bookroom, 2001), pp. 166–67.

42. J.G. Ballard, 'The car, the future', in *A User's Guide to the Millennium*, p. 263; J.G. Ballard, *Crash* (London: Vintage, [1973] 1995), p. 76.

43. Brian Harrison, 'The motorway effect', *Independent*, 19 June 1998.

44. 'Spaghetti Junction', *Birmingham Evening Mail*, 1 June 1965.

45. Chris Upton, 'Spaghetti wonder that grew and grew', *Birmingham Post*, 29 May 1999; 'Cliff Richard arrives in the city', *Birmingham Post*, 9 June 1973.

46. 'When 14 routes meet ... the shape of things to come', *Daily Mirror*, 13 May 1972.

47. Banham, 'Big Brum artwork', *New Society*, 13 July 1972, pp. 84–85.

48. Upton, 'Spaghetti wonder that grew and grew.'

49. Clive Aslet, *Landmarks of Britain: The Five Hundred Places that Made Our History* (London: Hodder and Stoughton, 2005), p. 306.

50. Alex de Rijke, *On the Road: The Art of Engineering in the Car Age* (London: Architecture Foundation/Hayward Gallery, 1999), p. 24.

51. Michael Pollan, *A Place of My Own: The Education of an Amateur Builder* (London: Bloomsbury, 1997), p. 118.

52. Stewart Brand, *How Buildings Learn: What Happens After They're Built* (London: Phoenix, 2nd edn 1997), p. 125.

3. Hatfield and the North

1. 'A word on the roads', *Chambers's Edinburgh Journal*, 19 April 1845, p. 242.

2. Robert Macfarlane, *The Wild Places* (London: Granta, 2007), p. 10.

3. Tom Lubbock, 'Simple pleasures', *Independent*, 25 September 2001.

4. 'Maps and map-reading for motorists: I', *The Times*, 1 September 1908.

5. Sean O'Connell, *The Car in British Society: Class, Gender and Motoring 1896–1939* (Manchester: Manchester University Press, 1998), p. 81.

6. Stephen L. Harp, *Marketing Michelin: Advertising and Cultural Identity in Twentieth-Century France* (Baltimore: Johns Hopkins University Press, 2001), pp. 83–84.

7. Andrew Emmerson and Peter Bancroft, *A, B, C and M: Road Numbering Revealed* (Harrow: Capital History, 2007), p. 21.

8. Hugh Davies, *From Trackways to Motorways: 5000 Years of Highway History* (Stroud: Tempus, 2006), p. 32.

9. Danny Sullivan, *Ley Lines: The Greatest Landscape Mystery* (Sutton Mallet: Green Magic, 2005), p. 23.

10. David Jeremiah, *Representations of British Motoring* (Manchester: Manchester University Press, 2007), p. 134.

11. Ian Nairn, *Your England Revisited* (London: Hutchinson, 1964), pp. 59–60.

12. Jessica Helfand, *Screen: Essays on Graphic Design, New Media and Visual Culture* (Princeton, NJ: Princeton Architectural Press, 2001), p. 102.

13. David Wainwright, 'Way ahead', *Guardian*, 4 July 1963; see also Jock Kinneir, *Words and Buildings: The Art and Practice of Public Lettering* (London: The Architectural Press, 1980), p. 44.

14. Rick Poyner, 'Margaret Calvert' (interview), in Rick Poyner (ed.), *Communicate: Independent British Graphic Design since the Sixties* (London: Laurence King, 2004), p. 82; Phil Baines, 'A design (to sign roads by): Kinneir, Calvert and the British road sign system', *Eye*, 34, 3 (Winter 1999), p. 32.

15. Brenda Colvin, 'The London–Birmingham Motorway: a new look at the English landscape', *The Geographical Magazine*, 32 (October 1959), pp. 245–46.

16. 'Lettering and legibility', *Design*, 152 (August 1961), p. 60.

17. Noel Carrington, *Industrial Design in Britain* (London: Allen and Unwin, 1976), p. 178; David Wainwright, 'Way ahead'.

18. Herbert Spencer, 'Mile-a-minute typography?', *Typographica*, 4 (December 1961), p. 3.

19. Baines, 'A design (to sign roads by)', p. 31; 'Marples gets a "rocket" on the A34', *Daily Mirror*, 5 July 1963.

20. Brooke Crutchley, *To Be a Printer* (London: Bodley Head, 1980), p. 134.

21. Simon Loxley, *Type: The Secret History of Letters* (London: I.B. Tauris, 2006), p. 200.

22. 'A better way back', *The Times*, 20 November 1962.

23. Crutchley, *To Be a Printer*, pp. 132, 135.

24. Louise Jury, 'Concorde beats Tube map to become Britain's favourite design', *Independent*, 17 March 2006.

25. Ministry of Transport, *Traffic Signs for Motorways: Final Report of Advisory Committee* (London: HMSO, 1962), p. 9.

26. Jan Struther, *Mrs Miniver* (New York: Harcourt, Brace, 1940), p. 115.

27. 'Notes of meeting held to discuss signposting of the London–Yorkshire motorway held at St Christopher House on 21st June 1962 at 2.30pm', National Archives, MT 95/384.

28. Raphael Samuel, 'North and south', in *Island Stories: Unravelling Britain: Theatres of Memory*, Volume II, ed. Alison Light with Sally Alexander and Gareth Stedman Jones (London: Verso, 1998), p. 165.

29. Reyner Banham, 'New way north', *New Society*, 4 May 1972, p. 241.

30. David Benson, 'I'll take the Spaghetti road and I'll be in Scotland afore ye', *Daily Express*, 25 May 1972; 'Happy holiday', *Daily Express*, 27 May 1972; 'Spaghetting away from it all ... at a crawl', *Daily Express*, 27 May 1972.

31. Ann Clywd, 'Painting out the English', *Guardian*, 30 June 1969; Martin Woollacott, 'Welsh wails', *Guardian*, 6 February 1970.

32. Gillian Lincsott, 'Clicking in Gaelic', *Guardian*, 4 October 1976.

33. 'Routemasters: The Blue and the Green', BBC Radio 4, 11 May 2004.

34. Eric Hobsbawm, *Age of Extremes: The Short Twentieth Century 1914–1991* (London: Michael Joseph, 1994), p. 403.

35. Edward Thomas, *The South Country* (London: Dent, [1909] 1984), p. 64.

36. Lewis Wolpert, *Six Impossible Things Before Breakfast: The Evolutionary Origins of Belief* (London: Faber, 2006), p. 3.

37. John Michell, *The New View over Atlantis* (London: Thames and Hudson, 1983), p. 23.

38. Iain Sinclair, *London Orbital* (London: Granta, 2002), pp. 40, 3; Iain Sinclair, *Dining on Stones (or, The Middle Ground)* (London: Hamish Hamilton, 2004), p. 116; Iain Sinclair, *Landor's Tower: Or the Imaginary Conversations* (London: Granta, 2002), p. 12.

39. Edward K. Miller, 'The smart way out of gridlock madness', *Ward's Auto World*, November 1990, p. 29.

40. 'This in-car music system reads maps as well', *Independent*, 24 June 1991.

41. Richard C. Francis, *Why Men Won't Ask for Directions: The Seductions of Sociobiology* (Princeton, NJ: Princeton University Press, 2004), p. 153.

42. Boris Johnson, *Life in the Fast Lane* (London: HarperPerennial, 2007), pp. 38–41; James May, 'Lost and found', *Daily Telegraph*, 3 September 2005; Simon Winchester, 'Why I loathe sat-navs', *Daily Mail*, 24 February 2007.

43. 'Map skills lost on younger generation', RAC News, 29 September 2006, at http://www.racnews.co.uk/ (accessed on 1 February 2007).

4. Please don't be rude on the road

1. George Gordon, Lord Byron, *Life, Letters and Journals of Lord Byron* (London: John Murray, 1844), p. 362.

2. Ian Burrell, 'Motorists go armed for war on the roads', *Sunday Times*, 5 June 1994.

3. Joel Best and Frank Furedi, 'The evolution of road rage in Britain and the United States', in Joel Best (ed.), *How Claims Spread: Cross-National Diffusion of Social Problems* (New York: Aldine de Gruyter, 2001), pp. 107, 122, 114.

4. 'Road-sense', *The Times*, 22 July 1919; 'Resolutions for the road', *The Times*, 2 January 1934; C.E.M. Joad, *A Charter for Ramblers: Or the Future of the Countryside* (London: Hutchinson, 1934), p. 32; 'War strain's effect on road manners',

Guardian, 5 March 1941; Reyner Banham, *Los Angeles: The Architecture of Four Ecologies* (Harmondsworth: Penguin, 1973), p. 215; 'Maniacs at the wheel', *Daily Mirror*, 12 April 1966.

5. Martin Amis, 'Road rage and me', *Guardian*, 7 March 1998.

6. Jean Baudrillard, *America* (London: Verso, 1988), pp. 54–55.

7. Sigmund Freud, 'Civilization and its discontents', in *Civilization, Society and Religion*, trans. James Strachey (London: Penguin, 1991), p. 305.

8. Tom Harrisson, Humphrey Jennings and Charles Madge, 'Anthropology at home', *New Statesman and Nation*, 30 January 1937, p. 155.

9. Sidney R. Jones, *English Village Homes and Country Buildings* (London: Batsford, 1936), p. 36.

10. David Matless, *Landscape and Englishness* (London: Reaktion, 1998), p. 64; 'Kingston by-pass opened', *Times*, 29 October 1927.

11. Earl of Cottenham, *Motoring To-Day and To-morrow* (London: Methuen, 1928), pp. 64, 116, 44; see also Earl of Cottenham, *Steering-Wheel Papers* (London: Cassell, 1932), p. 94.

12. 'Test for drivers opposed', *The Times*, 15 February 1929; 'The speed limit: whose opinion should prevail?', *Guardian*, 19 February 1929; Sean O'Connell, *The Car in British Society: Class, Gender and Motoring 1896–1939* (Manchester: Manchester University Press, 1998), p. 129; Ministry of Transport, *The Highway Code* (London: HMSO, 1931), p. 14.

13. Fougasse and McCullough, *You Have Been Warned: A Complete Guide to the Road* (London: Methuen, 1935), pp. 3, 10, 12; 'National safety congress', *Guardian*, 22 May 1936.

14. 'Mobile police', *The Times*, 22 February 1937; 'Televising road sins to the public', *Daily Mirror*, 21 January 1939.

15. Ross McKibbin, *Classes and Cultures: England, 1918–1951* (Oxford: Oxford University Press, 1998), p. 98; 'Accidents on the roads', *The Times*, 2 August 1934.

16. 'Printer's errors', *The Times*, 25 January 1930; 'Road sense and courtesy', *Daily Mirror*, 23 August 1934; see also 'Roundabouts', *Daily Mirror*, 18 April 1929.

17. 'Road hog – Don't be rude on the road', Central Office of Information, 1960; 'New approach to road safety', *Guardian*, 8 January 1963.

18. 'Lancashire constabulary: Motorway behaviour on motorway six during the period 24th September 1959 to 23rd October 1959', National Archives, MT 121/227.

19. Hansard, HC Deb, 17 July 1959, vol 609, cols. 733–43.

20. Hugh Barty-King, *The AA: A History of the First 75 Years of the Automobile Association 1905–1980* (Basingstoke: Automobile Association, 1980), pp. 214–15; 'M1 not for picnics', *Observer*, 8 November 1959.

21. Tony Brooks, 'The hazards of M1', *Observer*, 8 November 1959; J. Austin Crawley, 'A thousand miles a week', *Guardian*, 1 December 1959; 'M1 law-breakers', *Daily Mirror*, 10 November 1959; Patrick Mennem, 'I try out the speed road', *Daily Mirror*, 5 December 1958; 'Mr Marples thinks again about bridges', *Guardian*, 23 December 1959.

22. 'Motorways', *The Times*, 29 June 1963; Mark Arnold-Foster, 'Going slow on M1 is so soothing', *Observer*, 1 November 1959.

23. *The Secret Life of the Motorway*, Episode 1, 'Falling in love', BBC4, 21 August 2007.

24. *Jazz Britannia*, Episode 1, 'Stranger on the shore', BBC4, 1 January 2006; The Beatles, *The Beatles Anthology* (London: Cassell, 2000), p. 83.

25. Victor Knight, '40 mph roads', *Daily Mirror*, 4 February 1960; Reyner Banham, 'Freewheeling the LA way', *Guardian*, 4 November 1968; Banham, *Los Angeles*, pp. 217, 213.

26. E.P. Thompson, 'The peculiarities of the English', in *The Poverty of Theory and Other Essays* (London: Merlin Press, 1978), pp. 36–37.

27. Peter G. Hollowell, *The Lorry Driver* (London: Routledge and Kegan Paul, 1968), pp. 184–85.

28. 'Fools like me', *The Times*, 16 July 1960; 'Flashing headlights not a code for motorists', *Guardian*, 29 May 1962.

29. Quoted in Kristin Ross, *Fast Cars, Clean Bodies: Decolonization and the Reordering of French Culture* (Cambridge, MA: MIT Press, 1995), p. 61.

30. Karl Marx, *Capital: A Critique of Political Economy*, Vol III: *The Process of Capitalist Production as a Whole* (London: Lawrence and Wishart, [1894] 1972), p. 253.

31. 'Listen in to Bernard Buckham', *Daily Mirror*, 15 May 1939.

32. Elizabeth Day, 'Prosecute motorway road hogs', *Sunday Telegraph*, 22 August 2004.

33. Much of this information is taken from Hunter Davies, *The Eddie Stobart Story* (London: HarperCollins, 2002), pp. 36, 74–78, 101–2, 150–53.

34. 'Hans Monderman', *The Times*, 11 January 2008.

35. David Millward, 'Is this the end of the road for traffic lights?', *Daily Telegraph*, 4 November 2006; see also Tom Vanderbilt, *Traffic: Why We Drive the Way We Do (and What It Says About Us)* (London: Allen Lane, 2008), pp. 191–96.

36. 'Our London correspondence: Lord Cecil's remedies for dangerous speeds', *Guardian*, 21 August 1928; 'Lord Cecil's road bill', *The Times*, 16 February 1929.

37. 'Transport Bill proposal for road humps to cut speed and improve safety', *The Times*, 15 April 1981; Jason Groves, 'Poison chalice from Lembit', *Sunday Express*, 21 October 2007.

38. Steven Morris, 'Blunkett becomes butt of judge's anger', *Guardian*, 4 October 2003.

39. Commission for Architecture and the Built Environment, *Living with Risk: Promoting Better Public Space Design* (London: CABE, 2007), p. 59.

40. Michael Pinsky's website at http://www.michaelpinsky.com/lost_o/losto.html (accessed on 3 February 2008).

41. Mick Hamer, *Wheels Within Wheels: A Study of the Road Lobby* (London: Routledge and Kegan Paul, 1987), pp. 64, 94.

42. Martin Cassini, 'In your car no one can hear you scream! Are traffic controls in cities a necessary evil?', *Economic Affairs*, 26, 4 (December 2006), pp. 75–76.

43. Martin Cassini, 'The light idea', *Traffic Technology International*, June/July 2007, p. 24; *Newsnight*, BBC2, 14 January 2008.

44. Martin Cassini's website at http://www.freewebs.com/ mjcassini/inyourcar.htm (accessed on 5 February 2008).

45. 'In Your Car No-one Can Hear You Scream', at http:// uk.youtube.com/ (accessed on 5 May 2008).

46. Jon Lee Anderson, 'The dictator', *New Yorker*, 19 October 1998.

47. Jack Katz, *How Emotions Work* (Chicago: University of Chicago Press, 1999), pp. 28, 21.

48. Cassini, 'The light idea', p. 23.

5. 22 years in a Travelodge

1. Julio Cortázar and Carol Dunlop, *Autonauts of the Cosmoroute: A Timeless Voyage from Paris to Marseille*, trans. Anne McLean (New York: Archipelago Books, [1983] 2007), p. 92.

2. Julio Cortázar, 'The Southern Thruway', in *All Fires the Fire and Other Stories*, trans. Suzanne Jill Levine (New York: Pantheon, 1973), p. 29.

3. Cortázar and Dunlop, *Autonauts of the Cosmoroute*, p. 48.

4. 'Snack bar opens on motorway', *The Times*, 16 August 1960.

5. Tom Phillips, *The Postcard Century: 2000 Cards and Their Messages* (London: Thames and Hudson, 2000), p. 286.

6. T.R. Fyvel, *The Insecure Offenders: Rebellious Youth in the Welfare State* (Harmondsworth: Penguin, 1963), pp. 67–68; Suzanne Greaves, 'Motorway nights with the stars', *The Times*, 14 August 1985.

7. Greaves, 'Motorway nights with the stars'; Nick Mason, *Inside Out: A Personal History of Pink Floyd* (San Francisco: Chronicle Books, 2005), p. 67; Ronnie Wood, *Ronnie: The Autobiography* (London: Macmillan, 2007), p. 47; Terry Rawlings, *British Beat 1960–1969* (London: Omnibus, 2002), p. 2.

8. Humphrey Lyttelton, *It Just Occurred to Me … The Reminiscences and Thoughts of Chairman Humph* (London: Robson Books, 2006), pp. 6–7; David Lawrence, quoted in Alain de Botton, 'Take a holiday on the M1', *The Times*, 27 September 2008; David Lawrence, 'Somewhere – Nowhere: A special Classic Cafes introduction to the motorway service café', Classic Cafes website at http://www.classiccafes.co.uk/ motorway_panel.htm (accessed on 1 August 2008); David Lawrence, *Always a Welcome: The Glove Compartment History of the Motorway Service Area* (Twickenham: Between Books, 1999), p. 41.

9. 'Motorway wine has no alcohol', *Guardian*, 8 January 1964; 'Frenchmen park a wine bar by the "dry" restaurant', *Daily Mirror*, 26 April 1969.

10. D. Hearn, 'Motorway service areas', in Joyce C. Davis (ed.), *Motorways in Britain Today and Tomorrow* (London: Institution of Civil Engineers, 1971), p. 84; Bev Nutt, 'Research report on motorway service areas', *Traffic Engineering and Control*, 9, 2 (June 1967), p. 92.

11. 'Keeping the motorway away', *Architects' Journal*, 18 June 1969, pp. 1614–15; Lance Wright, 'Food, petrol – but no joy', *Architectural Review*, 151 (June 1972), p. 384.

12. Lawrence, *Always a Welcome*, p. 59.

13. Stephen J. Mennell, *All Manners of Food: Eating and Taste in England and France from the Middle Ages to the Present* (Urbana, IL: University of Illinois Press, 2nd edn 1996), pp. 286–87; Peter Hardy, 'Eat before you drive', *Daily Express*, 10 April 1978; 'Egon Ronay stirs it again for motorway cafes',

Guardian, 10 April 1978; Robin Young, 'Second bite at M-way cafes proves unappetizing', *The Times*, 10 April 1978.

14. Jeremy Gates, 'Is this a £60,000 case of motorway madness?', *Daily Express*, 7 September 1978; Department of Transport, *Report of the Committee of Inquiry into Motorway Service Areas* (London: HMSO, 1978), p. 20.

15. Department of Transport, *Report of the Committee of Inquiry*, p. 5.

16. Bernard Levin, 'Get the knives out, we're back to that Great British Disaster, the "caff"', *The Times*, 15 November 1977.

17. Clough Williams-Ellis, *England and the Octopus* (Portmeirion: Golden Dragon Books, [1928] 1975), p. 162.

18. Williams-Ellis, *England and the Octopus*, p. 141; David Jeremiah, 'Filling up: The British experience, 1896–1940', *Journal of Design History*, 8, 2 (1995), p. 100; Arthur H. Pollen, 'Ugliness on country roads', *The Times*, 22 February 1927; 'Fading beauty of the country', *The Times*, 13 May 1929.

19. Williams-Ellis, *England and the Octopus*, pp. 162, 97, 104.

20. J.B. Priestley, *English Journey* (Harmondsworth: Penguin, [1934] 1977), pp. 10, 67, 371, 375–77.

21. John Moore, 'The Cotswolds', in Clough Williams-Ellis (ed.), *Britain and the Beast* (London: J.M. Dent, 1937), p. 88.

22. Clough Williams-Ellis, 'Editor's introduction', in Williams-Ellis (ed.), *Britain and the Beast*, p. xiv.

23. Ian Nairn, *Your England Revisited* (London: Hutchinson, 1964), p. 9; Ian Nairn, *Outrage* (London: Architectural Press, 1955), pp. 393, 366, 363, 372.

24. Osbert Lancaster, *The Penguin Osbert Lancaster* (Harmondsworth: Penguin, 1964), p. 110; Nairn, *Outrage*, pp. 371, 386–87.

25. 'Artist-engineers in industry', *The Times*, 9 July 1955; John Betjeman, *First and Last Loves* (London: Arrow, 1960), pp. 11–12.

26. Peter G. Hollowell, *The Lorry Driver* (London: Routledge and Kegan Paul, 1968), p. 217.

27. B. Dunning, 'The impact of the motorways', *Country Life*, 20 October 1966, pp. 978–79, quoted in Peter Merriman, *Driving Spaces: A Cultural-Historical Geography of England's M1 Motorway* (Oxford: Blackwell, 2007), p. 202.

28. 'Giving a tow', *The Times*, 4 February 1960.

29. Mark Cocker, *Birders: Tales of a Tribe* (London: Vintage, 2002), p. 72.

30. Simon Calder, *Hitch-hikers' Manual Britain* (Oxford: Vacation Work, 1979), pp. 13–14, 17–24, 103, 106.

31. *The Secret Life of the Motorway*, Episode 2, 'The honeymoon period', BBC4, August 2007.

32. David Evans, *A History of Nature Conservation in Britain* (London: Routledge, 1992), pp. 165–66.

33. J.M. Way, 'Wildlife on the motorway', *New Scientist*, 47 (10 September 1970), pp. 536–37; Richard Mabey, *The Roadside Wildlife Book* (Newton Abbot: David and Charles, 1974), p. 34.

34. Sue Clifford and Angela King, *England in Particular: A Celebration of the Commonplace, the Local, the Vernacular and the Distinctive* (London: Hodder and Stoughton, 2006), p. 226.

35. J. Michael Way, *Grassed and Planted Areas by Motorways* (Monks Wood: Institute of Terrestrial Ecology, 1976), p. 17; see also Richard Mabey, *The Unofficial Countryside* (London: Collins, 1973).

36. Lyttelton, *It Just Occurred to Me*, p. 149.

37. Mark Cocker, *Crow Country: A Meditation on Birds, Landscape and Nature* (London: Jonathan Cape, 2007), pp. 98, 56; see also Roger Deakin, *Wildwood: A Journey Through Trees* (London: Hamish Hamilton, 2007), p. 54.

38. Tessa Hadley, *The Master Bedroom* (London: Jonathan Cape, 2007), p. 2.

39. Jon Henley, 'Diary', *Guardian*, 14 February 2007. This survey was conducted under the PTES's former name of Mammals Trust UK.

40. Michael Blastland and Andrew Dilnot, *The Tiger That Isn't: Seeing Through a World of Numbers* (London: Profile, 2008), p. 134.

41. Richard Mabey, 'Food – it's the stuff that's all around you', *The Times*, 20 September 2003.

42. Oliver Duff, 'Roadkill chef makes an offer Miliband can't refuse', *Independent*, 2 February 2007.

43. Margaret Baker, *Discovering M1* (Tring: Shire Publications, 1968), p. 3.

44. George Orwell, 'The lion and the unicorn: socialism and the English genius', in *The Collected Essays, Journalism and Letters of George Orwell*, Volume II: *My Country Right or Left, 1940–1943*, eds Sonia Orwell and Ian Angus (Harmondsworth: Penguin, 1970), p. 98.

45. 'Factory roofs at Slough', *The Times*, 30 November 1932.

46. Martin Pawley, 'Where the big sheds are', in *The Strange Death of Architectural Criticism: Martin Pawley, Collected Writings*, ed. David Jenkins (London: Black Dog, 2007), p. 226; Pawley, 'Stansted and the triumph of the big sheds', in *The Strange Death of Architectural Criticism*, pp. 260–61.

47. Stephen Spender, 'The Pylons', in *Selected Poems* (London: Faber, 1965), p. 34.

48. Anthony Gormley, 'Foreword', in Sefryn Penrose, *Images of Change: An Archaeology of England's Contemporary Landscape* (Swindon: English Heritage, 2007), p. 7; Lynn Barber, 'The interview: Anthony Gormley', *Observer*, 9 March 2008.

49. Charles Madge, 'The press and social consciousness', *Left Review*, 3, 5 (July 1937), p. 284.

50. Mike Jackson, *M5 Sights Guide* (Worcester: Severnpix, 2004), pp. 40, 1.

51. Simon Goddard, *The Smiths: The Songs That Saved Your Life* (London: Reynolds and Hearn, 2002), p. 218.

52. Willy Russell, *The Wrong Boy* (London: Doubleday, 2000), pp. 9–10.

53. Colin Davies, *The Prefabricated Home* (London: Reaktion, 2005), pp. 173–74.
54. Geoffrey Wansell, 'Milky bar kid who ruled over a £4bn empire', *Daily Mail*, 1 March 2007; 'Speech opening M25 service station, 6 June 1987', in Christopher Collins (ed.), *Margaret Thatcher: Complete Public Statements on* CD-ROM (Oxford: Oxford University Press, 1999).
55. 'Disgusted in Tunbridge Wells', *Economist*, 15 July 1995, p. 19.
56. David Nicholson-Lord, 'No-go areas of motorway life', *Independent*, 18 October 1992.
57. '22 years in a Travelodge', Travelodge press release, 4 September 2007.
58. Alain de Botton, *The Art of Travel* (London: Hamish Hamilton, 2002), pp. 48–56.

6. Fast cars, slow lanes

1. Boris Johnson, 'Motorists warned on M25 race', *The Times*, 2 July 1988; see also 'Speed, Greed and the M25', BBC Radio 4, 20 October 2007.
2. Patrick Barkham, 'Why speed cameras need safety cameras', *Guardian*, 11 July 2006; Malcolm Macalister Hall, 'We're mad as hell ...', *Independent*, 27 April 2004; Matthew Davis, '£500K war on Gatsos', *Sunday Star*, 24 June 2007.
3. Eric Hobsbawm, *Bandits* (London: Weidenfeld and Nicolson, 2nd edn 2000), p. 20; Jeremy Clarkson, 'Hurrah for the Gatso vigilantes', *Sun*, 6 September 2002; Jeremy Clarkson, 'Time to stop giving points for speeding', *Sun*, 1 November 2003.
4. Wolfgang Schivelbusch, *The Railway Journey: Trains and Travel in the 19th Century*, trans. Anselm Hollo (Oxford: Basil Blackwell, 1980), p. 60.
5. Michael Balint, *Thrills and Regressions* (London: Hogarth Press, 1959), pp. 24–9.
6. Paul Virilio, 'The Primal Accident', in Brian Massumi (ed.), *The Politics of Everyday Fear* (Minneapolis: University of

Minnesota Press, 1993), pp. 213–14; Paul Virilio, *Unknown Quantity* (London: Thames and Hudson, 2002), pp. 24–25.

7. Wolfgang Sachs, *For Love of the Automobile: Looking Back into the History of Our Desires*, trans. Don Reneau (Berkeley, CA: University of California Press, 1992), pp. 119–20.

8. Charles Jarrott, *Ten Years of Motors and Motor Racing* (London: G.T. Foulis, [1906] 1956), p. 171.

9. Piers Brendon, *The Motoring Century: The Story of the Royal Automobile Club* (London: Bloomsbury, 1997), pp. 84, 86.

10. Scott A.G.M. Crawford, 'Sir Malcolm Campbell', *Oxford Dictionary of National Biography* [online database]; Brendon, *The Motoring Century*, p. 86.

11. Sean O'Connell, *The Car in British Society: Class, Gender and Motoring 1896–1939* (Manchester: Manchester University Press, 1998), p. 135; 'Forcing motorists to slow down', *Guardian*, 13 December 1928; Hansard, HL Deb, 26 April 1932, vol. 84, col. 147; M. Culpin, 'The psychology of motoring', in *Practitioner*, 831 (September 1937), p. 213, cited in O'Connell, *The Car in British Society*, p. 100.

12. W.M. Whiteman, *The History of the Caravan* (London: Blandford Press, 1973), p. 58; Earl of Cottenham, *Steering-Wheel Papers* (London: Cassell, 1932), p. 88.

13. 'Identity card summons as test case', *The Times*, 15 February 1951; 'Protest on car speed check by radar', *The Times*, 26 January 1957.

14. Robert Edwards, *Stirling Moss: The Authorised Biography* (London: Cassell, 2001), p. 259.

15. Gavin Green, 'L.J.K. Setright: Iconoclastic motoring writer', *Independent*, 19 September 2005.

16. L.J.K. Setright, *Long Lane with Turnings: Last Words of a Motoring Legend* (London: Granta, 2006), pp. 59, 135.

17. L.J.K. Setright, *Drive On: A Social History of the Motor Car* (London: Palawan Press, 2002), p. 131; Stefan Collini, *Absent Minds: Intellectuals in Britain* (Oxford: Oxford University Press, 2006), pp. 377, 379; Geoffrey Wheatcroft, 'Portrait:

A.J.P. Taylor', *Prospect*, 120 (March 2006) at http://www.
prospect-magazine.co.uk/ (accessed on 12 June 2008).

18. Basil Cardew, 'Stop this hysteria over M1', *Daily Express*, 16
November 1959.

19. Eric St Johnston (County Police Headquarters, Hutton,
Preston) to Harold Watkinson, 5 January 1959, National
Archives, MT 121/22; 'Pitfalls in driving on the motorways', *The
Times*, 23 June 1964.

20. 'On the wrong track', *Daily Mirror*, 15 June 1964.

21. '190 mph storm on the M1', *Daily Express*, 15 June 1964; '180
mph race cars on M1 – probe order', *Daily Mirror*, 15 June
1964.

22. *James May's 20th Century*, Episode 1, 'Honey, I shrunk the
world', BBC2, 10 July 2007.

23. 'High speeds on motorway, General Traffic Division, 15th
June 1964', National Archives, MT 112/57; 'Report of the inter-
departmental working party on speed limit policy 1966–67,
November 1967', National Archives, MT 112/91.

24. Anne Perkins, *Red Queen: The Authorized Biography of
Barbara Castle* (London: Pan, 2004), pp. 215, 226.

25. Perkins, *Red Queen*, p. 215; Brendon, *The Motoring Century*,
p. 290.

26. Jonathan Glancey, '100 years old and still driving us crazy',
Independent, 16 January 1996.

27. Carol Kennedy, *From Dynasties to Dotcoms: The Rise, Fall and
Reinvention of British Business in the Past 100 years* (London:
Kogan Page, 2004), p. 115.

28. Patrick Mennem, 'Barbara in wonderland', *Daily Mirror*, 11
September 1967; 'M6 Radar shows faster family driving', *The
Times*, 27 April 1966.

29. Michael Palin, *Diaries 1969–1979: The Python Years* (London:
Phoenix, 2007), p. 163.

30. 'Minister appeals to motorway drivers', Ministry of Transport
press notice, 15 November 1963, National Archives, MT
103/386.

31. Richard Sennett, *Flesh and Stone: The Body and the City in Western Civilization* (New York: Norton, 1994), pp. 255–56, 264.

32. Patrick Hamilton, *The Siege of Pleasure* in *Twenty Thousand Streets Under the Sky: A London Trilogy* (London: Vintage, [1935] 1998), p. 297; RIBA, *Road Architecture: The Need for a Plan* (London: RIBA, 1939), p. 54; Geoffrey Boumphrey, *British Roads* (London: Thomas Nelson, 1939), p. 156, quoted in Peter Merriman, *Driving Spaces: A Cultural-Historical Geography of England's M1 Motorway* (Oxford: Blackwell, 2007), p. 65.

33. Quoted in Merriman, *Driving Spaces*, p. 66.

34. Brendon, *The Motoring Century*, pp. 263–66; L.T.C. Rolt, *The London–Birmingham Motorway* (London: Laing, 1959), p. 10.

35. 'Conversations: Will Self', *The Idler*, 2 (November 1993); see also Will Self, 'Mad About motorways', in *Junk Mail* (London: Penguin, 1996), pp. 131–32.

36. Department of Transport, *Transport Statistics Great Britain 1996* (London, HMSO, 1996), p. 184; Paul Vaughan, *Something in Linoleum* (London: Sinclair-Stevenson, 1994), p. 58; Brendon, *The Motoring Century*, p. 214; 'The worst week on the roads', *Daily Telegraph*, 4 January 1935; 'Slippery roads', *The Times*, 28 January 1929.

37. 'National safety congress', *Guardian*, 22 May 1936; Brendon, *The Motoring Century*, p. 252; Trevor Philpott, 'The road to disaster: a judgement on the A5', *Picture Post*, 12 February 1955, pp. 12–16.

38. James Drake, *Motorways* (London: Faber, 1969), p. 21; H.F. Ellis, 'M1 for murder', *Punch*, 28 October 1959, pp. 362–63.

39. 'Traffic behaviour on motorway M6 during the period 5th December 1958 to 4th January 1959', National Archives, MT 121/22.

40. Merriman, *Driving Spaces*, p. 198.

41. 'Police blame speed in fog for blocked motorways', *The Times*, 19 October 1965; Hansard, HC Deb, 21 January 1969, vol. 776, col. 444; Jak cartoon, *Evening Standard*, 15 September 1971.

42. J.G. Ballard, *The Kindness of Women* (London: HarperCollins, 1991), p. 177; J.G. Ballard, *Miracles of Life: Shanghai to Shepperton: An Autobiography* (London: Fourth Estate, 2008), p. 240; J.G. Ballard, 'The car, the future', in Ballard, *A User's Guide to the Millennium: Essays and Reviews* (London: HarperCollins, 1996), p. 263.

43. Ballard, *The Kindness of Women*, pp. 181–83, 217.

44. J.G. Ballard, *Crash* (London: Vintage [1973] 1995), p. 19; Martin Amis, 'J.G. Ballard', in *Visiting Mrs Nabokov and Other Excursions* (London: Penguin, 1994), p. 81.

45. 'M-way "ghouls" attacked', *Guardian*, 5 August 1972.

46. Department for Transport, *Transport Statistics Great Britain 2008* (London: HMSO, 2008), p. 138.

47. Geoffrey Hancock, 'The holiday journey', in Roy Hartley (ed.), *Motoring and the Motorist* (London: BBC, 1965), pp. 105–6.

48. Merriman, *Driving Spaces*, pp. 187–88.

49. Philip Larkin, 'Ambulances', in *Collected Poems*, ed. Anthony Thwaite (London: Faber, 1988), p. 132.

7. You can stuff your motorway

1. Paul Theroux, *Ghost Train to the Eastern Star: On the Tracks of The Great Railway Bazaar* (London: Hamish Hamilton, 2008), p. 11.

2. 'Road-on-stilts crash is their nightmare', *Sunday Citizen*, 28 March 1965; Mick Hamer, *Wheels Within Wheels: A Study of the Road Lobby* (London: Routledge and Kegan Paul, 1987), p. 53; Piers Brendon, *The Motoring Century: The Story of the Royal Automobile Club* (London: Bloomsbury, 1997), p. 286.

3. Attila Kotányi and Raoul Vaneigem, 'Elementary Program of the Bureau of Unitary Urbanism', in Ken Knabb (ed.), *Situationist International Anthology* (Berkeley, CA: Bureau of Public Secrets, 1981), p. 66.

4. *The Secret Life of the Motorway*, Episode 3: 'The end of the affair', BBC4, 23 August 2007; Sue McHarg, 'Double din on the new motorway', *Observer*, 2 August 1970.

5. John Davis, '"Simple solutions to complex problems": the Greater London Council and the Greater London Development Plan, 1965–1973', in Jose Harris (ed.), *Civil Society in British History: Ideas, Identities, Institutions* (Oxford: Oxford University Press, 2005), p. 258.

6. C.P. Snow, *The Two Cultures*, intro. by Stefan Collini (Cambridge: Cambridge University Press, [1959] 1993), pp. 11, xxxiii.

7. 'Oxford road plan', *The Times*, 14 July 1955; David Horan, *Oxford: A Cultural and Literary Companion* (Oxford: Signal, 1999), p. 23.

8. Bevis Hillier, *Betjeman: The Bonus of Laughter* (London: John Murray, 2004), p. 273; John Betjeman, 'Foreword', in Tony Aldous, *Goodbye, Britain?* (London: Sidgwick and Jackson, 1975), p. 7; Fred Inglis, 'Roads, office blocks and the new misery', in Peter Abbs (ed.), *The Black Rainbow: Essays on the Present Breakdown of Culture* (London: Heinemann, 1975), pp. 172, 174–75.

9. Department of the Environment, *How Do You Want to Live?: A Report on the Human Habitat* (London: HMSO, 1972), p. 103; David McKie, 'Motorway city of the seventies', *Guardian*, 17 April 1971.

10. John Roper, 'Little can be done about aircraft noise', *The Times*, 24 September 1970; Anthony Crosland, *The Future of Socialism* (London: Jonathan Cape, 1956), pp. 355, 357.

11. John Tyme, *Motorways Versus Democracy: Public Inquiries into Road Proposals and their Political Significance* (Basingstoke: Macmillan, 1978), pp. 1, 105.

12. 'Truth and courage … are they enough to hold back the bulldozers tearing the heart out of Britain?', *Daily Express*, 2 July 1976.

13. Stephen Hebron, *The Romantics and the British Landscape* (London: British Library, 2006), p. 92; Tony Aldous, *Goodbye, Britain?*, p. 163.

14. Tony Aldous, 'The battle for the relief of Winchester', *The Times*, 7 March 1973; John Thorn, *The Road to Winchester* (London: Weidenfeld and Nicolson, 1989), p. 125.

15. 'Archway inquiry', *The Times*, 23 September 1976.

16. Alan Whitfield, quoted in *The Secret Life of the Motorway*, Episode 3, 'The end of the affair'; *Twenty Years of British Motorways: Proceedings of the Conference Held in London 27–28 February 1980* (London: Institution of Civil Engineers, 1980), p. 85.

17. Margaret Thatcher, *The Path to Power* (London: HarperCollins, 1995), p. 3.

18. Margaret Thatcher, 'Speech opening final section of M25, 29 October 1986', in Christopher Collins (ed.), *Margaret Thatcher: Complete Public Statements on CD-ROM* (Oxford: Oxford University Press, 1999); Geoff Andrews, 'Thatcher drives home message over M25 critics', *Guardian*, 30 October 1986.

19. Department of Transport, *The M25 Orbital Motorway* (London: Central Office of Information, 1986), p. 12.

20. Terry Coleman, 'Ring of no confidence', *Guardian*, 30 October 1986.

21. James Lees-Milne, 'Otmoor and the M40', *The Times*, 8 February 1973.

22. Margaret Thatcher, 'Speech presenting 1989 Better Environment Awards for Industry, 16 March 1990', in Collins (ed.), *Margaret Thatcher: Complete Public Statements on CD-ROM*; Richard Mabey, *Landlocked: In Pursuit of the Wild* (London: Sinclair-Stevenson, 1994), p. 200.

23. 'Obituary of Lord Kelvedon MP', *Daily Telegraph*, 30 January 2007.

24. Christopher Hill, *The World Turned Upside Down: Radical Ideas During the English Revolution* (Harmondsworth: Penguin, 1975), pp. 39–56.

25. Geoffrey Lean, 'Transport takes a wrong turning', *Observer*, 15 August 1993.

26. Jim White, 'Frestonians forever. Yeah, cool', *Independent*, 20 November 1992.

27. Heathcote Williams, *Autogeddon* (London: Jonathan Cape, 1991), pp. 28, 64; 'Eco soundings', *Guardian*, 14 January 1994.

28. Sandy McCreery, 'The Claremont Road Situation', in Iain Borden, Joe Kerr, Jane Rendell with Alicia Pivaro (eds), *The Unknown City: Contesting Architecture and Social Space* (Cambridge, MA: MIT Press, 2002), p. 230.

29. Polly Ghazi and Roger Tredre, 'Anti-road demos hit by law on trespass', *Observer*, 19 June 1994; Lydia Slater, 'Too weak to walk, the sight of those glorious trees makes me burst into tears', *Daily Mail*, 20 May 1994.

30. Dillie Keane, 'The unhappy campers for whom the Bel tolls', *Mail on Sunday*, 7 August 1994.

31. Bel Mooney, 'Behold the spoil of war', *Guardian*, 15 February 1995.

32. See J. Michael Thomson, *Motorways in London: Report of a Working Party led by J. Michael Thomson* (London: Duckworth, 1969); 'Making motorways pretty', *Economist*, 29 May 1971, pp. 64–65; and M.J.H. Mogridge, *Jam Yesterday, Jam Today, and Jam Tomorrow?: Or How to Improve Traffic Speeds in Central London* (London: University College London, 1985).

33. Richard Mabey, *Beechcombings: The Narratives of Trees* (London: Chatto and Windus, 2007), pp. 93–95.

34. Mick Smith, *An Ethics of Place: Radical Ecology, Postmodernity and Social Theory* (Albany, NY: State University of New York Press, 2001), p. 142; Julian Cope, *The Modern Antiquarian: A Pre-Millennial Odyssey Through Megalithic Britain* (London: Thorsons, 1998), p. ix.

35. Adam Fresco, 'Last A30 tunneller emerges defiant', *The Times*, 31 January 1997.

36. Matthew Paterson, 'Swampy fever: media constructions and direct action politics', in Benjamin Seel, Matthew Paterson and Brian Doherty (eds), *Direct Action in British Environmentalism*

(London, Routledge, 2000), pp. 151, 155; Aufbehen, 'The politics of anti-road struggle and the struggles of anti-road politics: the case of the No M11 Link Road campaign', in George McKay (ed.), *DiY Culture: Party and Protest in Nineties Britain* (London: Verso, 1998), p. 122.

37. *Road Raging: Top Tips for Wrecking Roadbuilding* (Newbury: Road Alert!, 1997), p. ii.

38. John Deans, 'You dreadful human beings', *Daily Mail*, 9 February 1995; Steven Norris, *Changing Trains: An Autobiography* (London: Hutchinson, 1996), p. 195; Colin Brown, '"Bury Swampy" remark fuels gaffe machine', *Independent*, 15 March 1997.

39. John Vidal, 'Eco soundings', *Guardian*, 25 November 1998.

40. Simon Hacker, 'Wrong turns', *Guardian*, 20 December 1999.

8. The end of the road

1. T.S. Eliot, 'Choruses from "The Rock"' [1934], in *Collected Poems 1909–1962* (London: Faber, 1963), p. 170.

2. 'Walking the walk, talking the talk: re-imagining the urban landscape: Graeme Miller interviewed by Carl Lavery', *New Theatre Quarterly*, 21, 2 (May 2005), p. 161.

3. Barbara Bryant, *Twyford Down: Roads, Campaigning and Environmental Law* (London: E.F. Spon, 1996), p. 216.

4. George Monbiot, *Heat: How to Stop the Planet Burning* (London: Penguin, 2007), p. 145.

5. Andrew Clark, 'Flyover takes its place in minister's family album', *Guardian*, 17 October 2002.

6. David Hughes and Ray Massey, 'War on the motorist', *Daily Mail*, 18 November 1999; Department for Transport, '£148m M25 Heathrow improvement scheme opens ahead of schedule', press release, 13 December 2005.

7. Ben Webster, 'Go-ahead for Heathrow expansion', *The Times*, 8 December 2006.

8. These figures are taken from Jonathan Leake, 'The road fix', *New Statesman*, 13 August 2007, pp. 12–14.

9. Ben Webster, 'Road pricing is a no-brainer, but forget the grand projects', *The Times*, 2 December 2006.

10. Ben Webster, 'Hardliners drive their campaign via No 10 website', *The Times*, 11 January 2007; Association of British Drivers website at http://www.abd.org.uk/env.htm (accessed on 1 June 2007).

11. Simon Bain, *Railroaded! Battle for Woodhead Pass* (London: Faber, 1986), p. 53.

12. 'Mulley hits back at objectors', *Guardian*, 23 August 1974.

13. Andrew Martin, 'The boys from the black stuff', *Independent*, 8 March 2001.

14. Helen McCormack, 'Return of the high-rise', *Independent*, 3 January 2005; David Ward, 'Suburbs banished by trans-Pennine city', *Guardian*, 20 January 2005.

15. See Alan Weisman, *The World Without Us* (London: Virgin, 2008), pp. 26–27; Oliver Rackham, *The History of the Countryside* (London: Dent, 1986), p. 257; and Ultan Cowley, *The Men Who Built Britain: A History of the Irish Navvy* (Dublin: Wolfhound Press, 2004), p. 170.

16. 'Walking the walk, talking the talk', p. 163; Robert Macfarlane, *The Wild Places* (London: Granta, 2007), p. 203.

17. W.G. Hoskins, *The Making of the English Landscape* (Harmondsworth: Penguin, [1955] 1985), p. 265.

18. A.N. Wilson, *Our Times: The Age of Elizabeth II* (London: Hutchinson, 2008), pp. 96–97; *Between the Lines: Railways in Fiction and Film*, BBC4, 9 October 2008.

19. Will Self, 'Scale', in *Grey Area* (London: Penguin, 1996), pp. 104–5, 123.

20. Rosemary Hill, *Stonehenge* (London: Profile, 2008), p. 80.

21. Rose Macaulay, *Pleasure of Ruins* (London: Weidenfeld and Nicolson, 1953), p. 6.

22. The School of Life website at http://www.theschooloflife.com/ (accessed on 7 October 2008).

23. Ben Harker, *Class Act: The Cultural and Political Life of Ewan MacColl* (London: Pluto Press, 2007), p. 142.

24. *The Secret Life of the Motorway*, Episode 1, 'Falling in love', 21 August 2007.
25. Eddie Little, 'The building of the Barton High-Level Bridge', *Manchester Region History Review*, 15 (2001), p. 28.

ACKNOWLEDGEMENTS

I have tried to make the notes as unintrusive as possible for the reader by conflating different references together and restricting referenced material to quotations, statistics and contentious or unusual information. Most of the other information contained in this book has been drawn from sources mentioned in the notes, newspaper archives or the Ministry of Transport files at the National Archives at Kew. I have also learnt a lot from the websites of road aficionados, particularly the pages of SABRE, the Society for All British Road Enthusiasts; Chris Marshall's wonderfully warm-hearted and informative *Chris's British Road Directory*; and *The Motorway Archive*, a site run by the Motorway Archive Trust and hosted by the Institution of Highways and Transportation.

The Mass-Observation material quoted in this book is reproduced with the kind permission of the Trustees of the Mass Observation Archive, and is copyright © the Trustees of the Mass Observation Archive. I am grateful to Faber & Faber Ltd for permission to reproduce extracts from 'Ambulances' from Philip Larkin's *Collected Poems*; and 'The Rock' from T. S. Eliot's *Collected Poems*. Also for 'The Pylons' from *New Collected Poems* by Stephen Spender © 2004. Reprinted by kind permission of the Estate of Stephen Spender. Permission to quote from Black Box Recorder's 'The English Motorway System' is gratefully received.

I would like to thank the following people for reading draft material, leading me to sources, providing information, accompanying (sometimes driving) me on road journeys and helping in other ways:

Jim Barnard, Jo Croft, John Davies, Alice Ferrebe, Elspeth Graham, Ben Hamilton-Baillie, Joanne Hollows, Camilla Hornby, Steve Jones, Sian Lincoln, Keith Marley, David McKie, Liam Moran, Michael Moran, Win Moran, Joanna Price, Helen Rogers, Gerry Smyth and Kate Walchester. Penny Daniel and Anna Wilson took great care in editing the manuscript. And I must reserve special thanks for my brilliant editor, Daniel Crewe, who has guided me calmly out of this project's various detours and dead-ends.

PICTURE CREDITS

1. The M1 near Luton, October 1959 © Popperfoto/Getty Images.
2. Two MG drivers wave at each other, October 1964 © British Motor Industry Heritage Trust.
3. Ernest Marples and Sir Owen Williams on the M1, October 1959 © PA Photos.
4. Lane indiscipline on the M1, October 1959 © Mirrorpix.
5. Pennine Tower restaurant, Forton services, M6 © RIBA Library Photographs Collection.
6. New 50 mph speed limit sign, August 1960 © Getty Images.
7. Felled trees on the Newbury bypass site, 1996 © Photofusion Picture Library/Alamy.
8. Motorway at night © David Pearson/Alamy.

INDEX